AF541217

WOMEN ENTREPRENEURSHIP IN RURAL AREAS

By

Dr. J. Jeya Ani
Assistant Professor
Research Dept. of Commerce
St.Xavier's College
Palayamkottai - 627 002
Tamil Nadu (India)

&

Dr. Lourdes Poobala Rayen
Selection Grade Lecturer
Research Dept. of Commerce
St. Xavier's College
Palayamkottai - 627 002
Tamil Nadu (India)

DPH

DISCOVERY PUBLISHING HOUSE PVT. LTD.
NEW DELHI-110 002

Published by:
Tilak Wasan
DISCOVERY PUBLISHING HOUSE PVT. LTD.
4383/4B, Ansari Road, Darya Ganj
New Delhi-110 002 (India)
Phone : +91-11-23279245, 43596064-65
Fax : +91-11-23253475
E-mail : discoverypublishinghouse@gmail.com
sales@discoverypublishinggroup.com
parul.wasan@gmail.com
web : www.discoverypublishinggroup.com

***First Edition:* 2014**

ISBN: 978-93-5056-474-5

Women Entrepreneurship in Rural Areas

Printed at:
Dynamic Printers
Delhi

Preface

In rural areas, there are very few employment opportunities; moreover, work as casual and seasonal labourers in agriculture or construction may not be an option for women. For those with little or no land, engage in non-farming activities, such as marketing, processing, and other micro-enterprises. Self-employment in small-scale businesses presents a constructive option for income generation. In many developing countries, a high percentage of small-scale businesses that cater to local needs are controlled or owned by women. Women's enterprises tend to be relatively small, have informal structures, flexibility, low capital needs, modest educational requirements, high labour intensity, and depend on local raw materials. They are also characterised by their dependence on family labour and limited technical and managerial skills. Commonly, these enterprises are not registered, maintain no business records and do not have access to credit from formal credit institutions. By facilitating women's access to tools and skills to improve, monitor and evaluate their progress as entrepreneurs, the paper enables them to set goals for themselves and to achieve their business objectives, both individually and by working in groups. Women entrepreneurs are encouraged to organize themselves in a business association. Thus, they can get into touch with like-minded women, exchange ideas and take part in policy preparation processes that determine the future of micro and small-scale enterprises.

Many countries are taking some initiatives to encourage the development of potential for susceptible women entrepreneurs. In spite of women being conventionally involved with various small and medium enterprises by different government and non-government organizations (NGOs), feminine entrepreneurial aptitudes have not been successfully raised to the required level. Hence, it is essential to prevent the resurgence of negative consequences through the application of some strict procedures in order to promote women's entrepreneurship development and strike a balance between maximization of women empowerment and sustainable development, so as to achieve higher quality of life.

This book presents the research on the topic 'Rural women entrepreneurship' which gives the profile of the rural women entrepreneurs and their enterprise. Moreover the entrepreneurial skills, motivating factors and the problems associated with them were also analysed in this book. This book will help the planners and the decision-makers who are involved in the development of rural entrepreneurship to review the existing policies and to make suitable suggestions to amend the provisions of the Act which governs the rural women entrepreneurship.

Authors

Contents

Introduction and Design of the Study

Women constitute around half the total world population of the world. In traditional societies, they were confined to the four walls of houses performing household activities. In modern societies, they have come out of the four walls to participate in all sorts of activities. The global evidences buttress that women have been performing exceedingly well in different spheres of activities like academics, politics, administration, social work and so on. Now, they have started plunging into industry and running their enterprises successfully. The Phenomenon of women entrepreneursnip is largely confined to metropolitan cities and big towns in India. Most of the women entrepreneurs operate small scale units. However, women entrepreneurs are found in rural areas also.

Mostly, the rural women entrepreneurs are engaged in home-made articles such as candle making, handicrafts, handloom (weaving) textiles, pickles, masala powder, agarbati, pappad, tailoring, pottery, petty shops, tiffin centre, snack bars, street vending (vegetables, flowers, fruits, etc.), packaging materials, milk items such as curd, butter milk, ghee, etc.

Women have the potential and the will to establish and manage business of their own. What they need is encouragement and support in the form of various self-employment generation programmes. There are different types of women entrepreneurs in rural areas with a very small investment. This helps them to have a regular and satisfied living with a small profit to manage the families on their own.

Every village has different types of entrepreneurs and these entrepreneurs operate in their own villages and also move out of their villages in search of potential buyers in other villages. This mobility provides greater amount of satisfaction to the people of other villages also.

ENTREPRENEURSHIP DEVELOPMENT IN INDIA

Any country, particularly a developing one, depends to a great extent on industrialisation for its progress. The small-scale sector which is relatively labour intensive and has a short gestation period, play a vital role in the process, in achieving national objectives like increasing production, providing more employment opportunities, minimizing regional disparities and reducing inequalities in income distribution.

In India, the emphasis on the small-scale industry has grown with the introduction of each five-year plan. A large number of innovative fiscal incentives and concessions and other supporting facilities are being provided to small entrepreneurs for strengthening the economic base, leading thereby to more intensive industrialisation. Such provisions include subsidies; credit on easy terms, planned training programmes, supply of machinery on hire purchase facility and technical counseling through the Small Industries Service Institute (SISI).

The National Institute of Small Industry Extension Training (NISIET, Hyderabad) conducts various motivation training programmes for potential entrepreneurs. The establishment of the National Science and Technology Entrepreneurship Development Board (NSTEDB), the setting up of the Entrepreneurship Development Cells (EDCs) in Engineering Colleges and Indian Institute of Technology, the creation of Science and Technology entrepreneurs Parks (STEP), the programme of Training of Rural Youth for Self-Employment (TRYSEM), the Self-Employment Programme for the Urban Poor (STEPUP), the Development of Women and Children in Rural Areas (WCRA) and the establishment of industrial estates are some of the very important measures introduced for the development of entrepreneurship.

WOMEN ENTREPRENEURSHIP

Women entrepreneurship is a recent phenomenon in India which came into prominence in late 1970's. Now we see that more and more women are venturing as entrepreneurs in all kinds of business and economic activities. Though at the initial stage, women entrepreneurship developed only at urban areas, in recent times, it has extended its wings to rural and semi-urban areas too.

In the seventies, women concentrated much on traditional activities only. But due to the spread of education and favourable government policies towards development of women entrepreneurship, women now, have changed their attitudes and diverted towards non-traditional activities too. They show favourable response to changing situations and get adjusted to them and have improved their position.

The Government and Non-government organizations are giving more prominence in promoting self-employment among women and building up women entrepreneurship. Special financial assistance is provided and training programmes are organized for women to start their ventures.

RURAL ENTREPRENEURSHIP DEVELOPMENT IN INDIA

The Rural Entrepreneurship Development Programmes (REDPs) in India have been institutionalised by the Entrepreneurship Development Institute of India, Ahmedabad. The civil society institutions, particularly the Non-Governmental Organizations (NGOs), are seen as agents who help state agencies in implementing the programmes. The motivation, training and the follow up component is the role state expects NGOs to undertake. EDP's are designed to support a person or group wishing to start a business. It inculcates in the entrepreneur the necessary entrepreneurial traits that develop the personnel, financial, technical, managerial and marketing capabilities and skills.

The Government acts as a catalytic force of the emergence of new entrepreneurs through provision of infrastructural and other facilities. India has diversified multi agency institutional credit structure comprising of commercial banks, co-operative banks and regional rural banks for the development of micro entrepreneurs.

RURAL ENTREPRENEURSHIP DEVELOPMENT PROGRAMMES (REDPs)

Under this programme, grant assistance is sanctioned to reputed Voluntary Agencies (Vas) and professional agencies for conducting REDPs. It envisages the agency to provide 2 years escort and follow-up support to the trained women. In addition to REDPs, master-craftswomen also sanction special training programmes covering skill up gradation, market-oriented training programmes and training of and by master-craftswomen.

The main objective of integrated rural development programmes is to increase the income generating power of the family who are below the poverty line to alleviate the poverty. 30 per cent women should be the beneficiaries in rural development programmes run by the government.

Entrepreneurship Development of Women through SHG

Strength and weakness, both are the different sides of the same coin. Hence, all involved group members of SHG must realise that they all work with their own individual strengths and weaknesses. No one should be blamed for ones weakness *i.e.,* all SHG members are equally responsible for success and failure of their entrepreneur. Self-help group can take a lead in any of the income generating activities by which group members can get employment and enhance their family socio-economic status. The group provides a platform to women for income generation with co-operative and mutual helping attitude.

What is Self-Help Group?

The definition of SHG as approved by National Bank For Agriculture and Rural Development [NABARD] the apex banking body in India, is "An SHG is a small, economically homogeneous and affinity group of rural poor voluntarily formed to save and mutually agree to contribute common fund to be lent to its members as per group decision for their socio-economic development".

As the name indicates, self-help group is an informal group of about 15-20 people from a homogeneous class, who come together for addressing their common problems. Group itself becomes a base to convey necessities and sort out social economical problems of their group members.

Main aim of SHG is to make group members self-sufficient and self-reliant (independent) by self-employment and empowerment through group dynamics.

Principle of SHG

'Unity is Strength'

Self-help group is a best way to get strengthen. Example: A single wooden piece can be easily broken, but a bundle of 15-20 wooden pieces can't be broken easily. Like this, group of people can easily sort out any of the problem, because group decisions carry more weightage than individual decision.

Characteristics of an Ideal SHG

According to MARADA [2000] well functioning SHG should have following structural features:

1. An ideal SHG comprises 15-20 members.
2. All the members should belong to the same socio-economic strata of society.
3. Rotational leadership should be encouraged for the distribution of power and to provide leadership opportunities to all the members.
4. Member should regularly attend meetings, save money and participate in all activities Voluntarily.
5. The procedure of decision-making in SHG should democratic in nature.

6. The group frames rules and regulations, which are required in its effective functioning.
7. Transparency in account keeping and accounts should be maintained and updated regularly.
8. An SHG should be socially viable institution.

Role of Self-Help Groups in Empowering Women

The self-help groups empower women and train them to take active part in the socio-economic progress of the nation and make them sensitised, self-made and self disciplined. The SHGs have inculcated great confidence in the minds of rural women to succeed in their day-to-day life. SHGs enhance the quality of status of women as participants, decision-makers and beneficiaries in the democratic, economic, social and cultural spheres of life. The SHGs bring out the capacity of women in molding the community in right perspective and explore the initiative of women in taking the entrepreneurial ventures. SHGs also organize women to cope with immediate purposes depending on the situation and need.

Participation of women in SHGs makes a significant impact on the empowerment in social aspect also. Participation helps women come out in open and discuss their problems. It also helps to bring about awareness among rural women about savings, education, health, environment, cleanliness, family welfare, social forestry, etc. Researches also reveal that increased participation of women in decision-making at all level will help to adjust the goals pursued through development.

Empowerment should be extremely induced so that women can exercise a level of autonomy. There should also be 'self-empowerment' so that women can look at their own lives. The process of 'learning by doing and earning' would certainly empower rural women. More and more rural women need to be involved in self-employment. Self-employment in agriculture, village and small industries and retail trade and services should be expanded. Self-employment is also conducive to the development of individual initiative and entrepreneurial talent and offers greater personal freedom.

The added advantage is that the institution of family remains undisturbed. The emergence of self-help groups in this context is a welcome development. The groups would provide a permanent forum for articulating their needs and contributing their perspectives to development.

Self-help group should be developed as an institution for financial intermediation as well as people's network rather than a vehicle for credit disbursal only.

Self-Help Group is able to overcome most of the practical problems encountered in the implementation of the various income generating programmes for the economic empowerment of women. SHGs have also been organized during last decade under various programmes of the government, *e.g.* District Poverty Eradication Programme, Aapni yojna, Development of Women and Children in Rural Areas, Krishi Vigyan Kendra, etc.

The number of SHGs existing at present in the country is estimated to be about 2,60,000. Out of these; about 90 per cent are women group. The cumulative number of SHGs linked to the bank till March 2002 is 4,61,478 and to the tune of 10,263 million rupees has been advanced to the SHG for income generating activities [NABARD, 2002]. As per the report of NABARD, SHG bank linkage programme has benefited 4 million families, covering an estimated 20 million very poor people during 2001-02.

The SHGs are a viable alternative to achieve the objectives of rural development and to get community participation in all rural development programmes. The possible outcomes of women's entrepreneur through SHGs at household level are self-employment, sustainable livelihoods, enhanced social dignity and better status of women. SHG would lead to benefits not only to the individual women and women's groups but also for the family and community as a whole through collective action for development. Empowerment is not just for meeting their economic needs but also for more holistic social development.

The success of a small-scale-enterprise depends on the following major factors:

- Inherent viability of the project, *i.e.*, technical, organizational, financial, commercial viability.
- The way a project is planned, *i.e.*, decisions regarding various project parameters such as where to locate, what technology to be used, what should be the capacity of the machineries etc.
- The meticulousness with which a project is implemented.
- The way of project managed.

Everything revolves around the enterprise. Therefore, the factors responsible for their emergence and growth must be analyses and supported.

Self-Help Groups

Organizing the poor into groups however is not an easy task. The Non-Governmental Organizations play a crucial role to identify the self interested persons, to form them into self-help groups and guide the members in farming the rules and regulations with regard to thrift and credit procedures and repayment ethics. They must train the members for group dynamics, income generating activities for credit support (Karbanda, 1991).

The concept of Self-Help Groups is not new for Indian society. India has a long tradition of people coming together voluntarily for performing various socio-cultural, religious and economic activities collectively. It is a voluntary association of women formed to attain certain collective goals. The formation of Self-Help Groups as an instrument for delivering credit is of recent origin (Misra, 1999).

For mobilising credit support for the poor at the grass root, especially for the women folk, SHGs is the most viable means. For income generation, better bargaining power and improvement in the quality of life, women have shown extraordinary dynamism in organizing themselves for group activities. Membership in a group gives women a legitimate forum beyond the private domestic sphere and inputs to which they lack access previously, it permits a gradual building of her capacity to interact effectively and redistribute economic opportunities (David, 1992).

Thus, Self-Help Group is a small, economic, homogeneous and affinity group of rural/urban poor, voluntarily formed to save and contribute to a common fund to be lent to the members as per group decision and for working together for social and economic uplift of their families and community (RASS, 1997).

3E's Empirical Model for Entrepreneurship Development through SHG

1. Emerging Stage

(a) *Identification of Common Interest area of SHG Members:* For the successful implementation of any enterprise it is necessary that entrepreneurial activity should be accepted by all the SHG members with interest. So they will work as volunteers, otherwise it becomes boredom that may be the cause of failure.

(b) *Identification of Indigenous Entrepreneurs:* Dr. Hasnain defines "Indigenous as a part of culture which is being necessarily followed by society and expressed in form of oral, social and physical behaviour". Such knowledge or experiences thus have been passed on from one generation to another by word of mouth, which are commonly known as indigenous knowledge. Indigenous Entrepreneurs that are based on the experience of people for generations together cannot be discarded just because they are being practiced from old age. Hence it is necessary to identify area specific indigenous enterprises before establishing the new venture.

(c) *Blending with Latest Technology:* Now-a-day, with the advent of science and technology, development taking place is being expanded. Indigenous practices, if integrated with scientific knowledge, will help in developing enterprises, which are more suitable, better problem solving, need based and easily acceptable, with in the available resources and surroundings. It will also help to bridge the existing technological gap.

(d) *Technical Guidance:* Technical guidance at every step is requires for success of any enterprise. The Government and Non-Government Organizations are giving emphasis on women entrepreneurship. Special financial assistance is provided and training programmes are organized for women to start their enterprise. There is a big list of Government and Non-Government agencies and programmes helping for the promotion of women entrepreneurship as below:

- Women's corporate finance corporation (WCFC).
- Federation of societies of women entrepreneur (FSWE).
- Small entrepreneurship development institute of India (SEDII).
- District industrial centre (DIC).
- Development of women and children in rural areas (DWCRA).
- Integrated rural development programme (IRDP).
- Prime Minister's Rozgar Yojana (PMRY).
- Training of rural youth for self-employment (TRYSEM) etc.

These institutes and programmes are providing technical guidance to their beneficiaries for self-employment and entrepreneurship development.

2. Establishment Stage

(a) *Linkage with Bank:* Small-scale enterprise development cannot be ensured without arrangement for financing. Adequate and timely supply of credit is essential for new entrepreneurs development.

Financial problems are being solved by National Bank for Agriculture and Rural Development [NABARD] through providing credit facilities to SHG's on the basis of 5 principles of "Development through credit";

- Credit must be used in accordance with the most suitable methods of science and technology.
- The terms and conditions of credit must be fully respected.
- Work must be done with skill so as to increase production and productivity.
- A part of the additional income generated by using credit must be saved.
- Loan installments must be repaid in time and regularly so as to ensure timely recycling of credit.

Banks are lending more freely to women entrepreneurs today. Yet, government has to lend more subsidies to women self-help groups.

(b) *Micro-Entrepreneurship Establishment:* In the present scenario, everywhere the cost of living has increased. Now time is demanding from women to undertake economic activity and utilise her inherent talents to support her family. Now the attitude of the society has also changed and working women is not seen with suspicious eyes like earlier.

Self-help group's women can engage in various traditional and non-traditional income generating activities *e.g.*: value addition of crops, dairying, medicinal plants, nursery, bee keeping, domestic industries like, preservation of locally available fruits and vegetables, papad badi making, masala making, handicrafts, embroidery, quilting, knitting, soft toy making, doll making, pottery, fancy items, candle making, chalk making, agarbatti making, tailoring and garment industry, dari weaving, soap and surf making, beauty parlour, baby crèche centres, etc. Such activity should be started which can be easily accepted by all the group members.

(c) *Explore the Consumers:* One cannot imagine about enterprise without its consumers. The existence and survival of any enterprise depends on consumers. To achieve consumer satisfaction, products must be made available in the right form, on the right time at the right place and in the right manner that would tempt the consumer to obtain their possession. Hence, the purpose of an enterprise in order to exist and survive is to create and keep its consumers. An entrepreneur may have two options before him like either to respond to market demand or create demand. The creation of demand was a purposeful invention of entrepreneur, who had to achieve their goal, *viz.*: profit. Profit on the other hands, is directly related to the satisfaction of consumer wants that are unlimited in nature. Enterprise therefore was recognised as an economic activity to exploit the endless wants and convert this opportunity into profit.

Hence, an entrepreneur should explore and identify the consumers for their produce before production because without knowing the demand and attitude of consumers towards the produce, production is useless.

3. Expansion Stage

(a) *Marketing:* Marketing as a process or a function originated and developed along with human civilization. A market, in general, may be described as a place or geographical area where buyers and sellers meet and function, goods or services are offered for sale and transfers of ownership of title occur. Clark and Clark defines it as "an area in which the forces lending to exchange of title to a particular product operate, and towards which and from which, the actual goods tend to travel. This obviously means that a market is a geographical area and is found where a commodity is concentrated for sale".

Packaging, branding, standardising are some other forms of processes carried on to increase the value and utility of products.

Generally women entrepreneurs will have small-scale business they have to strive hard to sell their products in the modern competitive world. Thus, women entrepreneur should enhance her knowledge and skills regarding marketing strategy. Success of a small-scale enterprise mainly depends on the local and near by market.

(b) *Identification of Problems;* Problems and constraints facing by women entrepreneurs should be identified and enlisted. Group discussion should be made on the existing problems for solution.

(c) *Sort out Problems by Group Dynamics:* Possible solutions and alternates should be identified and enlisted to solve the burning problems. Problem should be sort out by the group decisions. The frequent interaction among the members creates an atmosphere of mutual trust and encourages the members to participate in decision-making. Always keeping in mind the welfare of all the group members.

(d) *Embodies New Ideas and Innovations;* Old practices are always replaced by new ones due to some external or internal factors. However, societies are changing through time constantly by adopting new practices, it is necessary to embodies new ideas, innovations and appropriate technologies in the existing enterprise for its sustainable development. Technological advances in the environment create new needs for the small entrepreneur as far as adaptation and adjustment is concerned. She may need to learn how to adjust to the new technological environment surrounding her, or she may need to take a set of advance technologies and bring these to her own level in the small enterprise. Either way constant re examination is needed for possible utilisation and improvement of existing technologies.

Though a lot has been done to uplift and promote women but benefits are still not reaching to them. The condition of women workers are far from satisfactory and are worsened by their socio-economic heritage. Thus, it is necessary to recognise talent and abilities of women community for development of our national economy.

Problems and Constraints

Women entrepreneurs are facing so many problems at every stage in all over the country. The major ones are:

1. **Emerging Stage**
   (a) *Social Barriers:* In our man dominating society women entrepreneurs are always seen with suspicious eyes, situation in rural areas is too worse.
   (b) *Caste and Religions*: Though India is a secular country, so many castes and religions dominate with one another and it restrict women entrepreneurship.
   (c) *Lack of self-confidence and Risk bearing Capacity:* Women have lack of self-confidence and always feel that they may not be successful and hence hesitate to take risk. Their risk bearing capacity is always less than man.
   (d) *Psychological Factors;* Mostly women feel that she is 'women' and less effective than man. Secondly, Family and home maintenance is her moral duty if she is engaged in work than how can she manage both or play dual role? She has to strive hard to balance her family life with care and hence feels better to be housewife.
   (e) *Lack of Family Support;* Due to some taboos and restriction, which are still prevalent in our society woman is not getting enough support by her husband and family members to undertake any entrepreneurship.
2. **Establishment Stage**
   (a) *Lack of Technical and Practical Knowledge*: Women have lack of technical and practical knowledge, as they mostly live inside the four walls of home. Hence they hesitate to establish her own enterprise.

(b) *Financial Problems:* Women entrepreneurs have lack of property in her name so bank and other financial institution may hesitate to render big amount. Mostly women didn't have knowledge about credit facilities.

(c) *Middle Man Exploitation*: Women entrepreneurs have to face the problem of middleman more, as they generally depend on them. Middleman plays a role of bridge between the entrepreneur and consumer.

3. Expansion Stage

(a) *Marketing Problem:* Market for a small-enterprise in a developing country can be quite a problem considered that the small entrepreneur will be in competition not only with locally mass-produced goods but even imports. Small enterprises must therefore prove that in quality and price of their product they are comparable. Small enterprises can brand together and sell their products as one body through closely-knit associations or organizations. The Government too can take an active part in marketing specific products or assisting small groups of entrepreneurs in selling their products.

Both large and small-enterprises stand to gain if complementarily between them is fostered especially in the marketing aspects of their businesses. A large number of small enterprises manufacture goods for direct sale to a large industry. The Government can promote such complementarily as a strategy for small enterprise development.

Generally women entrepreneur will have lack of marketing skills as compare to man. Sometimes market is far away from their resident so they couldn't directly connected with market, this problem is mostly facing in rural and remote areas.

(b) *Lack of Information*: Women entrepreneurs have lack of information regarding advance and innovative technology. Even they lack of knowledge regarding government policies and subsidy to promote women entrepreneur. Hence, they can't widen their market.

Shri Nirmal Ganguli, Deputy Director Publication Division, New Delhi has stated the following problems of the small scale enterprise in the country:

Constraints related to regular, timely and adequate availability, inadequacy of financial assistance, quality and technology problems, lack of effective marketing back up, encroachment of the areas of reservation, slow progress of ancillary units, concerning of benefits in a number of cases by the larger units within the area of small scale sector as compared to tiny units which constitute the overwhelming majority of the modern small scale industrial sector and problems of sick units.

So far as the view of Mr. B. K. Dixit stated that, the problems of small-scale enterprise may broadly be classified in to internal and external causes. The internal causes are mainly at the unit level due to lack of product management. Some of them are inadequate technical know - how, outdated production process, absolute machinery, high cost of inputs, defective pricing policy, weak market organization, lack of market feedback and market research, poor sales promotional techniques, unimpressive brand and packaging, lack of professionalism, poor industrial relations etc. These problems make the unit gradually sick and turn them economically non-viable.

External problems are those, which are beyond the control of those managing the enterprise. Such causes are infrastructure bottlenecks, non availability of critical raw materials, power shortage, Government controls and policies, procedural delays in sanctioning licenses, natural calamities, wars, sympathetic strikes and so on.

Now it becomes necessary for the society and government to find remedies for the problems of women entrepreneurship. Already the central and state government has taken so many steps to solve the problems, but still these are far from women entrepreneurs.

Remedial Measures and Suggestions

To solve the problems facing by women entrepreneurs, some remedial measures undertaken and suggestions are given below:

1. *Governmental Efforts*: Government agencies, associations of women entrepreneurs and NGO's have carried on so many programmes for development of women entrepreneurship. India has been the pioneer in initiating Entrepreneurship Development Programmes, to identify, select, motivate, train and guide first generation entrepreneurs from all spheres of life. Now-a-day, Programmes for entrepreneurship development are being introduced in school and colleges to provide the impetus for youth seeking self-employment opportunities.
2. *Stress on Women Education*: Government has increased number of opportunities for women education and special programmes have been introduced. Yet it is necessary to increase the number of professional school for women.
3. *Financial Assistance*: Banks, financial institutions are lending more freely to women entrepreneurs today. Yet, Government has to lend more subsidies to women entrepreneurs.
4. *Enhance Practical and Technical Knowledge;* As it is necessary to provide practical and technical knowledge of the business, during their study levels, some schools and colleges are providing such knowledge during the education period. It should be increased and informal education on small-scale entrepreneurship development should also be given.
5. *Market Facilities*: As women entrepreneurs have to face severe marketing problems, they should be taken into consideration by the Government and steps should be taken to solve them. Markets should be developed in rural and semi urban areas so that women entrepreneur can sell them easily in the nearest markets more and more fairs and exhibitions should be arranged for women products.
6. *Infrastructural Development;* The development of transport and communication throughout the country will help for women entrepreneurs to market their products easily.

7. *Self-employment Training Programmes;* As self-employment breeds entrepreneurship, more and more self-employment programmes should be undertaken and proper training should be given to rural and urban youths including women.
8. *Transfer of Technology and Information*: As women entrepreneurs have lack of information as regards to their enterprise, it is necessary to start information bureaus, to help them in getting the required information.
9. *Research and Survey Programmes:* Emphasis should be given to conduct research and survey, to identify the problems and needs of women entrepreneurs. Then steps should be taken to solve the problems of women entrepreneurs.

Yet, the Government at centre and states has organized specific programmes for promoting women entrepreneurship and getting their talent useful to the society. But still, rural women are not getting benefits, due to ignorance and marketing problems. Hence there is an urgent need to popularise these programmes and proper marketing strategy should be planned and implemented, which will provide scope for women entrepreneurs.

SUSTAINABLE DEVELOPMENT OF SHG RURAL WOMEN ENTREPRENEURSHIP

The role of micro-credit is to; improve the socio-economic status of women in households and communities. The micro entrepreneurship is strengthening the women sustainable development and removes the gender inequalities. Self-Help Group's saving are extended as micro-credit to its members to promote the micro and small-scale-enterprises to alleviate poverty and to provide sustainable economic development of the community. Women constitute 90 per cent of total marginal workers of the country Rural women are playing a direct and indirect role both in farm operations and domestic chores. Besides they are capable to manage the livestock activities with their savings and are able to increase the income levels of their families, and community. Now-a-days rural woman are achieving sustainable development by associating with the technical knowhow and are able to cope up with the changing scenario of the production field. By acquiring new skills they are able to setting their own enterprises for their sustainable development and also they are able to develop other women of their villages. Majority of the SHG women of rural areas and urban areas are managing micro enterprises with livestock and domesticated activities because they can be managed with micro finances. Very few are associated with agriculture and its allied activities. It is evident that micro entrepreneurs will have continuous income and can contribute to their sustainable development.

ADVANTAGES OF ENTREPRENEURSHIP AMONG RURAL WOMEN

Empowering women particularly rural women is a challenge. Micro-enterprises in rural area can help to meet these challenges. Micro-enterprises not only enhance national productivity, generate employment but also help to develop economic independence, personal and social capabilities among rural women. Following are some of the personal and social capabilities, which were developed as result of taking up enterprise among rural women.

- Economic empowerment.
- Improved standard of living.
- Self-confidence.
- Enhance awareness.
- Sense of achievement.
- Increased social interaction.
- Engaged in political activities.
- Increased participation level in gram sabha meeting.
- Improvement in leadership qualities.
- Involvement in solving problems related to women and community.
- Decision-making capacity in family and community.

Economic empowerment of women by micro-entrepreneurship led to the empowerment of women in many things such as socio-economic opportunity, property rights, political representation, social equality, personal right, family development, market development, community development and at last the nation development.

AREAS OF MICRO-ENTERPRISE DEVELOPMENT

Depending on number of factors ranging from land-holdings, subsidiary occupations, agro climatic conditions and socio-personal characteristics of the rural women and her family members the areas of micro-enterprises also differ from place to place. The micro enterprises are classified under three major heads:

1. *Micro-Enterprise Development Related to Agriculture and Allied Agricultural Activities:* Like cultivating to organic vegetables, flowers, oil seeds and seed production are some of the areas besides taking up mushroom growing and bee - keeping. Some more areas can be like dehydration of fruits and vegetables, canning or bottling of pickles, chutneys, jams, squashes, dairy and other products that are ready to eat.
2. *Micro-Enterprise Development Related to Livestock Management Activities:* Like dairy farming, poultry farm, livestock feed production and production of vermi composting using the animal waste can be an important area in which women can utilise both her technical skills and raw materials from the farm and livestock to earn substantial income and small scale agro-processing units.
3. *Micro-Enterprise Development Related to Household based Operations*: Like knitting, stitching, weaving, embroidery, bakery and flour milling, petty shops, food preparation and preservation.

SMALL SCALE INDUSTRIAL POLICY SINCE INDEPENDENCE

Industrial Policy Resolution, 1948

Cottage and Small industries have a very important role in the national economy, offering as they do scope for individual, village or co-operative enterprises and means for rehabilitation of displaced persons. These industries are particularly suited for better utilisation of local resources and for the achievement of local self-sufficiency in respect of certain types of essential consumer goods.

Industrial Policy Resolution, 1956

The role of village and small-scale industries in the development of the national economy was stressed once again. The State has been following a policy of supporting cottage as well as village and small scale industries by restricting the volume of production in the large scale sector by differential taxation or by direct subsidies. While such measures will continue to be taken whenever necessary, the aim of state policy will be to ensure that the decentralised sector acquires sufficient vitality to be self-supporting, for its development is integrated with that of large scale industry. The State will, therefore, concentrate on measures designed to improve the competitive strength of small-scale producer.

Industrial Policy, 1977

The essence of the industrial policy 1977 was that the prosperity and distribution of income arising from abroad based growth of agriculture and related activities in rural areas can be achieved only when the basic demand for a wide range of industries producing articles of mass consumption is adequately met. The policy objective was to achieve was to achieve through a process of reinforcing the interaction of agricultural and industrial sectors, employment for larger number of the rural population who cannot be absorbed in the agricultural sector. Considering the vast rural manpower and the reservoir of highly technical personnel, the new industrial policy aims at placing man at the centre of planning and implementation of projects and schemes.

Industrial Policy Resolution, 1980

The emphasis is on fostering the complementarily between the small and large sectors so that the dichotomies between the two sectors do not distort the economic pattern.

An important element is raising of the investment in plant and machinery and have been fixed at Rupees two lakhs for tiny sector instead of Rupees one lakh, Rupees two lakhs for the small scale sector instead of Rupees ten lakhs and Rupees twenty five lakhs instead of Rupees fifteen lakhs for ancillaries. The basic thrust of this policy is to ensure a continuous growth of the small-scale sector without inhibiting the growth of other sectors. In this context, automatic growth for a large number of industries in the medium and large sector has been ensured so that they can grow without hindrance.

Policy Measure, 1991

Over the last few decades, small enterprises emerged as leaders in industrial sector. They also played a more significant role in creating balances for economic and social development in the country. In recognition of their significance and stature, the new government announced Policy Measure on 6th, 1991 for promoting and strengthening of small, tiny and village enterprises. Its objective is:

(i) To impart more vitality and growth impetus to the small scale sector.

(ii) To decentralise and delicense the sector.

(iii) To deregulate and debureaucratise the sector.

(iv) To review all status, regulations and procedures and effect suitable modifications where necessary

(v) To promote small-enterprises especially industries in tiny sector.

(vi) To motivate small and sound entrepreneurs to set up new green enterprises in the country.

STATEMENT OF THE PROBLEM

Women entrepreneurs face special problems and constraints like illiteracy, lack of vital information, fear to take risk, lack of experience and training, feeling of insecurity, etc. In addition, there are structural constraints in the form of inequality, limited purchasing power, condemnation by local elite, etc. The rural women entrepreneurs have also face competition from the urban entrepreneurs who make more attractive and cheaper products due to the use of modern technology, commercial production and marketing networks.

India is a country with the blessing of greater amount of human resource with diverse knowledge and skills. The self-imbibed knowledge and skills of the human community have contributed a lot to the humanity. The efficiency of the human community with its enormous amount of capability and potentiality brought new products into markets to satisfy the needs of people. The changing situation worldwide has created a gap for the small innovative entrepreneurs to fill in with their important contributions to the society. There is an opinion that the human efficiency is ignored specially in rural areas.

There is a common tendency among women entrepreneurs to act in any given situation with a real entrepreneurial attitude. They are capable of organizing and managing with less resource of theirs or through borrowing. The basic qualities of women entrepreneurs are:

(i) Desire to take up new ventures.

(ii) Transforming the desire into a business opportunity.

(iii) Taking moderate risk.

High potential and productivity capacity of the rural women entrepreneurs is to be strengthened by providing soft loan facilities with low rate of interest to help the rural entrepreneurs to promote and expand their business operations from one part of the village to another village. The entrepreneurial skills, if applied effectively will lead to substantial improvement in the economic and social status of the women entrepreneurs. Women entrepreneurship in turn empowers people through the values of equality, participation, accountability and transparency that lead to benefit not only to the concerned entrepreneur but also to the family and the community as a whole through collective action for development.

In order to improve the existing situation of the rural women entrepreneurs engaged in a particular economic activity within a given geographical area, it is of much importance to study the current status in terms of their living condition, financial soundness, social security, selling process, etc. Moreover, it is also essential to work out an integrated strategy to provide them with self-persistence and concern for quality work.

There is an opinion that the human efficiency is ignored specially in rural areas. This study is considered relevant in understanding the socio-economic conditions of the rural women entrepreneurs, their entrepreneurial skills, factors influencing them and the problems which affect the progress of women entrepreneurs and the steps to be taken to face the challenges in the newly emerging scenario.

OBJECTIVES OF THE STUDY

1. To study the profile of rural women entrepreneurship in Tirunelveli district.
2. To study the various schemes available to rural women entrepreneurs and also the institutional support given to them.
3. To analyse the socio-economic conditions of rural women entrepreneurs in the study area.
4. To assess the entrepreneurial skills essential for rural women entrepreneurs.
5. To identify the factors influencing rural women entrepreneurship.
6. To examine the major problems associated with rural women entrepreneurs.
7. To offer suggestions based on the analysis and interpretations of the study.

OPERATIONAL DEFINITIONS

The various operational definitions are given below:

Entrepreneurship

Entrepreneurship is equivalent to enterprise which involves the willingness to assume risks in undertaking an economic activity, particularly a new one. It may involve risk taking, decision-making, although neither risk nor decision-making may be of great significance.

Entrepreneur

The entrepreneur is a person endowed with the qualities of judgment, perseverance and knowledge of the world as well as of business; entrepreneur is treated as employer, master, merchant and undertaker but explicitly identified him with capitalist.

Women Entrepreneur

The Government of India has defined women entrepreneurs based on women participation in equity and employment of a business enterprise. Accordingly, a women entrepreneur is defined as "an enterprise owned and controlled by a women having a minimum financial interest of 51 per cent of the capital and giving atleast 51 per cent of the employment generated in the enterprise to women."

Rural Entrepreneurship

Rural Entrepreneurship can simply be defined as entrepreneurship emerging in rural areas. In other words, establishing industrial units in the rural areas refers to rural entrepreneurship.

REVIEW OF PREVIOUS STUDIES

In India women entrepreneurship started only after the 1970's and it picked up in the late 70's and 80's. This was particularly visible only in the metropolitan and state capitals in India. It took much longer time to percolate to the other cities and towns. Hence, research and publications in India in rural women entrepreneurship are not available. The little that is available is the pioneering work done by certain organizations and institutions engaged in the promotion of entrepreneurship. While much research work has been done on the subject of self-employment and small business ownership from different perspectives, studies on rural women entrepreneurship was not given much thrust. In this section, an attempt has been taken to review the previous studies carried out in relation to women entrepreneurship.

WOMEN ENTREPRENEURSHIP

In most countries, regions and sectors, the majority of business owner/managers are male. However, there is increasing evidence that more and more women are becoming interested in small business ownership and/or actually starting up in business. One consequence of this is that women are a relatively new group of entrepreneurs compared with men, which means that they are more likely to run younger businesses. However, improvements need to be realised in the rural areas where women still lag behind due to the lack of awareness to engage themselves in other activities.

Debal. K. Singharoy and Parava Agarwal (1987) in their study on self-employment for women have emphasised that self-employment are required for the best utilisation of the available but unexploited human resources. He also stressed that the spread of literacy and technical knowledge in rural areas will attract more and more women to self-employment projects and such a situation is bound to bring a sense of pride and dignity in the rural population.

Amitabh Kundu (1996) analysed the trend and found that a more or less stable worker population ratio implies an increase in employment of women at the rate similar to growth of female population. According to the census, employment growth for women was as high as 4.04 per cent per annum during 1981-91.

Kumar D. (2004) in his article says that global evidences suggest that women have been performing exceedingly well in different spheres of activities like academics, politics, administration, social work and so on. Now they have started plunging into industry and also running enterprises successfully.

Archana Sinha (2004) talks about women's participation and she amply reveals that women constitute half of our population and play a vital role in the development of the family, the community and the nation. It has been widely recognised that unless women's potential is properly developed, no transformation and economic development is possible. Therefore, to accelerate the growth of the nation, it is very important to create opportunities for socio-economic development of women in rural India.

Revathy K. (2004) analysis a study on economic development of women and reveals the fact that women's empowerment and their full participation on the basis of equality in all spheres of society are fundamental for the achievement of equality, development and peace.

Ganapathi R. and Sannasi. S (2008) says that it is imperative to note the participation of women in economic activities as self-employed individuals. Many of the traditional occupations open to women were mainly based on creed and the nature of self-employment was based on the standard of living. The country needs to mobilise and utilise fully all its resources including human resources. It is essential even for the objective of raising the status of women which is now accepted as an indicator of a society's stage of development.

SOCIO-ECONOMIC PROFILE OF WOMEN ENTREPRENEURS

Rural women increasingly run their own enterprises, yet their socio-economic contributions and entrepreneurial potential remain largely unrecognised and untapped. They are concentrated in informal, micro-size, low productivity and low-return activities. Enabling and gender responsive policies, services and business environments are crucial to stimulate the start up and upgrading of women's businesses and thereby help them to generate decent and productive work, achieve gender equality, reduce poverty and ensure stronger economies and societies.

Sharma (1965) considered increased investment of human capital especially education, a source for successful and good entrepreneurs who were aware of their social responsibilities.

Bhatia (1974) came out with a conclusion that people from various castes and occupation participated in manufacturing and succeeded in it. Capital and experience in trading were reported to have accounted for their transition and success.

Rani (1978) found that women had additional income. Some women considered it as a career oriented and innovative; some were not very highly educated or well to do women entrepreneurs considered it as a source of revenue. Some women considered entrepreneurship as a hobby and ventilator for their psychological independence.

Desphande (1982) observed that the political system was responsible for dormancy of entrepreneurship. Financial help from family and father's occupational status were significantly related to entry. Industrial entrepreneurship was a result of collective ambitions and aspirations of the family.

Archana and Rehana (1985) noted that women in typical careers have acted as high as men in the same careers, while women who belonged to traditionally feminine professions scored low. The most important reason for low need for achievement among women is fear of success.

Hadiman (1985) realised that castes with traditions of manufacturing cloths either failed or remained static, while castes with entrepreneurial traditions succeeded in becoming entrepreneur.

Subbi and Shobha Reddi (1985) stated that the reasons for their high success are they are at the age of 50 years, having technical education from agricultural background, having investment more than ten lakhs of rupees, having previous experience in service and employing limited company type of ownership.

Mathur and Anamika (1987) found that men and women do not differ significantly with regard to innovative trait and internal control. They also found that women are in no way inferior to men in terms of intelligence, foresight, curiosity and healthy sense of self.

Nandi (1973) observed that while some necessary traits of good entrepreneur were generally found in all regions and cultures, some other traits varied from region to region and culture to culture in their importance.

Annadurai, *et al.* (1991) pointed out that 47 per cent of the rural people had shown interest in developing new skills or improving their skill status, more than that significantly about 30 per cent of them had shown their interest in becoming entrepreneurs. Majority of the rural people who fell in 18-30 years of age group and those who engaged in non-agricultural activities and business were found to be interested in becoming entrepreneurs.

Rani (1992) mentioned that there is a significant association among economic status and the time spent towards managing the enterprise as well as on training. The high and middle income groups received a better training compared to low-income group.

Sharma and Singh (1994) revealed that education, social participation, farm mechanisation and socio-economic status of marginal farmers were significantly correlated with the level of knowledge and extent of adoption as well. The farm mechanisation and socio-economic status were unequally the key determinants of farm entrepreneurship.

Patel (1995) indicated that the farmers with high entrepreneurial behaviour adopted new practices in agriculture and related fields. The farmers with high entrepreneurial behaviour adopted new practices in agriculture and related field earlier than farmers with low entrepreneurial behaviour.

Nanda (1999) conducted impact studies of Self-Help Groups and found that the outstanding impact of the linkage programme could be the socio-economic empowerment of the poor more particularly the women.

Sameer Gupta *et al*. (1999) identified that the reason for lack of entrepreneurship in the State of Jammu and Kashmir is lack of proper entrepreneurial education and training at graduate level. They observed that there is a close relationship between behavioural rigidity and entrepreneurial bent.

Sekhar (1999) identified that the youth in general are choosing or emulating wrong examples in their lives. The mass media whose influence on social behaviour is quite significant should be prevailed upon to increase their focus on developmental issues and social concerns related to human resources development. Non-Governmental Organizations must train the youth, employ them and ensure that there is differentiation of occupations.

Kamar Jahan *et al.* (2000) found out that the women entrepreneurs in Tamil engaged in three important activities namely manufacturing, trade, commerce and services. The manufacturing include food-based, cloth-based, etc. The trade and commerce include retail trade in food items, fruits, vegetables, flowers, etc. The services include community, social and personal repair services like beauty parlour, tailoring, money lending and pawn broking, etc.

Neelaveni, *et al.* (2000) found that the age as a significantly and negatively associated variable with developmental priorities. As age increases, their energy declines and hence their attention in management of activities in agribusiness declines. This might be the possible reason for the above trend. As mass media consumption and extension contact increase, their exposure to new technology in agribusiness management increases thereby their attention in management of activities of agribusiness similarly increased.

Sarwade *et al.* (2000) found that the rural entrepreneurs started their enterprises as a part time activity in small villages while it is a main business in the large villages. The fathers of the most rural entrepreneurs were businessmen and they are engaged in the same line of business or allied line of business. Majority of the rural entrepreneurs purchase their materials once in a month. The major problem of the rural entrepreneur is credit sale because the demand characteristics for a product are closely connected with agricultural income.

Vibha Sinha (2000) revealed that the hand of women burning to entrepreneurship has been growing many-fold in the region. Most of the women who entered this were first generation women entrepreneurs who joined this field primarily to remain busy and fulfill ambition. Women have shown to have high single-mindedness of purpose to achieve perfection in quality of their products and services and establish their business well.

Surapa Raju (2000) revealed that the pull category of women entrepreneur is younger than the push category. Most of the pull category women are upper caste and in push category most of them are BCs and SCs. The average monthly incomes of pull and push entrepreneurs are increased before and after starting the enterprises 4.0 and 1.2 times respectively. The percentage contribution of push entrepreneur's income is nearly 69 per cent whereas in the case of pull category it is only 34 per cent.

Thangamani and Umapriya (2001) identified that 56 per cent women obtained a profit of ₹ 500 and below 34 per cent of women gained ₹ 501 to ₹ 1,000/- Only 10 per cent of women had a profit of ₹ 1,001 to ₹ 1,500. In total 88 per cent of the women expressed that they had gained profit of ₹ 500/- and below. It was found out that sixty two per cent utilised the profit for the expansion of business by investing more on the purchase of raw-materials whereas 24 per cent women utilised for the family expenditure and 14 per cent utilising the profit for the education of their children.

Gayatridevi Patil and Uma Gaurmath (2002) found that an educated women would be in a better position to collect, interpret utilise and relate information in day to day life. Though their participation in social institutions was very low, their indirect participation either as a member or office bearer might have contributed to gain knowledge. Mass media are important sources of information. Women who were exposed to mass media gained better knowledge.

Kalyani and Chandralekha (2002) observed that the socio-economic and demographic characteristics have a significant impact on the involvement of women entrepreneurs particularly when it comes to enterprise management. Many of them do receive help from their family members in carrying out various kind of work.

Manimekalai (2002) mentioned that the significant correlation between women's education and their role in decision-making are identified in the area of child care, respondent's education, recreation, dress and family savings. Similarly, there is significant correlation between women's contribution to household income and their role in decision-making regarding child care, respondent's education, recreation, dress and family savings.

Nomesh Kumar and Narayanasamy (2002) identified that the farmers who adopted sustainable agriculture had high entrepreneurial behaviour like innovativeness, decision-making ability, achievement motivation, risk taking ability, information seeking ability, co-ordinating ability and leadership ability. Because of this, high entrepreneurial behaviour farmers adopted sustainable agriculture practices.

Raveendran, *et al*. (2002) revealed that the dummy variable of state was significant to determine annual savings of the group. Age of the groups in months had an interesting influence on the savings of the group and it influenced negatively. The significantly influencing variable on the annual savings of the SHG are annual loan disbursement, age of the group and average annual saving.

Ajit Singh, *et al*. (2003) found that the participation of rural youth is highest in terms of vegetable growing/kitchen gardening, growing of fruit plants, growing of ornamental plants, fodder chaff cutting and feeding and watering the animals. The participation of rural youth is high in agricultural and social activities. The important reason for their active participation is to enrich their knowledge and keeps them as healthy.

Mythili (2003) concluded that the successful women entrepreneurs become inspiration to others. They can become big industrialists and participate in global economy. They can help the charity trust and patronise them. The social inequalities are mitigated by keeping a good relationship with the surroundings. The economic prosperity that they are going to bring out is from the socialistic pattern of society.

Rajesham C.H and Raghava .D(2003) concluded that the promotion entrepreneurship for women will require even greater reversal of traditional attitudes than the mere creation of jobs for women. This means that we should first wait for society. But it implies that the programme should go beyond subsidies and credit allocation to attitudinal range, group formation, training and other support services but also practical application of the academic knowledge regarding management like marketing and finance of a business enterprise.

Manipal (2004) in his article 'Social Development of Rural Women in India' discusses the social development status of women particularly in terms of their general health and nutrition, sex ratio, education and physical quality because the aspects of their development and capacity building are reproductive actors in Indian society and economy.

ENTREPRENEURIAL SKILLS AND MOTIVATING FACTORS

The society of women is the foundation of good manners; of course a pre-requisite to achieve brilliant results especially for success in business. The increasing trend developed among the women to be self-employed suggests that time is not far away when women factor would also have an important role in the economic growth of the country. Possessing the natural gift of politeness, women entrepreneurs, and if provided the level ground, are expected to bring new milestones to this country. Women entrepreneurs in the developing world make a large and often unrecognised contribution to their countries' economic development. They employ other people, provide valuable services, and play a vital role in the development of emerging market economies worldwide. In the developing economies women entrepreneurs is a diverse group ranging from those who manage large conglomerates to those who operate roadside restaurants.

Characteristics reflected in research of women entrepreneurs show a woman who is highly motivated, initiates action and activity without direction has a high internal focus of control, and propensity toward achievement. Women's decision processes indicate a highly personal, subjective process. Studies reveal that there are multiple general individual characteristics of women business owners that promote their creativity and generate new ideas and ways of doing things.

It is quite well known that women have certain natural skills that are beneficial to companies they work for. Some of these include: *(i)* ability to organize, *(ii)* risk taker, *(iii)* innovative, *(iv)* being team leader, *(v)* being empathetic, *(vi)* thoughtful, *(vii)* supportive, *(viii)* loyal, *(ix)* consensus building and *(x)* compassionate. These are the skills that any leader should possess.

According to Marshall (1949) the factors influencing entrepreneurship are ready to take venture, undertake its risks, bring together the capital and the labour required, arrange or engineer its general plan and superintendent its minor details.

Knight (1957) pointed out that the entrepreneurship involves three factors, ability, willingness and power to give such guarantees. According to him, the entrepreneur is the economic functionary who undertakes responsibility as by its very nature cannot be insured, non-capitalised and non-salaried.

Sharma (1970) stated that people with higher level of motivation work harder, learn faster and are more self-reliant. They manipulate environment to suit their own needs. They have high aspirations and are very mobile when considering economic opportunities. These people are oriented towards saving and investing for the future. They are like to be entrepreneur, risk takers and innovators with desire to excel personal accomplishment.

Rao (1983) stated that most of entrepreneur started their enterprises on their own initiative and were motivated by their familiarity with the industry and expectation of high profits which guided them in choosing the line of manufacture.

Khan (1985) concluded that in the long run, economic growth is more likely to be determined by motivation, attitudes and skills of local entrepreneurs than by any other support factors.

Govindappa *et al*. (1996) inferred that better economic background, previous experience, conductive government policy and availability of infrastructure facilities were the important factors for growth and development of entrepreneurship in rice milling industry.

Aravindha and Renuka (2002) revealed the important factors which motivated the women towards entrepreneurship are self-interest and inspiration. The identified facilitating factors are self-experience, interest, family's help and support. The main conflicts in work role pertained to inability to expand the enterprise and optimum utilisation of available skills non-availability of time to spend with family and being a good spouse were the conflict areas faced in the performance of the home role.

Rachana and Anjali (2002) concluded the achievement value along with entrepreneurial success is the most essential predictor variables in predicting entrepreneurial success. The study has identified some psychological and socio-cultural variables that are highly correlated with entrepreneurial success. The significant positive correlation is identified between the basis of profit with individualism and achievement value whereas negative correlation is indentified with collectivism and the focus of control.

Dil Bagh Kaur, *et al.* (2003) concluded that besides providing technical and financial assistance, it is essential to educate rural women and to extend entrepreneurial management and marketing skills also, to enhance their confidence and competence so that they would become self-reliant.

Poonam Sinha (2003) concluded that there are several factors for the emergence of women entrepreneurship in the north east such as family background, motivating and facilitating factors, ambition, attitudes of family/society, etc. Women of the region have enough potential to take up entrepreneurship as a career. There is a strong need of support to be given by the organization working for promotion of entrepreneurship in general and women entrepreneurship in particular. Determined efforts from women entrepreneurs supported by congenial climate can bring about substantial results. This can also bring positive change and develop the region. Socio-economically women entrepreneurship can go a long way in speeding up industrialisation of rural areas and small towns.

Archana Sood (2004) in her study concludes that women empowerment particularly as applicable to rural women has a much greater positive influence in factors governing sustainable development. Women play a direct and exclusive role in child and family care, general health and sanitation, agriculture, articulture, forestry, animal husbandry, food, fuel and water.

ENTREPRENEURIAL PROBLEMS

Barriers, some real, some perceived and some self-imposed, confront women entrepreneurs. In the area of international business obstacles include limited business experience, inadequate education and lack of access to international networks. Societal, cultural and religious attitudes also impede women in business. Other challenges faced by all enterprises and women in particular are; financing, globalisation of social and economic environments, marketing, and management. Transition economies can pose difficult hurdles such as banking, legal aspects, political contacts, customs tariffs, bureaucracy that daily invents new mechanisms for the simplest procedures, and extortion.

Kaplan S.S. (1990) mentioned the plight of women workers over the years has staggered from bad to worse with social conditions continuing to be conservative, exploitative and anti-women in character.

Murty and Purnachandra Rao (1990) mentioned the issues in small business sector are in three dimensions namely: *(i)* financing, *(ii)* accounting and *(iii)* behavioural. The financing issues includes the provisions of capital access to credit facilities, non-availability of capital from any dependable outsider source, self-financing and credit through public banking whereas the accounting issues are related with score-keeping activity of every financial decision or transactions. The behavioural dimension focus on lack of access to resources and exploitation by large business units, group solidarity, flexibility, etc.

Wagh (1997) found the dual responsibility of women was one of the major constraints for women entrepreneur as they had to look after their families as well as enterprises. Lack of motivation from family, society and less social contact also affected the development of women entrepreneurs.

Neelam Yadav, *et al*. (1998) mentioned the lack of security, maternity and medical leave facilities, job guarantee, cuts in wages if absent from job, seasonal nature of employment, long hours of work were major constraints. Limited mobility in women is the greatest handicap of female labour. The self-employed women suffer from lack of finances, a fixed place for business and a stable market for their products.

Lalitha Rani (2000) identified the two major problems faced by the women entrepreneurs are dual career and wrong evaluation of the product by the customers. Securing financial aid, marketing have also been listed as other issues which posed a problem for the women entrepreneurs. The social barriers like comments by husbands, relatives and criticism by the immediate society are the societal barriers for women entrepreneurs.

Shailendra Singh and Saxena (2000) revealed that the women entrepreneurs operate in an environment characterised by a relatively traditional culture, low economic opportunity and low spatial accessibility. Added to that, their personal characteristics and social factors also pose challenges. These include shyness, lack of achievement, lack of motivation, low risks-taking, low educational level, unsupportive family environment being a woman, lack of information, and experience and problem of liquidity and finance.

Sivaloganathan (2000) identified the problems faced by women entrepreneurs in India are inequality, family background, low wages, inadequate training, Government policies, exploitation of middlemen, problem of finance scarcity of raw materials, stiff-competition, high cost of production, low mobility, social attitudes, low ability to bear risk, lack of education, low need for achievement, project related problems, family ties, shortage of power, inadequate infrastructure facilities and socio-economic constraints.

Ajantha Borgohain Raj Kowar (2001) found the entrepreneurs taking up industry form of entrepreneurship in large number. The highest number of entrepreneurship under the group of activities allied to Agriculture is in Poultry farming and lowest in Dairy. Under the group of activities allied to industry, the highest number of entrepreneurship is in knitting and embroidery and the lowest is in crusher plant and phenyl manufacturing. The main problems faced in the development of rural entrepreneurship are illiteracy of the people and inadequate infrastructure facilities.

Shilla Nangu (2001) identified the general problems faced by the micro-enterprises (SMEs) are low demand for SMEs goods and services, lack of tools and equipment for production, uses of outdated technology and lack of credit facilities. The results show that there is great gap between the non-financial services required by SMEs and the actual services received or given.

Archana Sinha (2002) in her study stated that, in India, women constitute a sizeable section of rural work force. The realisation of women's full potential is crucial to the overall socio-economic development and growth of a society. However, this realisation will require a real revolution in people's attitudes and behaviour. It will be a revolution that place gender at the heart of policy-making and planning in all areas of development and that will awaken the full awareness among the people. With regard to their multi-dimensional responsibilities, it is required to strengthen the status of rural women economically to enable them to stand in society on their own with confidence.

Dil Bagh Kaur, *et al*. (2003) observed that much of the enterprising spirit is being dampened by the social factors prevailing in rural society. Some common factors identified in rural Tamil Nadu are prevailing conventional customs, norms of modesty, norms of male dependents, illiteracy, lack of knowledge and inadequate information in de-motivating to start their own new venture.

Vasumathi, *et al*. (2003) highlights two important matters. *First*, small entrepreneurs are affected by stress caused by achievement and affiliated need related stressors. Power-need related stressors were not significant to affect them. *Second*, entrepreneurs adopt silent, less-expensive, tradition bound stress reduction strategies in preference to other types of copying styles.

Ponnarasu. S (2004) attempts to touch upon certain aspects of women and explained that the holistic concept of development should perceive women as an integral part of development. He highlights that we need to realise that women is issues cannot be compartmentalised and isolated as secondary issues in development as the feature of development and society lies in the future of women, of course, equally with men.

Gandhan Siva Ramakrishna, *et al*. (2007) made a comprehensive study and observed that the future development of society lies in the status of women. One reality is that women of the society not only form a major section of the society but also hold greater responsibilities than men. Hence, it is the women who matters because if one woman is empowered through education, health and information then the whole family recognise these benefits spread over the world. Thus, the empowerment of women is a part of human resource department and cannot be treated independently.

Kanka S.S. (2007) stated that the women entrepreneurs face two types of problems *one*, general problems faced by all entrepreneurs such as finance, scarcity of raw materials, stiff competition, etc., and *second*, problems specific to women are male dominating society, family ties, lack of need achievement, education, risk bearing abilities, etc.

The above said reviews show the clear-cut picture of the relationship between profile of entrepreneurs and their involvement and performance in enterprising. Apart from that, it provides more information on the skills and constraints faced by the entrepreneurs. Even though there are so many studies related to entrepreneurs, only few studies are focusing women entrepreneurs. So that, the present study focus on various aspects of rural women entrepreneurs, their skills and also the problems encountered by them.

SCOPE OF THE STUDY

In order to improve the existing situation of the rural women entrepreneurs engaged in a particular economic activity within a given geographical area, it is of much importance to study the current status in terms of their the socio economic conditions of rural women entrepreneurs and the steps to be taken to face the challenges in the newly emerging scenario. Moreover, it is also essential to work out the skills which provide them with self-persistence and concern for quality work. The entrepreneurship is generally understood as a pursuit of opportunity without limiting oneself to the accepted norms of an organization. The forces which motivate a person to start an enterprise need to be examined. In addition to this, the present study also examines the various skills necessary for the entrepreneurs to perform entrepreneurial activities in a desirable manner. While performing entrepreneurial activities, the factors which influence the entrepreneurs will be assessed to know its influence. The study also focuses the problems faced by the rural women entrepreneurs.

METHODOLOGY

The methodology adopted in the present study was described through the choice of study area, the collection of data, the sampling technique adopted, the period of study, hypothesis and the tools of analysis.

Choice of the Study Area

The Tirunelveli district was purposively selected as study area by the researcher for the following reasons:

- There were no recent exclusive studies about the rural women entrepreneurship in Tirunelveli district.
- Familiarity to the culture, local dialect and infrastructural facilities available would help the researcher to develop good rapport with the respondents and hence, the better and valid responses could be received.

- Development of women entrepreneurship is increasing nowadays and the number of rural areas is more in Tirunelveli district.

Sampling Procedure

The study is based on proportionate random sampling. The sample size of 300 women entrepreneurs were selected giving representation to all the nineteen blocks of the area under study. The list of entrepreneurs maintained by the District Industries Centre, Entrepreneurial Development Centre and the traders association were used to identify the rural entrepreneurs.

Table 1.1: Block-wise Distribution of Rural Women Entrepreneurs

S. No.	Name of the Block	Rural Population	No. of Women Entrepreneurs
1.	Manur	113283	785
2.	Palayamkottai	130652	2257
3.	Sankarankoil	89171	657
4.	Meelaneellithanallur	84755	322
5.	Kuruvilulam	94891	391
6.	Tenkasi	84526	742
7.	Alangulam	94700	746
8.	Keelapavur	111559	659
9.	Vasudevanallur	62535	649
10.	Senkottai	52752	625
11.	Ambasamudram	66888	645
12.	Cheranmahadevi	47579	889
13.	Pappakudi	55947	946
14.	Kadayanallur	62604	641
15.	Kadayam	84596	645
16.	Nanguneri	86899	492
17.	Kalakadu	44160	679
18.	Valliyoor	95331	1285
19.	Radhapuram	89407	1041
	District average	**1552235**	**15096**

Source: Census of India 2011.

Collection of Data

The present study was based on primary as well as secondary data. Interview schedule was used to collect the primary data from the sample respondents. For this, a pilot study was made and with that response, final interview schedule was prepared to collect the information required for the study. With a view to identify the rural women entrepreneurs, the researcher has made an in-depth review of the previous studies undertaken related to the topic of the present study. Further, the researcher had preliminary discussions with the officials of the District Industries Centre and a few well informed women entrepreneurs registered in the District Industries Centre, Entrepreneurial Development Centre, Other associations, etc. In the light of information gathered, the researcher had prepared the interview schedule and had also identified twenty factors which had influenced the growth of women entrepreneurs.

The secondary data were collected from the published as well as unpublished reports, handbooks, action plans and pamphlets from the office of the Director of Industries and Commerce, various books, journals, magazines, websites, etc.

Period of the Study

The study was conducted during the period 2010-12. The primary data were collected from Jan 2011 to June 2011 to find out number of women entrepreneurs and their location in the district and the remaining period was utilised to study the nature, skills, factors motivating and the problems faced by them.

Hypotheses

- The sources of inspiration of rural women entrepreneurs are independent of socio-economic variables.
- The level of entrepreneurial skills of rural women entrepreneurs is independent of their socio economic variables such as age, educational qualification, occupation, income and experience.

- There is no significant difference among the mean scores of entrepreneurial skills and different dimensions of various skills of women entrepreneurs with respect to the social variables such as educational qualification, marital status, nature of family, family occupation, respondent's occupation and years of experience.
- The level of problems of women entrepreneurs is independent of their socio-economic variables such as educational qualification, occupation, income and the years of experience.
- There is no significant difference among the mean scores of problems in total and in different dimensions of various problems of women entrepreneurs with respect to socio-economic variables such as age, educational qualification, marital status, nature of family, family occupation, respondent's occupation and years of experience.

Tools of Analysis

The collected data were analysed properly with the help of proper tools for the effectiveness of this study. The tools employed are percentage analysis, ANOVA, Chi-square test, Co-efficient of Variation, 't' Test for one sample (variable), 't' Test for Independent Sample, Factor Analysis, Scheffe's Test, etc.

Chi-Square Test

Chi-square test was applied to test the effect of various Socio-Economic factors such as educational qualification, occupation of family, occupation of respondents, and family monthly income and level of sources of information to become an entrepreneur, socio-economic factors and level of entrepreneurial skills, and socio-economic factors and problems faced by the entrepreneurs.

χ^2 is useful to establish and measure the existence of the association between any two attributes. This χ^2 takes only positive value and is given by the formula:

$$\chi^2_{(r-1,\, c-1)} = \sum_{i-j} \frac{(O_{ij} - E_{ij})^2}{E_{ij}}$$

Where

O_{ij} – Observed value in the ijth cell.

E_{ij} – Expected value in the (ij)th cell.

R = number of rows in the contingency table.

C = number of columns in the contingency table.

On the assumption of independence of attributes,

$$E_{ij} = \frac{(A_i)(B_j)}{N}$$

Where

A_i = total of ith row.

B_j = Total of jth column.

N = Total number of observations.

If $\chi^2_{(calc)} < \chi^2_{(5\%)}$ for (r-1)(c-1) degrees of freedom, then it is accepted that the two attributes A and B are independent or there is insignificant association between them at 5 per cent level. But if $\chi^2_{(calc)} > \chi^2_{(5\%)}$ then it is accepted. There is significant association between them at 5 per cent level.

Factor Analysis

Factor analysis is a technique by which a data set is analysed by creating one or more factors, each representing a cluster of interrelated variables within a data set. The concentration variables are converted to logarithms and R-mode factor analysis was performed, which involved a comparison of the relations among variables in terms of samples.

Co-efficient of Variation

The arithmetic mean was found out by adding the individual scores for all the respondents for each variable and the sum was calculated by the number of respondents. The standard deviation was only the square root of ratio between the sum of squares of deviation and the number of observation.

$$\text{Co-efficient of variation} = \frac{\sigma}{\bar{X}} \times 100$$

Where

σ = Standard deviation.

$\bar{x}$ = Arithmetic mean.

't' Test for one Sample (Variable)

$$t = \frac{\bar{X} - \mu}{\left(\frac{\sigma}{\sqrt{n}}\right)}$$

Where

$\bar{x}$ = Arithmetic mean.

σ = Standard deviation.

μ = Neutral value.

n = Number of sample.

't' Test for Independent Sample

$$t = \frac{\left|\bar{X}_1 - \bar{X}_2\right|}{\sqrt{\frac{\sigma_1^2}{n_1} + \frac{\sigma_2^2}{n_2}}}$$

Where

$\bar{x}_1$ = Mean of the first group.

$\bar{x}_2$ = Mean of the second group.

σ_1 = standard deviation of the first group.

σ_2 = standard deviation of the second group.

n_1 = Number of sample in the first group.

n_2 = Number of sample in the second group.

Analysis of Variance

Analysis of Variance (ANOVA) is a mathematical technique for partitioning the total variation of a set of data in such a manner that it identifies the component sources of variation. This technique enables the researcher to test the hypothesis concerning the equality of more than two population means. The objective of the analysis of variance is to locate important independent variables in a study and to determine how they interact and affect the response. ANOVA test is used to test whether there is any significant difference in the level of entrepreneurial skills of the respondents and the socio and economic factors.

$$F = \frac{\text{Mean Squares (Between)}}{\text{Mean Squares (Within)}}$$

Scheffe's Test

Whenever 'F' ratio is found to be significant for the means scores, Scheffe's test is followed as a post-hoc test to determine which of the paired mean differences is significant.

$$\text{CI (Confidential Interval)} = \sqrt{(k-1)F_{table}} \times \sqrt{MSW_{value} \times \left(\frac{1}{n_1} + \frac{1}{n_2}\right)}$$

Where

k = Number of groups.

F_{table} = Table value of F-ratio.

MSW_{value} = Mean of Squares (Within) value.

n_1 = no. of sample in the first group.

n_2 = no. of sample in the second group.

LIMITATIONS OF THE STUDY

The present study was based mainly on the information given by the sample rural women entrepreneurs. The sample respondents were not having any proper records. Hence, the extent of the reliability of the financial data provided by rural women entrepreneurs may be subjected to personal bias.

REFERENCES

1. Kanka. S.S, "Entrepreneurial Development", Sultan Chand and Sons, New Delhi, 1996, p. 19.
2. Verma. S.B, "Entrepreneurship and Employment", Deep and Deep Publications Pvt Ltd., New Delhi, 2005, p. 37,38.
3. Vasant Desai, "Entrepreneurial Development: Principles, Programmes and Policies", Himalaya Publishing House, 1991, Vol. 1, pp. 42.
4. Sathiabama. K, "Rural Women Empowerment and Entrepreneurship Development", Research papers, Rural Institute, Dindigul, April 2010.

5. Kanka S.S., "Entrepreneurial Development", Sultan Chand and Sons, New Delhi, 1996, p. 18.
6. Debal K. Singharoy and Parava Agarwal (1987), "Self-Employment for Rural Women", *Yojana* 33, 24-26.
7. Amitabh Kundu, "Trends and Pattern of Female Employment: A Case of Organized Informalisation", Gender and Employment, Vikas Publishing House, New Delhi.
8. Kumar D., "Status of Women in India", Kisan World, Vol. 31, No. 1, Jan 2004, p. 26.
9. Archana Sinha, "Rural Women in Dynamics of Agriculture and Food Security", *Kurukshetra*, Vol. 52, No. 9, July 2004, p. 10.
10. Revathy K. (2004), Economic Empowerment of Women", Kisan World, Vol. 43, No. 8, p. 32.
11. Ganapathi R. and Sannasi. S, "Women Entrepreneurship – The Road Ahead", *Southern Economist*, Jan 15, 2008, p. 36.
12. Sharma S.P., "The emergence of Industrial Entrepreneur: A Sociological Process", *Indian Journal of Commerce*, 18(65), December, 1965, pp. 369-373.
13. Bhatia. B.S, "New Industrial Entrepreneur: Their Argues and Problems", *Journal of General Management*, 2(1), August 1974, pp. 69-70.
14. Rani. C, "Potential Women Entrepreneurship – A Study", *Sedme* Vol. XII, No. 3, 1978.
15. Desphande. M.V, *Entrepreneurship for Small Industries*, Deep and Deep Publications, New Delhi, 1982.
16. Archana. T.K. and Rehana. G, "Achievement, Motivation and Job Satisfaction", *Productivity*, 24(3), 1985, pp. 231-287.
17. Hadiman, "*Dynamics of Industrial Entrepreneur*", Asish Publishing House, New Delhi, 1985, p. 155.
18. Subbi and Shobha Reddi (1985), " Successful Entrepreneurship – A Study", *Productivity*, 26(1), 1985, pp. 21-27.
19. Mathur. P and Anamika, "Difference of Personality Traits among Male and Female Successful Entrepreneurs" Paper presented at the 29th Annual Conference of Indian Academy of Applied Psychology, Walatin, March 2-25, 1987.
20. Nandi Asish, "Entrepreneurial Cultures and Entrepreneurial Men", *Economic and Political Weekly*, 8(47), November 1973, pp. 98-106.

21. Annadurai. M, Dil Bagh Kaur and Sharma. V. K, "Rural Entrepreneurship: A Study among Rural People in Tamil Nadu", *Ashigam*, 15(122), 1994, pp. 53-62.
22. Rani. C, "Potential Women Entrepreneurs" in Kalbagh, (ed.), *Women in Enterprise and Profession*, Discovery Publishing House.
23. Sharma. R.C and Singh. A.K, "Determination of Entrepreneurship in Agriculture", *Productivity*, 35(3), October-December 1994, pp. 536-539.
24. Patel. M.M, "Role of Entrepreneurship in Agricultural Development", *Kurushetra*, 43(1), 1995, pp. 41-44.
25. Nanda Y.C., " Linking banks and Self-Help Groups in India and Non-Governmental Organization: Lesson Learned and Future Prospects", *National Bank News Review*, 15(3), 1999, pp. 1-9.
26. Sameer Gupta and Neeru Rohmetra, "Behavioural Rigidity and Entrepreneurial Justifications of Potential Entrepreneurs", *Indian Management*, 38(11), November 1999, pp. 37-39.
27. Sekhar K., "Indian Rural Youth Some Issues", *Kurushetra*, 47(7), April, 1999, pp. 36-41.
28. Kamar Jahan. K and Veerasekaran. R, "Women Entrepreneurs in Urban Informal Sector", *Rural India*, October 2000, pp. 199-201.
29. Neelaveni S., Rambabu. P and Venkataramaiah. P, "An Analysis of the Developmental Priorities of Farm Women in Agribusiness Management (ABM)", *The Andhra Agriculture Journal*, 47 (3 and 4), 2000, pp. 245-248.
30. Sarwade W.K. and Balasheb Ambedkar, "Retail Trade Structure in Rural Area", *Indian Journal of Marketing*, Vol. 30 (8-10), August-October 2000, pp. 26-36.
31. Vibha Sinha, "Emerging Socio-Psychological Profile of Successful of Women Entrepreneurs – A Case of Jammu and Kashmir", *Sedme*, 27(2), June 2000, pp. 29-40.
32. Surapa Raju S., "Pull *vs.* Push Women", *Indian Economic Panorama*, 10(3), October 2000, pp. 40-45.
33. Thangamani. K and Umapriya. V, "Impact of Micro-Enterprises Undertaken by Women Beneficiaries of Loan Fund Scheme of Avinas Nomesh Kumar. N and Narayana Swamy. B. K., "Entrepreneurial Behaviour of Farmers Adopting Sustainable

Agriculture in India", *Mysore Journal of Agriculture,* 36(1), January-March 2002, pp. 87-90. Hilingam Trust", *Journal of Extension Education,* 12(1), January-March, 2001, pp. 3048-3055.

34. Gayatridevi Patil and Uma Gaurmath ," Rural Development Programmes: A Study of Women Beneficiaries", 32(4), October-December 2002, pp. 87-94.
35. Kalyani W. and Chandralekha K., "Association between Socio-economic Demographic Profile and Involvement of Women Entrepreneurs in the Enterprise Management", *The Journal of Entrepreneurship,* 11(2), 2002, pp. 219-245.
36. Manimekalai N., "A Comparative Study of Working Women and Housewives", *Social Welfare,* 49(5), August 2002, pp. 29-38.
37. Raveendran. N, Snehalatha Mathew, Ajjan. Nroups in Tamil Nadu and Kerala", *Indian Journal of Training and Development,* 32(3), July September, 2002, pp. 133-137.
38. Ajith Singh, Amandip Kaur and Anjana Kabra, "Participation of Rural Youth in Agricultural and Allied Activities", *Rural India,* 66(9), September 2003.
39. Mythili S., "Women Entrepreneurs: A New Social Order", *HRD Times,* 5(8) 2003, pp. 14-16.
40. Rajesham C.H. and Raghava D., "Emerging in Women Entrepreneurs in India – Some Observations", *Indian Journal of Marketing,* pp. 22 and 25.
41. Manipal "Social Development of Rural Women in India", *Kurukshetra,* Vol. 52, No. 9, July 2004.
42. Marshall. A, *Principles of Economics,* 8th Edition, McMillan Co, New York, 1949.
43. Knight H.F., *Risk Uncertainty and Profit,* 8th Edition, Impression Heighten Mifflin Co., New York, 1957.
44. Sharma K.N., "A Study of Entrepreneurs in Kanpur City", *Research Cell Bulletin,* A. No. 4, 1970.
45. Rao, "Entrepreneurship Development among Technical Personnel: A Few Observations", *Sedme,* 10(3), September 1983, pp. 33-36.
46. Khan. R. R, Entrepreneurial Management School of Management Studies, Paramakudi Taluk.
47. Govindappa G. T, Manojkumar and Halasagi. S, "Entrepreneurship in Agro-processing Industry – A Case Study", *National Bank News Review,* 12(4), January-March, 1996, pp. 26-34.

48. Aravindha and Renuka, "Women Entrepreneurs – An Exploratory Study", *Public Opnion,* 47(5), Feburary 2002, pp. 27,28.
49. Rachana Chattopadhyay and Anjali Ghosh, "Predicting Entrepreneurial Success: A Socio-Psychological Study", *The Journal of Entrepreneurship,* 11(1), January-June 2002, pp. 21-31.
50. Dil Bagh Kaur, Annadurai. M. and Sharma V. K., "Rural Women Entrepreneur", *Abhigyan,* 20(4), January-March 2003, pp. 27-31.
51. Poonam Sinha, "Women Entrepreneurship in the North East Indian Motivation, Social Support and Constraints", *Indian Journal of Industrial Relations,* Vol. 38, No. 8, April 2003.
52. Archan Sood (April 2004), "Sustainable Rural Development – Focuses in Women", *Kurushetra,* Vol. 52, No. 6, pp. 30.
53. Kaplan S.S., "The Income, Wages and Working Conditions of Women Worker in Unorganized Sector", *Social Welfare,* 36(2), 1990, pp. 29-35.
54. Murthy M.S.G.K. and Purnachandra Rao R., "Business Sector, Entrepreneurship and Economic Development – A Policy Framework", *Indian Economic Panorama* 9(2), July 1999, pp. 26-28.
55. Wagh S.P., "Entrepreneurs Club: A Movement of New Industrial World", *Sedme,* 24(4), December 1997, pp. 55-59.
56. Neelam Yadav, Saroj Kashyap and Asha Rani, "Working Women and their Constraints – A Comparative Study", *Indian Journal of Social Research,* 39(1), January-March 1998, pp. 41-51.
57. Lalitha Rani, "Enterprise Development: Employment Avenues for Women", *Monthly Public Opnion Survey,* 45(12), September 2000, pp. 26-27.
58. Shailendra Singh and Saxena. S.C, "Women Entrepreneurs of Eastern U.P – Challenges and Strategies of Empowerment", *Indian Journal of Industrial Relations,* 36(10), July 2000, pp. 67-77.
59. Sivaloganathan. K, "Women Trepreneur: Problems and Prospects", *Indian Economic Panorama,* 12(2), July 2002, pp. 40-41.
60. Ajantha Borgohain Raj Kowar, "A Study on Development of Rural Entrepreneurship with Reference to the Dibrugarh District of Assam", *Finance India,* 15(1), March 2001, pp. 195-200.

61. Shilla Nangu and Chawla. A.\S, "The Non-financial Services Required by Small and Micro-Enterprises (SMEs)", *Indian Management Studies,* 5(2), October 2001, pp. 53-69.

62. Archana Sinha, "Types of SHGs and their Work", *Social Welfare,* February 2002, p. 14.

63. Dil Bagh Kaur, Annadurai. M and Sharma. V.K, "Rural Women Entrepreneurs: A Study in Rural Tamil Nadu", *Abhigyan,* 20(4), January-March 2003, pp. 27-31.

64. Vasumathi. A, Govindarajalu S., Anuradha. E.K and Amutha. R, "Stress and Coping Styles of an Entrepreneur: An Empirical Study", *Journal of Management Research,* 33(1), April 2003, pp. 43-50.

65. Ponnarasu S. (Dec 2004), "Women Empowerment: A Success in Twenty First Century", *Kisan World,* Vol. 31, No. 12, p. 13.

66. Kanka S.S., *"Entrepreneurial Development"*, S. Chand Publications, New Delhi, 2007.

2

Promotional Assistance to Rural Women Entrepreneurs

In rural areas, there are very few employment opportunities; moreover, work as casual and seasonal labourers in agriculture or construction may not be an option for women. For those with little or no land, engage in non-farming activities, such as marketing, processing, and other micro-enterprises. Self-employment in small-scale businesses presents a constructive option for income generation. In many developing countries, a high percentage of small-scale businesses that cater to local needs are controlled or owned by women. Women's enterprises tend to be relatively small, have informal structures, flexibility, low capital needs, modest educational requirements, high labour intensity, and depend on local raw materials. They are also characterised by their dependence on family labour and limited technical and managerial skills. Commonly, these enterprises are not registered, maintain no business records and do not have access to credit from formal credit institutions.

CHALLENGES FOR A WOMEN ENTREPRENEUR

Finance is the lifeblood of any enterprise and in absence of adequate financial aid, it becomes invariably impossible for any business to sustain. Women entrepreneurs are believed to stiffer a lot in raising and meeting the financial needs of their businesses. Adding to their woos, bankers, creditors and financial institutes are also never too much willing to provide financial assistance to women borrowers. They cite their lack of credit worthiness and business acumen as the main reason for their unwillingness.

Though a number of credit schemes are available for women, low awareness about these available schemes impedes many women in realising their dream of becoming an entrepreneur. Another major concern is that of banks providing only a minor relief in terms of interest rate. The other terms and conditions of the schemes happen to be similar to consumer loans. Also, the higher the loan amount, the more difficult it is to get loans. Bank officials often get skeptical when a woman comes asking for a loan of a higher amount to start a business. It also becomes a challenging task for a woman to convince a bank official about her business plan and that she would not default on the loan granted by the bank.

Women entrepreneurs have had tasted adequate amount of success in carving a niche for themselves. Nevertheless, the myth that financing a woman run business is a big risk still persists. They are still under the notion that women entrepreneurs can never handle pressure as great as men and this would eventually mean only failure. It is only when people come out of this myth will woman entrepreneurs thrive and they would be able to contribute to the economic development of the country and come with par with that of their male counterparts.

WOMEN NEED GRANTS

Women need grants because despite their business and career success, they are still disadvantaged – and have been for hundreds of years. Though they make up roughly 51 per cent of the world population, women are still a minority and face many related issues. Women are underserved and overlooked and suffer continuously from unfair practices such as gender discrimination, gender underestimation and even gender harassment.

Women grants, especially business grants for women, give them the upper hand to fight back, and prevail. This type of assistance enables them to recover from an unfair and unjust system that has existed for a long-time. The concept is very similar to affirmative action initiatives that help other minority groups.

Business grants help women either start or expand an existing home business or non-profit organization. Education grants help women pay for college – tuition, books, and even dorms. These types of opportunities make up the thousands of federal, state, and private grants for women that are designed to give them the tools and funding they need to be successful.

SCHEMES AVAILABLE TO RURAL WOMEN ENTREPRENEURS

National Level Poverty Alleviation Programmes

Recognising the fact that the development strategies aimed at industrialisation, infrastructure development and intensive agriculture had not impacted on the lowest three decibels of the Indian population, the Government of India made a concerted effort at alleviating poverty by formulating a variety of programmes spanning the gamut of wage employment to self-employment, during the 1970s and 1980s. These programmes were intended to benefit the poorest strata of society and many were targeted specifically at women.

These programmes could be classified as follows:

- Programmes to promote self-employment through subsidised credit, such as Integrated Rural Development Programme (IRDP), Scheme for self-employment of educated unemployment youth (SEEUY), and Self-Employment Programme for the Urban Poor (SEPUP). More recent thrift and credit initiatives are the Rashtriya Manila Kosh, Mahila Samriddhi Yojana (MSY).
- Programmes for self-employment targeted towards women such as Support to Employment Programmes for Women (STEP), Development of Women and Children in Rural Areas (DWCRA), and Indira Mahila Yojana.

- Programmes for group formation and training in productive skills, such as Mahila Mandals Programmes, Women's Development Programme (WDP) of the Government of Rajasthan, Training of Rural Youth for Self-Employment (TRYSEM), and Vocational Training Programme for Women'.
- Employment Schemes, such as Employment Guarantee Scheme (EGS) of the Government of Maharashtra, National Rural Employment Programme (NREP) and Rural Landless Employment Guarantee Programme (RLEGP), now amalgamated into the Jawahar Rozgar Yojana <JKY).
- Integrated development programmes, such as the Integrated Women's Employment and Development Project, Haryana.

Some of these programmes have been profiled below.

Support to Training-cum-Employment Programmes for Women (STEP)

In the Seventh Plan, Rs. 450 million was provided for the STEP programme under the Department of Women and Child Development and Ministry of Human Resources Development.

The Scheme was launched in 1987, aims to upgrade the skills of poor and assetless women, mobilise, provide training and subsequently employment on a sustainable basis in traditional sector of agriculture, small animal husbandary, fisheries, handlooms, handicrafts, khadi and village Industries, sericulture, social forestry, wasteland development etc. In addition to the training and employment support, the programme advocates gender sensitisation, Women in Development (WID) inputs and provision of support services.

There is flexibility of project design in the different sectors. Each project is suited to local and sectoral needs. Working capital for maintenance of productive assets is provided for supplementary activities leading to increased production. Old and new marketing channels are explored, For each project, 90 per cent assistance on a grant basis is provided by this Department and 10 per cent by the implementing agencies for a period ranging from one to four years, depending upon the activities to be undertaken. Projects extending beyond 1996 were not be considered.

STEP had the potential to reach the poorest of women and, through the involvement of NGOs, women in backward areas could be reached in greater numbers, Since inception of the programme, 29, projects benefiting 1,52 lakh women have been launched in the states of Bihar, Gujrat, Haryana, Kerela, Karnatka, Rajasthan, Tamil Nadu, Uttar Pradesh and West Bengal. So far women in dairy business have been receiving the maximum benefit under the programme, followed by handlooms, handicrafts and sericulture.

Integrated Rural Development Programme (IRDP)

The Integrated Rural Development Programme (IRDP) was launched on 20th October, 1980, as a major credit linked self-employment programme for poverty alleviation. The objective of the programme is to identify rural poor families, to augment their income and to enable them to cross the poverty line through acquisition of employment on a sustainable basis. Assistance is given in the form of subsidy by the Government and credit advances by financial institutions (such as commercial banks, co-operatives and regional rural banks), for income generating activities in the rural areas. The target group consists of small and marginal farmers, agricultural labourers and rural artisans having annual income below Rs. 11,000 per annum defined as a poverty line over the Eighth Plan. Further, to ensure better participation of women in the development process, it has been specified that at least 40 per cent of those assisted should be women.

Development of Women and Children in Rural areas (DWCRA)

DWCRA, a sub-component of IRDP, was launched as a pilot project in 1982-83 in 50 selected districts throughout the country. The objective of the programme is to "organize women in socio-economic activity growps with the dual objective of strengthening them" (Seventh Plan Document). This programme is collaborative effort of the Central Government, State Government and UNICEF.

Groups of 15-20 women are formed and a grant of Rs. 15,000 given to them as a revolving fund for purchase of raw materials, marketing, childcare, etc., Multi-purpose community centres are constructed for the women to carry out their economic activities. DWCRA also aims to increase these women's access to other government programmes and welfare services.

DWCRA is now in operation in 497 districts of the country with UNICEF still continuing to provide financial support. During 1994-95, 26,137 groups with a membership of 3.89 lakh women were formed to take up economic activities. DWACRA projects have been assisted by Council for Advancement of People's Action and Rural Technology (CAPART).

CAPART is a government organization and provides financial assistance as grants to NGOs in various fields. Funds under different Ministeries for different projects are appraised and routed through CAPART for NGO Funding. An amount of Rs. 300 lakh was given to CAPART for initiation of DWCRA projects by voluntary organizations. 1,316 DWCRA projects have been assisted by CAPART.

DWCRA has, however, come in for criticism from several quarters. Some aspects that have been criticized include:

- Inability of the programme to form viable, functioning, participatory groups, in part due to the large group size recommended and IRDP criteria followed for membership.
- Target orientation of DWCRA functionaries, often leading to notional groups on paper only whereby members come together only to avail of the revolving fund and loan facilities.

Training of Rural Youth for Self-Employment (TRYSEM)

TRYSEM is a supporting component of the IRDP. The main objective of this scheme is to equip rural youth with the necessary technical and entrepreneurial skills through a training institution or a master craftsman, so as to enable them to take up income generating activities. Out of the total number of beneficiaries under the scheme, at least 40 per cent should be women, To enable the participants to take up employment, a suitable tool kit costing not more than Rs. 800 is also provided. The scheme aimed at training about two lakh rural youth in the country every year in various skills. Training of rural women is also given due consideration under this scheme. A minimum of 33 per cent youth trainees are supposed to be women. In addition to this, TRYSEM also strengthens training institutions in each state for skills training of rural women-Monitoring and coordination of the scheme is done at the state level by Rural Development Departments; at the District level by the District Rural Development Agencies, and at the Block, by the Block Development Agencies.

While TRYSEM provides an opportunity for rural women to upgrade their skills, it has been criticized for lack of follow-up, stereotyped training, and lack of backward and forward linkages. If skills training were given in conjunction with other support like credit, raw material procurement, WED, marketing, business management etc., TRYSEM would be more successful. Although recent figures and gender break-down under TRYSEM are not available, at the end of the Sixth Plan it was found that only 49 per cent of TRYSEM trainees had been able to establish themselves in self-employment activities. Since its inception, *i.e.* 15th August, 1979, about 32.44 lakhs (up to Nov. 94) youths had been already trained under the scheme, out of which 14.29 lakhs (about 44%) are reported to be self-employed after the training. It is also heartening to note that about 44 per cent out of the total are women.

Socio-Economic Programme (SEP)

The Central Social Welfare Board had started the Socio-Economic Programme in 1958. Under this programme, financial assistance is extended to voluntary organizations to undertake a wide variety of income-generating activities providing opportunities for 'Work and Wage' to needy women like widows, destitute and disabled particularly those coming from economically backward and under-developed areas. The programme supports the setting up of industrial units, hand-looms and handicrafts units, dairy emits, and other allied economic activities like piggeries, sheep and goat-rearing, poultry, etc. A recent thrust of the programme is on identifying new sectors for income generating projects.

Rashtriya Mahila Kosh (RMK)

Rashtriya Mahila Kosh was set up as a registered society in March 1993. RMK is intended to meet the credit needs of poor women particularly in the informal sector, It is being managed by a governing board which has approved the policies and procedures for lending to women borrowers through the intermediation of NGOs and other women's organizations, like co-operative societies, women development corporations, etc., for which suitable eligibility criteria, such, as lending and credit management experience, and sound financial management have been prescribed.

According to the 1995 report of Department of Women and Child Development, an amount of Rs. 31 crores was released to the RMK during 1992-93 as the corpus fund. Credit up to Rs. 2,500 in the case of short-term loans, and Rs. 5,000 in case of long-term loans will be extended to borrowers through the medium of non-governmental organizations and other eligible organizations. The credit will be provided at 8 per cent interest per annum to these intermediary organizations, which in turn will lend to women borrowers at 12 per cent per annum.

Mahila Samriddhi Yojana (MSY)

In pursuance of Government's policy of empowering women by raising their socio-economic status, an innovative scheme of Mahila Samriddhi Yojna was launched on 2nd October, 1993. The scheme aims to promote self-reliance and a measure of economic independence among rural women by encouraging thrift.

Under the scheme, every adult rural woman is encouraged to have an account in the post office under the jurisdiction of her village. The Scheme has received a very enthusiastic response from both rural and tribal women, including from those living in the remote areas of the country, as reported by Department of Women and Child Welfare, New Delhi.

Indira Mahila Yojana (IMY)

Indira Mahila Yojna (IMY), launched on 20 August 1995, is a strategy to co-ordinate and integrate components of all sectoral programmes and facilitate their convergence to empower women. It proposes to bring out a mechanism by which there could, be a systematic co-ordination amongst various programmes, in a meaningful integration of various streams of funds available under different schemes to meet women's needs and at the same time ensuring that women's interests are taken care of under such scheme.

The major objectives of IMY include:

- To help women become self-reliant and independent by their economic empowerment through income generation activities and active participation in decision-making at various stages.
- To optimise the utilisation of scarce resources in speeding up the process of mainstreaming women in development programmes and issues of specific concern to women.
- To ensure convergence of sectoral services at the local, block and district levels through active involvement of women and sectoral departments.
- To create awareness in women through provision of information on different developmental programmes and issues of specific concern to women.

Vocational Training Programmes for Women

The major objective of the programme is to provide a wide range of training opportunities for women at the training institutes set up under the scheme. The training is extended in a three tier system *viz.;* basic skills, advanced skills and instructors' training in selected trades which has high employment potential. At present there is one National Vocational Training Institute (NVTI) at New Delhi and 10 regional institutes for women at Bombay, Bangalore, Trivandrum, Hissar, Calcutta, Tura, Allahabad, Vadodara, Indore and Jaipur. Part time and short-term courses are also organized by these training institutes based on the needs of the local industries. To keep pace with the changing technological environment, the training activities are being diversified to include training in new non-conventional areas like architectural draftsmanship, desk top publishing, food preservation, catering, beauty care, etc. These programmes are also regularly upgraded and updated as per the latest requirements the industries.

Prime Minister's Rozgar Yojana (PMRY)

The scheme launched in 1993 has been designed to provide employment to more than one million persons by setting up 7 lakh mico-enterprises during the Eighth Five-Year Plan through industry, services and business routes. Educated unemployed youth (as per the laid down criteria), within the age group of 18-35 years, are eligible for a bank loan, as well as a subsidy from government^ to set up enterprises under this scheme. Preference is given to weaker sections, including women. Projects up to Rs. 1 lakh are covered under the scheme in the case of individuals; if two or more eligible persons join together in partnership, a project with a higher cost is also covered, provided each person's share in the project is Rs. 1 lakh or less. To avail of this scheme, entrepreneurs are required to contribute 5 per cent of the project cost in the form of cash. No collateral is required to avail loan under the scheme. The subsidy is provided by the government at 15 per cent of the project cost, subject to a Ceiling of Rs. 75,000 per entrepreneur.

Assistance to Women Co-operatives

This is a scheme of central government and it gives 100 per cent financial assistance for organization and development of co-operatives which are exclusively run by women. The financial assistance is provided to the women co-operative societies through the state government. This is provided in the form of share capital amounting to Rs. 40,000 and a managerial subsidy of Rs. 20,000.

Science and Technology projects for Women

This scheme was introduced during the Sixth Plan by the Department of Science and Technology. The broad objective of the scheme is to reduce day-to-day drudgery of women through the introduction of a science and technology component. The projects taken up under the scheme seek to provide opportunities for gainful employment for women, especially those in rural areas; reduce the drudgery in their lives; improve environmental conditions and protect women from occupational hazards. The programme mainly caters for rural women belonging to less privileged groups. The annual budget of the programme is Rs. 1 crore.

Employment and Income Generating Training -cum-Production Units for Women

This scheme was started in 1982 by the Department of Women and Child Development in collaboration with the Norwegian Agency for International Development (NORAD). The main aim of the scheme is to extend training and employment opportunities for women in non-traditional and upcoming trades. It is urban slums, school drop outs, weaker sections, war widows and widows of employees of the public; joint and private enterprises.

National Commission for Women (NCW)

Under the Department of Women and Child Development, this statutory body called National Commission for Women was set up in 1992. The specific mandate of the Commission is to study and monitor all matters relating to the constitutional and legal safeguards provided for women; review the existing legislation and suggest amendments wherever necessary, and look into complaints involving deprivation of the rights of women, Similar commissions have been set up in the states of Assam, Maharashtra, Orissa, Punjab, Tamil Nadu, Tripura and West Bengal.

Employment and Income Generating Training -cum-Production Units for Women

This scheme was started in 1982 by the Department of women and Child Development in collaboration with the Norwegian Agency for International Development (NORAD). The main aim of the scheme is to extend training and employment opportunities for women in non-traditional and upcoming trades. It is aimed at poor rural women, women of urban slums, school dropouts, weaker sections, war widows and widows of employees of the public, joint and private enterprises.

The scheme is implemented through public sector undertakings, corporations, autonomous bodies and voluntary organizations. Trades in which women are trained include electronics, watch manufacturing/assembly, computers and computer programming, printing and binding, handlooms, weaving and spinning, garment making, etc.

Trade Related Entrepreneurship Assistance and Development for Women (TREAD)

In 1995, an inter-agency programme formulation mission led by the Government of India and comprising the Internationa] Trade Centre (ITC), UNDP and ILO, was undertaken in preparation for the proposed TREAD programme. The draft project proposal resulting from this mission is now available and the programme is slated to be launched shortly as a three-year programme reaching 100,000 women entrepreneurs in Delhi, Madhya Pradesh, Karnataka, Gujarat, Kerala and Assam.

The programme is intended to improve institutional capacities, provide trade information, guidance, counselling and follow-up with a view to creating a tailor-made package for selected product and market development activities and extension activities, to transfer marketable designs and production know – how together with marketing skills, packaging inputs and tie-ups with marketing organizations.

The planned client group comprises women at various levels of entrepreneurial development in rural and urban areas, with a specific focus on poor women in rural areas and urban slums (through the development of group level entrepreneurship), educated established entrepreneurs and new entrants or emerging entrepreneurs.

The programme will be implemented nationally by the Ministry of Industries, Government of India. An inter-agency task force comprising ITC, ILO, UNDP and representatives from selected national organizations (NSIC, NIESBUD, NISIET, Department of Women and Child Development), women entrepreneurs, co-operatives and selected NGOs, will assist the Government in monitoring and coordinating the programme.

Women's Development Corporations (WDCs)

This scheme was sanctioned by the Government of India in 1986-87 for setting the pace for self-employment among women and to mainstream them into the development process. The aim of these corporations is to provide technical, managerial, marketing and financial information for the weaker sections of women so that they can generate a sustained income for themselves. While all women belonging to the weaker sections of society are eligible for benefits which fall within the purview of the Corporation, priority is given to single women.

This scheme proposed the establishment of Women's Development Corporations in all states and union territories. Training imparted is to be through existing institutions, such as women's polytechnics and ITI's.

The main functions of the Corporations are:

(i) To identify women entrepreneurs.

(ii) To provide project formulation and technical consultancy services.

(iii) To promote marketing through co-ordination with the state marketing organizations.

(iv) To arrange training for the beneficiaries through existing institutions.

(iv) To promote and strengthen women's co-operatives and other institutions.

(v) To facilitate the availability of credit through banks and other financial institutions.

The Department of Women and Child Development contributed 49 per cent of the paid-up capital as financial assistance, while the State Government provided 51 per cent to set up corporations. In 1992-93, as per the decision of the National Development Council, the scheme was transferred to the State Sector. However, a provision of Rs. 5.14 crore was made for the year 1993-94 to liquidate the balance of the Central Government's equity share capital contribution as against the State Government's share capital released up to March 31, 1992.

Women's Development Corporations have been set up in several states (*viz.;* Kerala, Karnataka, Andhra Pradesh, Punjab, Haryana, Tamil Nadu, Goa, Himachal Pradesh, Jammu and Kashmir, Meghalaya, Orissa, Maharashtra, Gujarat, Madhya Pradesh, Uttar Pradesh, West Bengal and Manipur) and one union territory (Chandigarh).

An analysis of different state-level organizations established for women's development clearly reveals that the overall objective of such organizations is almost the same, but the specific objectives vary, both in terms of content and focus. Even the statutory standing of the corporations is not uniform.

While there is very limited data on the performance of the WDCs, qualitative data available from a World Bank study noted that:

- The Punjab, Maharashtra, Kerala and Tamil Nadu WDCs are reported to be functioning successfully.
- There is no fixed format for state-level reporting of WDCs which has led to a paucity of information regarding the same.
- The Andhra Pradesh WDC had assisted about 95,000 women and disbursed about Rs. 31 million as 20 per cent margin money, between 1975-76 and June 1987. However, it was reported that recovery of dues was poor: estimated at 25 per cent of dues in 1983-84, and less than 11 per cent in the three subsequent years.

- The Tamil Nadu WDC has had better results, with banks expressing satisfaction over women's repayment performance.
- The Punjab and Maharashtra corporations took the initiative of bringing together voluntary organizations and financial institutions to match grassroots organizations with sources of funds. They have also helped in establishing marketing facilities for voluntary agencies and small-scale women entrepreneurs.
- The National Commission for Self-Employed Women and Women in the Informal Sector, however, reports that the WDCs in most states are not satisfactorily reaching out to poor women and helping them to develop their productivity or income, although the WDCs have a better potential to do so than the State Welfare Departments.

Apart from the programmes detailed above, various ministries and departments have evolved different schemes which seek to promote entrepreneurship amongst women.

For instance, the Ministry of Agriculture, the Ministry of Labour, the Ministry of Social Welfare, and the Central Social Welfare Board have their own programmes which provide avenues of self-employment to needy women. Under the socio-economic programmes of the Central Social Welfare Board, many needy women have been able to acquire sewing machines, knitting machines, handlooms and other such equipment which they can use in their own homes for earning an income.

The *All India Handicrafts Board* conducts training programmes, assists in setting up training-cum-production centres, and gives guidance in marketing and designs, In organizing a variety of village industries, such as matchbox making, hand-made paper, pottery, fiber, bamboo and cane work, fruit processing and food preservation, the Khadi and Village Industries Commission has been able to reach large numbers of women.

INSTITUTIONS THAT PROVIDE ASSISTANCE TO WOMEN ENTREPRENEURS

There is a variety of specialised organizations which provide different types of support to women involved in economic activities. A few such institutions are profiled below:

Small Industries Development Organization (SIDO)

The government agency mainly concerned with training programmes for women, and promotion of employment and self-employment is the Small Industries Development Organization (SIDO) and its drain of Small Industries Service Institutes (SISI) spread all over the country.

Thus, the Small Industry Development Organization as a whole, acts as a policy formulating, coordinating and monitoring agency for the development of small-scale industries at the national level. It provides a wide range of extension services through its network of 27 Small Industry Service Institutes (SISIs), 37 SISI Extension Centres, 4 Regional Testing Centres, 19 Field Testing Stations, 3 Product-cum-Process Development Centres, 2 Central Footwear Training Centres, 2 Central Rooms, 1 Central Institute of Hand Tools and 4 Production Centres.

The Small Industries Service Institutes conduct training programmes for women entrepreneurs and actively assist women in setting up their own enterprises. SISI is also popular amongst women entrepreneurs for its continuing education programmes on small enterprise management.

During 1978-90 SIDO with its national network of 27 SISIs, conducted EDPs through which about 13,000 potential women entrepreneurs benefitted. These EDPs were a near-complete adaptation of the SIET Integrated model, with additional facilities for providing skills training.

To encourage entrepreneurs, SIDO has instituted national awards for outstanding SSI entrepreneurs. Women entrepreneurs get special consideration by adding 5 per cent mean weightage by virtue of their being women. SIDO is also responsible for executing schemes for providing self-employment to educated unemployed youth (both men and women), between the ages of 18-35 years. Under these schemes, eligible youth can get a composite loan for establishing industry, service and small business.

In order to meet the increasing need for counselling, and also to coordinate with various development agencies and state governments regarding the particular problems faced by women entrepreneurs, SIDO has recently established a 'Women's Entrepreneurial Cell' headed by a woman.

Others

Besides SIDO, a few national level organizations are also involved in promoting entrepreneurship in general though not specific to promotion and development of women entrepreneurship. These organizations are:

- National Science and Technology Entrepreneurship Development Board (NSTEDB).
- Department of Science and Technology (DST).
- National Research Development Corporation (NRDC).

The activities of SIDO are divided into three categories as follows:

(a) Coordination activities of SIDO

1. To coordinate various programmes and policies of various state governments pertaining to small industries.
2. To maintain relation with central industry ministry, planning commission, state level industries ministry and financial institutions.
3. Implement and coordinate in the development of industrial estates.

(b) Industrial development activities of SIDO

1. Develop import substitutions for components and products based on the data available for various volumes-wise and value-wise imports.
2. To give essential support and guidance for the development of ancillary units.

3. To provide guidance to SSI units in terms of costing market competition and to encourage them to participate in the government stores and purchase tenders.
4. To recommend the central government for reserving certain items to produce at SSI level only.

(c) Management activities of SIDO

1. To provide training, development and consultancy services to SSI to develop their competitive strength.
2. To provide marketing assistance to various SSI units.
3. To assist SSI units in selection of plant and machinery, location, layout design and appropriate process.
4. To help them get updated various information related to the small-scale industries activities.

Schemes Available Through Banks

Apart from credit facilities offered to women through special schemes, banks also hold entrepreneurship development training programmes with a special focus on the rural population and women as client groups. SIDBI, for Instance, out of a 102 EDPs held in 1994-95, held 66 of these exclusively for rural entrepreneurs; 30 were for women and 8 for other groups in the north-east and other backward areas?

Some of the bank-sponsored schemes are dealt with below. Unfortunately, information on performance aspects of these schemes is not readily available, even in the Annual Reports of individual banks, with the exception of SIDBI and NABARD.

Small Industries Development Bank of India (SIDBI)

For ensuring larger flow of financial and non-financial assistance to the small-scale-sector, the government of India set up the Small Industries Development Bank of India (SIDBI) under Special Act of Parliament in 1989 as a wholly owned subsidiary of the IDBI. The SIDBI has taken over the outstanding portfolio of the IDBI relating to the small-scale-sector.

1. *Schemes of Assistance for Women Entrepreneurs:* The objectives of the scheme for assistance to women entrepreneurs operated through SIDBI, are:
   (i) to provide training and extension services support to women entrepreneurs according to their skills and socio-economic status;
   (ii) to extend financial assistance on concessional terms to enable them to set up industrial units in the small scale sector.

At the institutional level, SCs, SIDCs, commercial banks, state co-operative banks and regional rural banks are eligible for support. This apart, all projects in the SSI sector promoted and managed by women entrepreneurs, including those in the cottage, village and tiny sector industries, are eligible.

The programmes for training, consultancy support and extension services for women entrepreneurs are organized through designated agencies, such as Technical Consultancy Organizations, the Entrepreneurship Development Institute of India, Central/State Social Welfare Boards, KVIC or other recognised training and management institutes.

Under the special re-finance schemes meant for women entrepreneurs, SIDBI extended assistance of Rs. 16.8 crore to 1,021 entrepreneurs in 1994-95. The average assistance per project was 1.6 lakh, which is reflective of the fact that the scheme was taken advantage of by women entrepreneurs taking up small projects in the tiny sector.

2. *Mahila Udyam Nidhi Scheme:* The main aim of the Manila Udyam Nidhi Scheme is to provide equity-type assistance to women entrepreneurs setting up new industrial projects in the small-scale-sector.

Eligible institutions were originally SFCs and IDCs. However, in 1994-95, public sector banks, private sector banks and urban co-operative banks were also made eligible for assistance under the scheme.

All new industrial projects in the small-scale sector, as well as service activities set up by women entrepreneurs which are eligible for finance as per SSI norms, are eligible for assistance under the scheme, provided the cost of the project does not exceed Rs. 10 lakhs.

Assistance is provided in the form of seed capital as a soft loan to meet the gap in equity, after taking into account the promoter's contribution to the project. No security or collateral needs to be provided by the borrowers for soft seed capital. The repayment period is 10 years, including moratorium up to 5 years. The anticipated debt-equity ratio is 3:1.

Projects eligible for assistance under this scheme would also be eligible for term loan assistance, with interest rates and repayment period in congruence with the 'Women Entrepreneur's Scheme'.

Daring 1994-95, 22 voluntary organizations were extended assistance of about Rs. 64 lakh for setting up training-cum-production centres in pottery, jute processing/ products, bee-keeping, cane and bamboo crafting, tailoring, block printing, book binding, file making, seri-culture related activities, ready-made garments, gem cutting, etc., in the states of Assam, Gujarat, Kerala, Manipur, Tamil Nadu, Uttar Pradesh and West Bengal. The assistance sanctioned under the scheme is expected to benefit about 3,000 women.

3. *Informal Lending:* Responding to the reality that a vast segment of the rural poor remain outside the reach of the institutional system, and recognising the need for creating and strengthening self-help groups (SHGs) of the poor, SIDBI has started extending support to voluntary organizations with a good *track* record which are working with special target groups in rural areas. A scheme of savings-cum-credit has been formulated and put into operation in 1994-95.

Through this scheme, the poor are encouraged to take up income generating activities and develop the savings habit. SIDBI extends revolving fund type of support to self-managed voluntary organizations. These voluntary organizations in turn lend to the poor or alternatively place funds with well organized self-help groups for on-lending to their needy members.

Assistance carries interest of 9 per cent per annum. Voluntary organizations are required to charge interest at a rate not more than 12 per cent (although this can go up to 15 per cent with the approval of the Governing Body) to the self-help groups.

During the year 1994-95, assistance of Rs. 94 lakh was extended to 16 voluntary organizations in the states of Andhra Pradesh, Assam, Bihar, Gujarat, Kerala, Maharashtra, Manipur, Orissa, Rajasthan, Tamil Nadu and West Bengal and having a total membership of 8,000 women.

Industrial Finance Corporation of India (IFCI)

(i) *Interest Subsidy for Women Entrepreneurs:* The main objective of this scheme is to provide incentives to women having business acumen and entrepreneurial traits, so that avenues of self-development and self-employment are created for them and they can contribute to the industrial development of the country.

Subject to eligibility criteria, all industrial projects whether in the rural, cottage, tiny or small-scale (Including ancillary) sectors (with a project cost up to Rs. 10 lakhs), if set up by a woman entrepreneur on her own with a minimum financial stake of 51 per cent in the unit, will be covered under the scheme. The scheme is operated through the State Financial Corporations (SFCs/State-level financial institutions performing the role of SFCs/banks) granting assistance to women entrepreneurs.

To be eligible for availing the subsidy under the scheme, a woman entrepreneur is required to fulfil a set of specified criteria.

The disbursement of the subsidy is made by IFCI upon receiving an application for interest subsidy under he Scheme from the woman entrepreneur concerned with due recommendations and certificates from tire SFC/Bank, as may be required. The actual disbursement of the subsidy is made to the SFC/Bank which acknowledges the amount and certifies that this has been utilised for setting off the interest on the loan amount granted to the unit.

National Bank for Agriculture and Rural Development (NABARD)

(i) *NABARD's 'Women's Cell':* NABARD has set up a 'women's cell' at its head office and nodal branches in each regional office so as to pay focused attention to policies pertaining to rural women. In 1993-94, the cell initiated the following measures as part of its overall strategy:

- Introduced *an* exclusive scheme of Assistance *to Rural* Women in the Non-Farm Sector (ARWIND) to meet the credit and support needs of rural women with umbrella support from voluntary agencies, NGOs, WDCs, co-operatives etc.
- Under the project, associated itself with the implementation of the Danish-aided project of the Government of India related to training packages for women's development, gender sensitisation programmes for district level functionaries and middle and senior level functionaries of banks are being held by the Government of India.
- Sanctioned 6 programmes exclusively for the development of rural women which included assistance for conducting training in catering and credit, sensitisation meetings for officers of NABARD and other banking institutions, and production of two video films on rural women. A total of 28 promotional programmes in the nature of training-cum-production centres, rural entrepreneurship development programmes, etc., were sanctioned exclusively for women in 1993-94.

(ii) *Self-Help Groups:* NABARD also launched a pilot project on self-help groups in collaboration with commercial banks, regional rural banks and co-operative banks. As on March 31, 1994, 620 groups had been linked with banks and loan amounts of Rs. 84.20 lakh and refinance of Rs. 45.93 lakh had been extended. Out of these 620 groups, as many as 332 groups were exclusively women.

Quick studies in three states indicated that the intervention led to use of credit for non-traditional economic activities, development of thrift and self-help among members, reduction in transaction cost for both banks and members of self-help groups, better recovery of loans, effective use of credit for purchase of income-generating assets, as well as empowerment of women. Further larger participation in the project was that of women, particularly from poor resource regions.

In addition to the above, refinance facilities are available through the National Bank for financing under the non-farm sector term/composite loans.

(Hi) Scheme covered under Automatic Refinance Facility (ARF): The following are the loan and financial facilities provided under ARF for various projects:

- Financing for setting up artisan units, tiny cottage and village industries – composite loans.
- Setting up of small-scale industrial units and tiny industries – term/composite loans.
- Refinance assistance for infrastructural and promotional support.
- Financial assistance for project formulation and consultancy services.
- Indirect finance through co-operative societies – composite loan.
- Financing of ISB component under IRDP and SC/ST action plan – composite loans.

Activities covered under schematic lending for which banks are required to submit proposals/schemes to NABARD for appraisal and sanction:

- Financing of registered institutions approved by KVIC/KVIB and those certified as eligible institutions for interest subsidy from KVIC – term/composite loans.
- Financing of industrial co-operative societies – term loans.
- Soft loan assistance towards margin money.

- Term loan assistance/composite loan for acquisition of societies ceded to commercial banks.
- Handloom sector – term loans.
- Sericulture sector – term loans.
- Coir sector – term loans.
- Handicrafts sector – term loans.
- Project finance for agro-industries – term Loans.

National Small Industries Corporation Limited

The National Small Industries Corporation (NSIC) Limited was set up by the Government of India in 1955 to promote and develop small-scale industries in the country. NSIC offers a package of assistance for the benefit of small-scale enterprises.

1. *Single Point Registration*: Registration under this scheme for participating in government and public sector undertaking tenders.
2. *Information Service*: NSIC continuously gets updated with the latest specific information on business leads, technology and policy issues.
3. *Raw Material Assistance*: NSIC fulfils raw material requirements of small-scale industries and provides raw material on convenient and flexible terms.
4. *Meeting Credit Needs of SSI*: NSIC facilitate sanctions of term loan and working capital credit limit of small-enterprise from banks.
5. *Performance and Credit Rating*: NSIC gives credit rating by international agencies subsidized for small enterprises up to 75 per cent to get better credit terms from banks and export orders from foreign buyers.

In the process, it extends help in the establishment of new, small and ancillary industries and in the modernisation of existing ones by supplying them with appropriate, modern and sophisticated machinery and equipment. The Corporation provides help to both potential and existing entrepreneurs through a set of schemes like machinery on hire purchase, internal marketing and export marketing assistance, product export, single point registration scheme, etc. These facilities are not women-specific but the women entrepreneurs do get encouragement to avail of facilities from the schemes.

Indian Bank

Indian Bank was one of the first nationalised banks to open a 'Women's Cell' for potential entrepreneurs. This cell acts as a counselling unit for women who wish to undertake entrepreneurial activity. It also acts as an intermediary between the bank and the beneficiary. This cell also provides information pertaining to training, products and loans available to women. Besides availing of facilities provided by this cell, the following schemes are also offered by Indian Bank;

- A loan amount up to Rs. 6,000 per beneficiary at 4 per cent interest The loan is given under the scheme of assistance to urban poor women for self-employment purposes.
- A term loan (SSI) scheme for women entrepreneurs with 1 per cent rate of interest.

Bank of India

The Priyadarshini Scheme of the Bank of India provides long-term and working capital assistance under the following categories:

- To the professional and self-employed, *e.g.*, chartered accountants, lawyers and doctors.
- To small businesses *e.g.*, beauty parlours, laundries and circulating libraries.
- To retail traders *e.g.*, fair price shops, general provision stores.
- To village or cottage and small-scale industries.
- To road transport operators *e.g.*, auto-rickshaws or taxi drivers.
- For allied agricultural activity.

The maximum loan amount sanctioned depends on the entrepreneur's needs, with limits of up to Rs. 2 lakhs for term loans and up to Rs. 1 lakh for working capital. Interest rates depend upon the quantum of the loan. Repayment schedules are fixed after taking into account the expected surplus income, and normally span a period of three to five years. The assets acquired with bank finance have to be hypothecated to the bank as security. The entrepreneur's contribution margin is about 20 per cent, depending upon the type of activity he/she intends to undertake.

State Bank of India

The State Bank of India has introduced a programme called the 'Stree Shakti Package' for financial enterprises set up by women entrepreneurs. An enterprise where the woman holds a minimum financial interest of 51 per cent of the share capital and gives at least 50 per cent of the employment generated to women, is eligible for assistance under this package.

Others

Schemes for deposit-linked loans for housing, money-back deposit schemes, deposit linked consumer credit for durables, State Bank Card Scheme, scheme for loans against public sector bonds, scheme for loans for installation of solar heating devices, scheme for loans for purchase of personal/home computers (Computer Loan Scheme) are some of the other schemes available to women for which employed/self-employed women are also eligible.

Employed/self-employed women can also avail of loan schemes for the purchase of consumer durables including computers. Pensioners can take loans for the payment of medical expenses (Medicaid). Schemes for loans to parents/guardians for education of children/wards (EDUCAID) are also available.

National Institute for Entrepreneurship and Small Business Development (NIESBUD)

The National Institute for Entrepreneurship and Small Business Development is an apex body established by the Ministry of Industry, Government of India, for coordinating and overseeing the activities of various institutions/agencies engaged in entrepreneurial development in small industry and small business.

Besides its many activities in promoting entrepreneurship in the country, NIESBUD has evolved model syllabi for conducting EDPs for various client groups including women. A syllabus for developing rural women as entrepreneurs was also designed by the Institute as per the recommendations of the National Level Standing Committee on Women Entrepreneurs, NIESBUD also organizes national and international training programmes exclusively for potential women entrepreneurs and women trainers/promoters in the area of entrepreneurship development. It also undertakes exploratory research in the field of women's entrepreneurship.

International Centre for Entrepreneurship and Career Development (ICECD), Ahmedabad

ICECD is an autonomous organization established by a group of professionals to promote women entrepreneurs through training, educational and research initiatives at both the national and international level. Some of the areas that ICECD works in include gender issues, women's economic empowerment, management capability building in government and non-governmental organizations, awareness generation for enterprise establishment, credit delivery and support, and technology identification and transfer. ICECD has had experience in developing a large number of women for economic self-sufficiency in rural and urban areas of many developing countries. Based on its experience it has also developed a few training manuals such as Group Entrepreneurship for Rural Women and Trainers' Manual.

Technical Consultancy Organizations (TCOs)

Technical Consultancy Organizations have been established in almost all the States. Presently 21 such organizations are functioning in the country.

The main objective of the TCOs is to help potential and existing entrepreneurs obtain a variety of information on different projects. TCOs conduct Entrepreneurship Development Training Programme as well, some of which are especially for women. In addition, some of the TCOs have a specialised 'Women Cell'.

Research and Technology Foundation (RTF)

RTF is a voluntary organization registered under the Indian Trust Act of 1888. It aims at fostering the development and growth of rural, small and medium enterprises. As part of its efforts in entrepreneurship development, it attempts to motivate women for greater participation in cottage and rural small and medium enterprises through EDPs, and by setting up their units and providing escort services. It also provides assistance in the field of technological upgradation, research and development, marketing, credit, training under PMRY and development of rural enterprises.

Women Entrepreneur's Wing of National Alliance of Young Entrepreneurs (NAYE)

The Women Entrepreneur's Wing is an integral part of the National Alliance of Young Entrepreneurs (NAYE). More than 45,000 entrepreneurs in different parts of the country have registered with NAYE and are forging ahead with confidence and determination, steadily moving into higher technology areas. NAYE constantly lobbies with the Central and State governments for special facilities and incentives to be provided to women entrepreneurs in the form of land and sheds, easier access to credit, providing up-to-date technologies and arranging for training, production management and marketing.

Federation of Indian Chambers of Commerce and Industry (FICCI Ladies Organization)

FICCI is the oldest and the strongest association of business, commencing operations in India in 1928. Its membership has increased from 400 in 1980 to 1,600 In 1984. FICCI has a separate women's cell which held its first Entrepreneurship Development Programme for women in 1986. It has also organized several training courses specifically for women entrepreneurs, under the ILO's, Improve Your Business (IYB) programme.

Indian Council of Women Entrepreneurs (ICWE)

ICWE, located in New Delhi, is an integral part of the entrepreneurship movement in. India and renders valuable services for the advancement of women's entrepreneurship in the country.

The Working Women's Forum (WWF)

WWF, a grassroots initiative headed by Jaya Arunchalam, has organized about 57,000 business women in Tamil Nadu, Karnataka and Andhra Pradesh. All of them run their own small enterprises. The organization was started in 1978 and the main issues addressed by WWF at the time were: *(i)* lack of organization amongst women in the informal sector; *(ii)* lack of consciousness amongst these working women which caused them to be exploited by middle-persons; and *(iii)* lack of access to cash or credit for productive and increased employment.

In the city of Madras, more than half the women micro entrepreneurs in the unorganized sector are affiliated to WWF. Their unity has provided them with access to credit sources. WWF has intervened in exploitative situations, especially in instances where poor women entrepreneurs were at tire mercy of middlemen, so that today these women are confident entrepreneurs in their own right.

WWF has a simple operating strategy for enabling women to avail of credit facilities. To start with, groups of 20 are formed with two leaders chosen in each group. The leaders act as loan guarantors and are responsible for collecting dues. 2,500 fisher women in the coastal village of Adirapalam, in Tanjore District of Tamil Nadu, have been organized in this way. Credit facilities were provided to them within the first three years. 1,500 fisherwomen were given loans to remove them from the clutches of middle-persons. They have also been exposed to the modernisation of traditional fishing operations.

In Andhra Pradesh, WWF has made an impact through working with the lace-makers of Narsapur District. The lace-making industry is heavily dependent on women for labour. In Narsapur, these women were exploited through provision of low wages and long hours of work, which in turn resulted in various occupational illnesses. Since lace-making is mainly an export-oriented industry, these women once organized, were able to pressurize exporters linked with them for an increase in wages, *i.e.*, from Rs. 5.00 to 8.00 per reel.

In Karnataka, WWF has mainly been working with women in the agarbatti industry. WWF organized 200 such workers from different areas in Bangalore and as a group, pressurized middle men to double their wages: from Rs. 2.70 to Rs. 5.50 per day. Bid! making women in Vellore were also unionised, and the union had a membership of 1,500 within a span of eight months.

Within the first three years, WWF was able to organize over 7,000 women into groups and more than 5,600 women were given loans. WWF enabled these women to become self-employed with, the subsidies and credit-flow generated through WWF's own funding resources.

The goal of WWF is first to unionise the workers working in small industries, and then to steer them on towards self-employment through loans, know-how, enterprise creation and moral support. It is an ongoing struggle to inspire poor, illiterate, deprived and exploited women into becoming entrepreneurs.

Association of Women Entrepreneurs of Small-Scale Industries (AWESSI)

Another pioneering effort to organize women entrepreneurs in Southern India is the Association of Women Entrepreneurs of Small-Scale Industries, founded in Madras in 1984. Ms. *Flossy* Raj, founder President of the Association and member of the World Assembly of Small and Medium Entrepreneurs (WASME), conceived the idea of a women entrepreneurs' association in the 1970s.

AWESSTs goal is to promote, protect and encourage women entrepreneurs and their interests in the Southern parts of India. It does this by cooperating with Central and State government services and other government agencies, and by promoting measures for the furtherance and protection of small-scale industries.

The Association attracts a cross-section of women and its members are mostly above the age of 30, with educational levels averaging at SSLC.

Ms. Raj points out that there are two major obstacles that women must overcome in small-enterprises: *(i)* the generally biased assessment about the technical eligibility of women to enter entrepreneurship, and *(ii)* their ability to repay loans. Banks refuse to even consider loan applications until a working site is allotted. Thus, women entrepreneurs must face this severe test of establishing their financial credibility, when the banks insist that they must pay the first deposit within a month of the allotment. Subsequent payments are often to be made within three months. The State Bank of India favours rural schemes, and this leaves urban women entrepreneurs at a loss when they feel the need of a bank loan.

District Industries Centres (DIC)

The District Industries Centres (DIC's) programme was started in 1978 with a view to provide integrated administrative framework at the district level for promotion of small-scale industries in rural areas. The DIC's are envisaged as a single window interacting agency at the district level providing service and support to small-entrepreneurs under a single roof. DIC's are the implementing arm of the central and state governments of the various schemes and programmes. Registration of small industries is done at the district industries centre and PMRY (Pradhan Mantri Rojgar Yojana) is also implemented by DIC. The organizational structure of DICS consists of General Manager, Functional Managers and Project Managers to provide technical services in the areas relevant to the needs of the district concerned. Management of DIC is done by the state government.

The main functions of DIC are:

1. To prepare and keep model project profiles for reference of the entrepreneurs.
2. To prepare action plan to implement the schemes effectively already identified.

3. To undertake industrial potential survey and to identify the types of feasible ventures which can be taken up in ISB sector, *i.e.*, industrial sector, service sector and business sector.
4. To guide entrepreneurs in matters relating to selecting the most appropriate machinery and equipment, sources of it supply and procedure for importing machineries.
5. To provide guidance for appropriate loan amount and documentation.
6. To assist entrepreneurs for availing land and shed equipment and tools, furniture and fixtures.
7. To appraise the worthness of the project-proposals received from entrepreneurs.
8. To help the entrepreneurs in obtaining required licenses/ permits/clearance.
9. To assist the entrepreneurs in marketing their products and assess the possibilities of ancillarisation.
10. To conduct product development work appropriate to small industry.
11. To help the entrepreneurs in clarifying their doubts about the matters of operation of bank accounts, submission of monthly, quarterly and annual returns to government departments.
12. To conduct artisan training programme.
13. To act as the nodal agency for the district for implementing PMRY (Prime Minister Rojgar Yojana).
14. To function as the technical consultant of DRDA in administering IRDP and TRYSEM programme.
15. To help the specialised training organizations to conduct Entrepreneur development programmes.

In fine DIC's function as the torch-bearer to the beneficiaries/entrepreneurs in setting up and running the business enterprise right from the concept to commissioning. So the role of DIC's in enterprise building and developing small-scale sector is of much significance.

KVIC in India

The programmes of KVIC are implemented directly and its agencies like State KVI Boards, Co-operatives, individuals and directly aided institutions. At the inception of the Commission, there were only two State KVI Boards, 242 registered institutions and 60 co-operatives under the purview of KVIC. At present the organizational structure has strengthened to a level of 30219 co-operative societies and 7.85 lakhs individual artisans. The KVIC has so far covered more than 2.40 lakhs villages in the country.

During 1997-98 the overall Khadi and Village Industries production achieved was to the tune of Rs. 45 19.31 crores and sales were effected to the level of Rs. 5065.28 crores. The employment opportunities were provided to 56.50 lakh persons and their earnings during the 'ear were to the extent of Rs. 1546.34 crores.

ROLE OF KVIC IN TAMIL NADU

Implementing Agencies

In Tamil Nadu the Khadi and Village Industries programmes are implemented mainly through Tamil Nadu State Khadi and Village Industries Board and Tamil Nadu Palmgur development Board, apart from KVIC's directly aided institutions. There are 99 registered institutions under KVIC in Tamil Nadu. In Tamil Nadu, the performance under KVI Sector during 1998-99 third terms of production to the tune of Rs. 558.3 I crores; sales 583.01 crores; employment opportunities 'ere provided to 10.57 lakh persons.

MARGIN MONEY SCHEME OF KVIC

Introduction

A High Power Committee on Khadi and Village Industries headed by the Prime Minister recommended in May, 1994, among other things accelerated growth of rural employment generation programmes. Accordingly, KVIC has formulated a Scheme for financing projects with investment limits up to Rs. 25 lakhs for rural industrialisation and employment generation. Under the scheme, a portion of the project cost is being provided as Margin Money by way of back-end subsidy.

Though KVIC has introduced the Margin Money Scheme during 1996, with necessary modifications again this scheme is introduced during October, 1997. Further for smooth implementation of the scheme, Commission has already placed lump sum Margin Money in advance with Nodal branch of each Public Sector Banks at Mumbai. The total amount deposited is Rs. 132 crores, covering 27 Public Sector Banks.

The Reserve Bank of India has already approved and circulated the contents of the Scheme vide Ref. RPCJ) No. PLNFSIBC. 13106.0612(d) 1997-98 dated 28th July, 1997.

Consequently the Public Sector Banks have already issued Circulars for their branches for adoption of the Scheme of KVIC.

Further R.B.I. has vide their circular/letter addressed to all Regional Offices of R.B.I., the need for extending invitations to representative of KVIC to SLBCIDCC meetings and the Agenda for these meetings should include periodical review of financing of Khadi and Village Industries Sector. In this regard, R.B.L has already advised the S.L.B.C. convenors.

The Salient Features of the Scheme

The Bankers are at liberty to finance in identification of beneficiaries and viable schemes as per the banking norms and KVIC's criteria. In this endeavour, KVIC/KVIB would render all cooperation to the banks in selection of beneficiaries and schemes.

(a) About the Scheme

Margin Money Scheme (MMS) Through Public Sector Banks

The Scheme envisages that;

25 per cent of the project cost for the projects up to Rs. 10 lakhs will be provided as 'Margin Money'.

For projects above Rs. 10.00 lakhs and up to Rs. 25.00 lakhs, rate of Margin Money will be 25 per cent of Rs. 10.00 lakhs plus 10 per cent of the remaining cost of the project.

In the case of weaker section beneficiary *viz.;* SC/ST/OBC/Women/Physically Handicapped/Ex-servicemen and

Minority Community beneficiary/Institution and for Hill, Border and Tribal Areas, North Eastern Region, Sikkim, Andaman and Nicobar Islands, Lakshadweep, Margin Money grant will be at the rate of 30 per cent of the project cost up to Rs. 10.00 lakhs and above this amount up to Rs. 25 lakhs it will be 10 per cent of the remaining cost of the project. Project cost will include one cycle of Working Capital.

Margin Money Scheme is applicable for viable village Industry projects (Khadi and Polyvastra are kept out of its purview).

The Bank will initially sanction 90 per cent of the Project cost in case of General category of beneficiary/institution and 95 per cent of the project cost in case of Weaker Section beneficiary/institution and disburse full amount suitably for setting up of the project.

(b) The Beneficiaries

Individual/Entrepreneurs for projects up to Rs. 10.00 lakhs.

Institutions/Co-operative Societies trusts for projects up to Rs. 25.00 lakhs.

(c) Modalities of the Scheme Financed through Banks

(i) KVIC has placed a lump sum deposit of Margin Money in advance with the corporate office of each Bank or a Nodal Branch designated by the Banks in Savings Bank Account in the name of KVIC.

(ii) Banks will ensure that each project fulfills the criteria of 'Village Industries', 'Per Capita Fixed Investment', and 'Own Contribution' and is located in 'Rural Area'.

(a) *Village Industry Means*: Any industry located in rural area which produces any goods or renders any services with or without the use of power and in which the fixed capital investment per head of an artisan or a worker does not exceed Rs. 50,000/- A list of village industries under purview of KVIC is also furnished.

(b) *Rural Area Means*: An area which comprises any village or includes an area outside the Municipal limits, the population of which does not exceed 20,000.

(iii) Banks will appraise projects technically as well as economically and take their own credit decision on the basis of viability of each project.

(iv) Banks must ensure investment of 'own contribution' of the entrepreneur/individual/institution! Co-operative Society etc. @ 10 per cent of the total cost of the project for General category and 5 per cent in the case of the Weaker Section beneficiary/ institutions *viz.*; SC/ST/OBC/Women Minorities! Ex-servicemen and Physically Handicapped persons, North Eastern Region, Sikkim, Andaman and Nicobar Islands, Lakshadweep, Hill, Border and Tribal Areas are treated as Weaker Section areas.

(v) Once the Margin Money is released in favour of the loanee, it should be kept in Term Deposit Receipt for 2 years at branch level in the name of the beneficiary/institution. Interest accrued on such deposit will be utilised to service partial interest burden on the loan disbursed to the beneficiary/ institution.

(vi) Since 'Margin Money' is to be provided in the form of back-ended Subsidy (Grant), it will be credited to the borrower's loan account after 2 years from the date of first disbursement to the borrower/ institution.

(In case, the Bank's advance goes 'bad' before 2 years period is over, Margin Money will be adjusted by the banks to liquidate loan liability of the borrower either in part or full).

(vii) In case any recovery is effected subsequently by the Bank from any source whatsoever, such recovery will be utilised by the Bank for liquidating their outstanding dues first. Any surplus will be remitted to KVIC.

(viii) Margin Money will be one time assistance from KVIC. For any enhancement of Credit Limit, the KVIC's Margin Money assistance will not be available.

(i) *KHADI:* (Cotton, Silk and Woollen) and Dann carpet (Exclusively for sikkim and North East States).

(ii) *Village Industries:* Village industries/schemes under the purview of KVIC group in seven major groups are as under:

Group - I: Mineral Based Industry

1. Cottage Pottery Industry.
2. Lime Stone, Lime shell and other lime products industry.
3. Stone cutting, crushing, carving and engraving for Temples and Buildings.
4. Utility articles made out of stone.
5. Slate and Slate pencil making.
6. Manufacture of plaster of paris.
7. Utensil washing powder.
8. Fuel briqueting.
9. Jewellery out of Gold, Silver, Stone, shell and synthetic materials.
10. Manufacture of Gulal, Rangoli.
11. Manufacture of Bangles.
12. Manufacturer of paints, pigments, varnishes and distemper.
13. Manufacturer of Glass toys.
14. Glass Decoration - cutting, designing and polishing.
15. Gem cutting.

Group - II: Forest Bases Industry

1. Handmade paper.
2. Manufacture of Kattha.
3. Manufacture of Gums and resins.
4. Manufacture of Shellac.

5. Cottage Mafch Industry, manufacture of fireworks and Agarbattis.
6. Bamboo and cane work.
7. Manufacture of paper cups, plates, bags, and other paper containers.
8. Manufacture of exercise book binding, envelope making, register making, including all other stationery items made out of paper.
9. Khus tattis and broom making.
10. Collection, processing and packing of forest products.
11. photo framing.
12. Manufacture of jute products (under fibre Industry).

Group - III: Agro-Based and Food Industry

1. Processing, packing and marketing of cereals, pulses, spices, condiments, masala etc.
2. Noodles making.
3. Power atta chakki.
4. Daliya making.
5. Mini rice shelling unit.
6. Pa1mgur making and other plam products industry.
7. Manufacture of cane gur and Khandasari.
8. Indian sweets making.
9. Raswanti - Sugarcane Juice catering Unit.
10. Bee-keeping.
11. Fruits and Vegetable processing, preservation and canning including pickles.
12. Ghani oil industry.
13. Menthol oil.
14. Fibre other than coir.
15. Collection of forest plants and fruits for medicinal purpose.
16. Processing of maize and ragi.
17. Pith work, manufacture of pith mats, and garlands etc.

18. Cashew processing.
19. Leaf cup making.
20. Milk products making unit.
21. Cattle feed, poultry feed making.

Group - IV: Polymer and Chemical Based Industry

1. Flaying curing and tanning of hides ad skins and ancillary industries connected with the same and cottage leather industry.
2. Cottage soap Industry.
3. Manufacture of rubber goods (dipped latex products).
4. Products out of Rexin, PVC, etc.
5. Horn and Bone including Ivory products.
6. Candle, Camphor and sealing wax making (Mytanufacture of packing items of plastics.
7. Manufacture of Bindi.
8. Manufacture of mehandi.
9. Manufacture of Essential Oils.
10. Manufacture of shampoos.
11. Manufacture of Hair Oil.
12. Detergent and washing powder making (non-toxic).

Group - V: Engineering and Non conventional Energy

1. Carpentry.
2. Blacksmithy.
3. Manufacture of household aluminium.
4. Manufacture and use of manure and methane.
5. Vermiculture and waste disposal.
6. Manufacture of paper pins, clips, safety pins, stove pins, etc.
7. Manufacture of decorative bulbs, bottles, glass.
8. Umbrella assembling.
9. Solar and wind energy implements.
10. Manufacture handmade utensils out of brass.
11. Manufacture of handmade utensils out of copper.

12. Manufacture of handmade utensils out of bell metal.
13. Other articles made out of brass, copper and bell metal.
14. Production of radios.
15. Production of cassette player whether or not fitted with radio.
16. Production of cassette recorder whether or not fitted with radio.
17. Production of voltage stabilizer.
18. Manufacture of electronic clocks and alarm time pieces.
19. Carved wood and artistic furniture making.
20. Tin smithy.
21. Motor winding.
22. Wire net making.
23. Iron grill making.
24. Manufacture of rural transport vehicles such as hand carts, bullock carts, small boats, assembly of bicycles, cycle rickshaw, motorised carts, etc.
25. Manufacture of musical instruments.

Group - VI: Textile Industry (Excluding Khadi)

1. Polyvastra which means any cloth woven on handloom in India from yarn handspun in India from a mixture of manmade fibre with either cotton, silk or wool or with any two or all of them or from a mixture of manmade fibre yarn handspun in India with either cotton, silk or woollen yarn handspun in India or with any two or all of such yarn.
2. Manufacture of Lok vastra cloth.
3. Hosiery.
4. Tailoring and preparation of readymade garments.
5. Batic works.
6. Toys and doll making.
7. Thread balls and woollen balling, lacchi making.
8. Embroidery.
9. Manufacture of surgical bandages.

10. Stove wicks.
11. Embroidery of fabrics.

Group - VII: Service Industry

1. Laundry.
2. Barbar.
3. Plumbing.
4. Servicing of Electronics wiring and electronics domestic appliances and equipments.
5. Repairs of diesel engines, pumpsets etc.
6. Tyre vulcanising unit.
7. Agriculture servicing for sprayers, insecticides, pumpsets, etc.
8. Hiring of sound system like loud speaker, amplifier, mike, etc.
9. Battery charging.
10. Art board painting.
11. Cycle repair shops.
12. Masonary.
13. Band troupe.
14. Motorised local boat (fibre glass) for goa only.
15. Motor Cycle to fly as taxi (for Goa only).
16. Musical instruments (for Goa only.
17. Dhabas (Not serving liquor).
18. Tea stall.

Small Industries Service Institutes (SISI)

The small industries service institutes have been set up in state capitals and other places all over the country to provide consultancy and training to small-entrepreneurs both existing and prospective.

The main functions of SISI include:

1. To serve as interface between central and state government.
2. To render technical support services.
3. To conduct entrepreneurship development programmes.

4. To initiate promotional programmes.

The SISIs also render assistance in the following areas:

1. Economic consultancy/information/EDP consultancy.
2. Trade and market information.
3. Project profiles.
4. State industrial potential surveys.
5. District industrial potential surveys.
6. Modernisation and in plant studies.
7. Workshop facilities.
8. Training in various trade/activities.

Small-Scale Industries Board (SSIB)

The government of India constituted a board, namely, Small-Scale Industries Board (SSIB) in 1954 to advice on development of small scale industries in the country. The SSIB is also known as central small industries board. The range of development work in small-scale industries involves several departments/ministries and several organs of the central/state governments. Hence, to facilitate co-ordination and inter-institutional linkages, the small-scale industries board has been constituted. It is an apex advisory body constituted to render advice to the government on all issues pertaining to the development of small-scale industries. The industries minister of the government of India is the chairman of the SSIB. The SSIB comprises of 50 members including state industry minister, some members of parliament, and secretaries of various departments of government of India, financial institutions, public sector undertakings, industry associations and eminent experts in the field.

State Small Industries Development Corporations (SSIDC)

The State Small Industries Development Corporations (SSIDC) were sets up in various states under the companies' act 1956, as state government undertakings to cater to the primary developmental needs of the small tiny and village industries in the state/union territories under their jurisdiction. Incorporation under the companies act has provided SSIDCs with greater operational flexibility and wider scope for undertaking a variety of activities for the benefit of the small sector. The important functions performed by the SSIDCs include:

- To procure and distribute scarce raw materials.
- To supply machinery on hire purchase system.
- To provide assistance for marketing of the products of small-scale industries.
- To construct industrial estates/sheds, providing allied infrastructure facilities and their maintenance.
- To extend seed capital assistance on behalf of the state government concerned provide management assistance to production units.

NGO Initiatives

There are many voluntary organizations and non government organizations who provide assistance to women. Some of which offer interest-free loans for purchase of equipment that the women may require in order to set up her entreprise. Also loans/grants to meet working Capital requirements to carry on small business ventures like vegetable vending, rice, fish vending, setting up general stores etc., are provided. A few of such organizations involved in promoting women enterpreneurship are listed below:

(a) *Udyogini:* Udyogini, a Non-Government Organization's main objectives are to strengthen skills and empower poor, marginalised women so as to enable them to sustain their ventures and improve their economic and social status. It also aims to strengthen development organizations working at grassroot level with women's groups involved in micro-enterprise initiatives. It is supported by the Economic Development Institute of the World Bank to carry out WEMTOP (Women's Enterprise Management Training Outreach Programme). The programme aims at developing and strengthening NGOs and voluntary organizations in terms of institution building, traning of trainers, and delivery of training to women which is carried out in turn by the NGOs.

(b) *Social Alliance of Women Entrepreneurs* (SAWE): SAWE which is Kerala based, is a non-government organization set-up in 1990 to socially and economically uplift poor rural women. It has been providing the following services to women; income generation activities, self-employment activities as well as skill development training in garment making, mushroom cultivation, screen printing, motor rewinding, etc.

The organization is run by volunteers, with experts being called in for programmes. There are 200 members of the association, cansisting of beneficiaries and volunteers.

(c) *Rural Development and Self-Employment Training Institute (RUDSET):* RUDSET Institutes are located in 11 centres in rural India. These institutes are actively associated with development of self-employment programme and entrepreneurship development training and support to entrepreneurs in rural areas. The institutes conduct skill development training programmes in a number of fields, both agro-based and others. These programmes are tailored to the needs in the region in which the institute is located. A few women-specific programmes are also conducted.

(d) *Marketing Organization of Women Entrepreneurs (MOOWES):* MOOWES, based in Madras, has been set up with the objective of promoting women entrepreneurs by providing marketing services to them. It regularly holds exhibitions of products made by women who are its members. In addition, the organization is now planning its own showroom in Madras.

(e) *Consortium of Women Entrepreneurs of India (CWEI):* The Consortium of Women Entrepreneurs of India has been created, keeping in mind the need of women, to explore new marketing linkages and exchanges of technology within the country and overseas. The aim of the Consortium is to act as an alternate trading organization (ATO) linking with nodal agencies in India and abroad for direct marketing, both in the domestic and export markets as well as in product and design development.

(f) *Ladies' Wing of Indian Merchants' Chamber:* The Ladies Wing was initiated and established by Indian Merchant's Chamber in 1966 in Bombay. Thc activities of the wing inspire, motivate and encourage women to share the business opportunities presented by the new age. Inspiration comes from eminent personalities from various fields invited to express their views and experiences in their chosen fields. The Wing is claimed to be one of the most dynamic organizations in the Wsestern Region, – with more than 1, 000 members which include entrepreneurs, managers executives, professionals and women from business families.

(g) *FISME Federation of Indian Women Entrepreneurs (FFIWE):* EFTWE is an autonomous national-level women entrepreneurs' organization whose main functions are networking and providing a package of services to the associations of women entrepreneurs in different parts of the country, Another major objective of FFIWE is to help secure women their rightful place in the national economy and also to strengthen international co-operation. It also aims to affiliate associations of women entrepreneurs from various districts and states of he country so that they can avail of the various facilities and services provided to women entrepreneurs. Individual women entrepreneurs are also eligible for general membership.

Assistance to women is also provided by voluntary organizations, some of which offer interest-free loans for the purchase of equipment that the woman may require in order to set up her enterprise. Also, grants/loans to meet working capital requirements to carry on small business ventures like vegetable vending, rice, fish vending, setting up general stores, etc., are provided.

(h) *Self-Employed Women's Association (SEWA):* SEWA (Ahmedabad) was established in 1972 and has emerged as a pioneering organization championing the cause of the poor self-employed women. SEWA is presently an autonomous, registered trade union, although it functioned under the women's wing of the Textile Labour

Association until April, 1981. With the Gandhian philosophy guiding SEWA's efforts, SEWA organizes women in the informal sectors by trade, so that problems unique to each occupation can be addressed by the women collectively. SEWA women are primarily engaged in trades such as vegetable vending, farm labour, handloom weaving, selling door to door articles of daily necessity, block printing and bamboo-weaving.

Each member of SEWA can avail of the services of three organizations: the SEWTA Union, the SEWA Bank and the SEWA Manila Trust. The Union supports the organization of trade groups and helps in the continued struggle against various vested interests. The Bank provides banking and credit facilities, and the Mahila Trust extends facilities for legal aid, social security, productivity training and education.

The creation of banking and credit facilities for poor self-employed (and mostly illiterate) women, was one of the important developmental efforts spearheaded by SEWA. The Mahila Sahakari (Women's Co-operative) Bank was registered in 1974 and is the only one of its kind in the country. This Bank has belied all reservations of the organized banking structure regarding provision of credit to poor, illiterate and self-employed women, and has become a viable financial unit with share capital and deposits from its members. The myth that poor women have low loan repayment rates, has also been shattered by SEWA's experience. In fact, SEWA's experience with banking and credit has proved that such inputs are vital in the struggle of poor women to be freed from the clutches of money-lenders and to succeed in their bid to be self-reliant.

Apart from the above, SEWA provides support to its members in a variety of ways. For instance, a package of information, awareness and bargaining skills are made available by SEWA personnel through their numerous services, such as counselling, skill enhancement courses, and the large bank which enables self-employed women to become assertive and demand their fair share in the market. SEWA's efforts have received local, national and international recognition.

STEPS TAKEN BY GOVERNMENT TO DEVELOP WOMEN ENTREPRENEURS

The growth and development of women entrepreneurs required to be accelerated because entrepreneurial development is not possible without the participation of women. Therefore, a congenial environment is needed to be created to enable women to participate actively in the entrepreneurial activities. There is a need of Government, Non-Government, promotional and regulatory agencies to come forward and play the supportive role in promoting the women entrepreneur in India. The Government of India has also formulated various training and development cum employment generations programme for the women to start their ventures. These programmes are as follows:

Steps taken in Seventh Five-Year Plan

In the seventh five-year plan, a special chapter on the 'Integration of women in development' was introduced by Government with following suggestion.

(i) *Specific Target Group:* It was suggested to treat women as a specific target groups in all major development programmes of the country.

(ii) *Arranging Training Facilities:* It is also suggested in the chapter to devise and diversify vocational training facilities for women to suit their changing needs and skills.

(iii) *Developing New Equipments:* Efforts should be made to increase their efficiency and productivity through appropriate technologies, equipments and practices.

(iv) *Marketing Assistance:* It was suggested to provide the required assistance for marketing the products produced by women entrepreneurs.

(v) *Decision-making Process:* It was also suggested to involve the women in decision-making process.

Steps taken by Government during Eight Five-Year Plan

The Government of India devised special programmes to increases employment and income-generating activities for women in rural areas. The following plans are lunched during the Eight-Five-Year Plan:

(i) Prime Minister Rojgar Yojana and EDPs were introduced to develop entrepreneurial qualities among rural women.

(ii) 'Women in agriculture' scheme was introduced to train women farmers having small and marginal holdings in agriculture and allied activities.

(iii) To generate more employment opportunities for women KVIC took special measures in remote areas.

(iv) Women co-operatives schemes were formed to help women in agro-based industries like dairy farming, poultry, animal husbandry, horticulture etc., with full financial support from the Government.

(v) Several other schemes like integrated Rural Development Programmes (IRDP), Training of Rural youth for Self-employment (TRYSEM) etc., were started to alleviated poverty. 30-40 per cent reservation is provided to women under these schemes.

Steps taken by Government during Ninth Five-Year Plan

Economic development and growth is not achieved fully without the development of women entrepreneurs. The Government of India has introduced the following schemes for promoting women entrepreneurship because the future of small-scale industries depends upon the women entrepreneurs:

(a) Trade Related Entrepreneurship Assistance and Development (TREAD) scheme was lunched by Ministry of Small Industries to develop women entrepreneurs in rural, semi-urban and urban areas by developing entrepreneurial qualities.

(b) Women Component Plant, a special strategy adopted by Government to provide assistance to women entrepreneurs.

(c) Swarna Jayanti Gram Swarozgar Yojana and Swaran Jayanti Sekhari Rozgar Yojana were introduced by government to provide reservations for women and encouraging them to start their ventures.

(d) New schemes named Women Development Corporations were introduced by government to help women entrepreneurs in arranging credit and marketing facilities.

(e) State Industrial and Development Bank of India (SIDBI) has introduced following schemes to assist the women entrepreneurs. These schemes are:

(i) Mahila Udyam Nidhi.

(ii) Micro-Cordite Scheme for Women.

(iii) Mahila Vikas Nidhi.

(iv) Women Entrepreneurial Development Programmes.

(v) Marketing Development Fund for Women.

Consortium of Women entrepreneurs of India provides a platform to assist the women entrepreneurs to develop new, creative and innovative techniques of production, finance and marketing.

There are different bodies such as NGOs, voluntary organizations, Self-help groups, institutions and individual enterprises from rural and urban areas which collectively help the women entrepreneurs in their activities.

Evaluation of Tenth Five-year Plan

Goals, Objectives and Strategy of the Tenth Plan

The prime goal of rural development during the Tenth Five-Year plan was the development of rural people by alleviating poverty through the instrument of self-employment and wage employment programmes, by providing community infrastructure facilities such as drinking water, electricity, road connectivity, health facilities, rural housing and education and promoting decentralisation of powers. The vision has been to make Tamil Nadu the best State in the country by way of creating growth opportunities in rural areas and eradicating rural poverty. Poverty reduction was to be attempted by organizing the rural masses into self-help groups and the establishment of micro-enterprises, training, credit linkages, market support, etc., and by substantial flow of investment in physical infrastructure like roads, water supply and social infrastructure like health, education and nutrition.

The strategy adopted in the Tenth Plan targeted not only at addressing the issue of material deprivation but also the issue of security against vulnerability and risk exposure of individual rural families. To accelerate the growth of Rural Economy, the focus of the State was improving rural infrastructure providing better quality of living for the rural poor through partnerships with NGOs, Community based Organizations and Panchayat Raj Institutions with the department of Rural Development providing logistic support.

Performance of the State: Programme-wise

(i) *Wage Employment Programme:* Economic transformation was sought to be established for the rural households by safeguarding the family from exposure to vulnerability through wage employment programme, which included food grain component also. Through the programme of Sampoorna Grameen Rozgar Yojana (SGRY), 16.41 lakh MTs of rice were distributed at a subsidised rate as part of wages, to provide the minimum food requirement of the family. 474104 assets were created and 2352.70 lakh man-days of employment were provided for the rural poor.

(ii) *Guaranteed Employment: Tamil Nadu Rural Employment Guarantee Scheme (TNREGS):* During the last two years of the plan period, a new scheme providing for guaranteed employment for 100 days in a year to needy households was introduced in 6 districts of the state. While the state could not make inroads to effectively garner the benefits and utilise the allocation in 2005-06, better progress was shown in the second year of the scheme which was the final year of the Plan period.

(iii) *Economic Empowerment Scheme:* To provide for economic empowerment the Swarnajayanthi Gram Swarozgar Yojana programme was implemented throughout the plan period, the objective being to ensure appreciable increase in the income of the family over a period of time. This objective was sought to be achieved by interalia organizing the rural poor women in Self-Help Groups, building their skills and capacity for a specific activity and providing them with income generating assets through mix of subsidy and credit. The 'thrift and credit' functions of the groups were encouraged by providing a revolving fund and infrastructure was provided for common economic activities.

(iv) *Housing Programme:* Housing sector continued to be one of thrust areas during the Tenth plan. Providing pucca concrete roofed houses improved the quality of living of rural poor while ensuring shelter security at the same time. The performance of the state towards providing houses under the Indira Awaas Yojana (IAY) scheme can be gauged. The unit cost of the house provided by Government of India (GOI) is Rs. 25,000 for ordinary soil and Rs. 27,500 for difficult terrains. The expenditure is shared in the ratio of 75:25 between GOI and GOTN. Since the Central allocation during the Tenth plan period could not meet the huge pending demand for houses the Government evolved a special housing programme involving credit, subsidy and beneficiary contribution at a unit cost of Rs. 10,000 each. This new scheme was implemented only during the last two years of the plan period with focus on up-gradation of houses of SHG members. A total no. of 1,00,905 SHG members benefited in this scheme.

(v) *Quality of Living Programme:* Since improvement of the quality of living was one of the objectives of the Tenth plan, the state brought into implementation schemes that laid emphasis on providing better amenities for the rural poor through improved road connectivity.

Rural Connectivity – Pradhan Mandri Gram Sadak Yojana (PMGSY)

Rural road connectivity promotes access to services and opportunities and is a key ingredient in any sustainable poverty reduction programme. Through the PMGSY, the Government provided connectivity to all unconnected rural habitations with the population of thousand and above by all weather roads. Before the end of the Tenth plan, an effort was made to connect all habitations with 500+ population also.

Several other schemes to focus on improving the quality of life of the people living in rural areas through provision of vital infrastructure formed part of the Tenth plan strategy. Constituency development schemes like the Member of Parliament Local Area Development Scheme (MPLADS) with the discretion of allotment resting with the elected representatives resulted in infrastructure development of the village.

(vi) *Total Sanitation Programme*: Focusing on improving the quality of living in the rural areas the total sanitation programme was effectively implemented over the Tenth plan period. With the direct relationship existing between water, sanitation and health, the strategy of the total sanitation programme was to emphasise more on Awareness Building, Human Resource Development and Community Driven Initiatives for better sanitary facilities. Location specific awareness campaigns with location specific technology options formed part of the strategy that involved PRIs, Co-operatives, SHGs and NGOs. During the plan period, nearly 763.43 crores were spent on creating 714 rural sanitary marts and on construction of toilets. Nearly 97.2 lakhs individual households have been provided with toilets along with 82221 schools and 70472 Anganwadis which have also been covered under this programme. Nearly 13064 integrated sanitary complexes have been constructed to take care of needs of women alone.

Objective, Goals and Strategies for the Eleventh Five-Year Plan

The bottlenecks identified in implementation of the various programmes during the Tenth five-year plan are sought to be addressed in the Eleventh Five-Year plan. Basically most of these programmes are implemented through the units of local self-government. The Panchayat Unions and the Rural Development Department extend technical and administrative support for implementation of these schemes. It has also been noticed that though the objectives of rural transformation are being achieved by and large, there is an urgent need for improving the implementation machinery.

(a) Objectives

- To enhance the quality of living of the rural poor through creating adequate and appropriate infrastructure in the rural areas and providing equitable access to them.
- To provide increased livelihood opportunities in the rural areas.
- To strengthen the Self-Help Group movement with focus on empowering women and youth.
- To Strengthen grass root democracy and make the panchayati raj institutions vibrant, responsive service delivery agents.
- To provide an adequate financial resource base for the rural local bodies to function effectively.

(b) Strategy

Though the strategy for Eleventh Five-Year Plan differs from programme to programme to achieve the Goal/ Objectives, the thumb rule adopted is by and large, better implementation of various Central Schemes, Shared Schemes and State Programmes with full utilisation of programme allocation. The programme-wise strategies are discussed in detail.

Wages to labourers are paid partly in cash and partly in the form of rice, which is given through fair price shops. The Government of Tamil Nadu has fixed the minimum wage at Rs. 80 per day. The Centre and State contribute to the cash portion of the scheme in the ratio 75:25. The cost of the food grains is borne by Government of India and the transportation charges are borne by the State Government. This scheme will be implemented in 19 Districts only since SGRY has already been merged with the National Rural Employment Gurarantee Scheme (NREGS) in the 10 districts of Cuddalore, Dindigul, Nagapattinam, Sivagangai, Tiruvannamalai, Villupuram, Thanjavur, Tiruvarur, Tirunelveli and Karur Districts.

Over the Eleventh Five-Year Plan period around Rs. 1100 crore is likely to be pumped into the rural areas to generate nearly 775 lakh mandays of employment. Under the wage employment/food security scheme (SGRY) in these 19 districts.

Rural Employment Guarantee Programme

The National Rural Employment Guarantee Act, 2005 (NREGA) guarantees 100 days of employment in a financial year to any rural household whose adult members are willing to do unskilled manual work. This Act is an important step towards the realisation of the right to work. It is also expected to enhance people's livelihoods on a sustained basis, by developing the economic and social infrastructure in rural areas.

The Tamil Nadu Rural Employment Guarantee Scheme, introduced in 2005-06 in six districts has been expanded to ten districts in 2007-08. In these districts, this programme will substitute the SGRY programme. It is expected that the scheme will cover the entire state during the Plan period. The Village Panchayat will issue job cards to every registered household. Work should be given within 15 days to persons who apply for the same, failing which an unemployment allowance shall be payable by the State Government at the rate prescribed in the Act. Payment of the statutory minimum wage and equal wages for men and women are other notable features of the scheme.

Self-Employment Sector

Swarnajayanthi Gram Swarojgar Yojana will continue to be a flagship programme for holistic approach to self-employment providing sustainable income to the rural poor who are below poverty line by organizing them into SHGs, providing training, credit linkages and infrastructural assistance including marketing assistance in the rural areas. 10 per cent of the scheme fund is allocated for the training component, 20 per cent for the infrastructure component and 70 per cent for revolving fund-cum-subsidy component. The SHGs, after the first grading, are provided with a revolving fund of Rs. 25,000 (bank loan of Rs. 15,000 and Rs. 10,000 as subsidy). After the second grading, the successful groups are provided with economic assistance, the maximum eligible subsidy being 50 per cent of the project cost with a ceiling of Rs. 1.25 lakh.

In order to implement the scheme in a more purposeful manner during the Eleventh Five-Year Plan period, a directory of reputed training institutions will be prepared and an elaborate Activity Mapping exercise will be done throughout the State identifying two leading activity clusters in each block. The expected outlay over the plan period would be around Rs. 500 crore for this scheme inclusive of Central and State Shares with the credit target of at least Rs. 650 crore in the Eleventh Five-Year Plan.

Entrepreneurship Development Training and Skill Training For Women (EDP)

During Eleventh Five-Year Plan, it is proposed to impart skill training of longer duration *i.e.*, more than a month, with better quality and also incorporating a five-day capsule of Entrepreneurship development training. This skill training will be imparted through reputed institutions.

Youth Self-Help Groups: Focus in Eleventh Plan Period

The success of the women SHGs has revealed the tremendous potential available in society, which can be tapped for the development of society by well-designed Government programmes. With this objective in mind and to provide employment to unemployed youth, formation of youth groups will be focused in the Eleventh Plan period.

Advancing Self-Help Groups

Self-Help Groups, an unit for collective action for the development of its constituent members have also become the vehicle of development process by providing space for convergence of development programmes. The strategy to develop the skills of the SHG members would revolve round the following areas.

- Issuing Identity Cards for all SHG members to approach different offices and institutions.
- Providing literacy and basic accounting skills to all SHG members.
- Acquiring skills from within the village community for local requirements.

- Updating acquired skills to keep pace with technological advancement and new demands.
- Balancing local availability of opportunities and opportunities through migration.
- Creation of rural production centres for local consumption needs.
- Developing healthy competition between SHGs in the form of awards to best performing SHGs during Pongal.

Integrated approach requires participation of the state, private organizations, Non-Government Organizations and the local community whose roles are outlined below.

Role of the State

- Creating suitable learning opportunities for the rural youth to acquire livelihoods skills.
- Enacting suitable laws to facilitate the participation of private, non-governmental and community based organizations in the skill building process.
- Create forums for the above mentioned organizations to express their views and to design an integrated strategy for skill building.

Role of Private Organizations

- Provide financial support for skill building and provide employment to the youth. They can support the vocational institutes run by the community based organizations in their promotion and also spend for training the youth; later they can recruit the trained youth from the institutes.
- Expressing the demand for skills to the NGOs, community based organizations and the State agencies.

Role of NGOs

- Promoting Community based, community owned vocational institutes in rural areas.
- Facilitating linkages between the State, private and the community.

Role of Community

- Understanding the present situation and using the emerging opportunities. They should not stick on only to the traditional livelihoods and should be ready to accept the change.
- Expressing their demand for relevant skills through their own institutions (community based) at appropriate forums.

Tamil Nadu Volunteers Research Centre (TNVRC)

The Women Development Corporation has constituted the TNVRC as an institution for strengthening the Non-Governmental Organizations and for building their capacities in developmental work. This institution will be utilised for various NGO related development activities in the village including programmes of Tamil Nadu State Aids Control Society through SHGs.

3

Socio-economic Profile of Rural Women Entrepreneurs

Rural women increasingly run their own enterprises, yet their socio-economic contributions and entrepreneurial potential remain largely unrecognised and untapped. They concentrate in informal, micro-size, low productivity and low-return activities. Enabling and gender responsive policies, services and business environments are crucial to stimulate the start up and upgrading of women's businesses and thereby help to generate decent and productive work, achieve gender equality, reduce poverty and ensure stronger economies and societies.

The socio-economic profile of the women respondents shows the personal factors that lead to entrepreneurial development. The social factors related to the family and the community has a bearing on entrepreneurship. The economic factors act as a base for financial support to develop the entrepreneurship. In the present study, the profile of the respondents is taken into account to provide the background of the respondents.

AGE OF THE RESPONDENTS

The age is one of the important aspects of self-development since the resistance to change is relatively lesser at the young age compared to the older age. The youngsters are generally interested to learn new things and take the risk in thin life which is highly essential for the entrepreneurship. At the same time, the aged are having more knowledge and experience in their own field. Since, the age of the respondents influences the entrepreneurship; it is included in the present study.

Table 3.1: Age-wise Distribution of Respondents

S. No.	Age (in years)	No of Respondents	Percentage
1.	Upto 25	28	9.3
2.	26-35	167	55.7
3.	36-45	72	24.0
4.	Above 45	33	11.0
	Total	**300**	**100.0**

Source: Primary Data

Table 3.1 furnishes the age-wise distribution of respondents. The dominant age group among the respondents is 25 to 35 years and 36 to 45 years which constitute 55.7 and 24 per cent respectively. The number of respondents who are upto 25 years of age constitute 9.3 per cent to the total. It is inferred from Table 3.1 that most (80%) of the respondents are in the age group of 25 to 45 years. It implies that the entrepreneurs are involving themselves in the entrepreneurial activities in the age group of 25 to 45 years and the youngsters who are in the age group upto 25 years also started involving themselves in entrepreneurship.

SOCIAL CLASS OF THE RESPONDENTS

The social class represents the caste of the respondents. The caste is also an important social factor that influences entrepreneurship. The caste of the respondents leads the respondents to have some knowledge on enterprises and

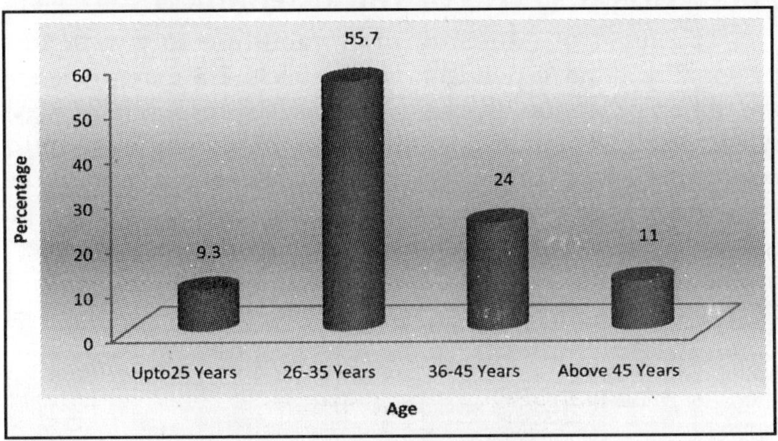

Fig. 3.1: Age-wise Distribution of Respondents

willing to start and manage the enterprise. Even though the caste behaviour can be moulded with the help of education, exposure and multi-media development, still it plays its own role towards entrepreneurship. In the present study, the caste is grouped into forward class, backward class, most backward class and scheduled caste/tribe.

Table 3.2: Community-wise Distribution of Respondents

S. No.	Community	No. of Respondents	Percentage
1.	FC	31	10.3
2.	BC	181	60.4
3.	MBC	52	17.3
4.	SC/ST	36	12.0
	Total	**300**	**100.0**

Source: Primary Data

Table 3.2 represents that 60.4 per cent of the total respondents are belonging to backward class followed by this 17.3 per cent are belonging to most backward class. The number of respondents belonging to Schedule caste/Schedule tribe and FC together constitutes 22.3 per cent. The most dominant class among the rural women entrepreneurs is backward class.

EDUCATIONAL STATUS OF THE RESPONDENTS

The level of education may facilitate to enrich the personality of the respondents in all aspects. The entrepreneurs are not an exception. By the education, the respondents may wider their scope of operation, aware of the economic opportunities, etc. In the present study, the level of education is confined into high school, higher Secondary, degree and others. The status of education of the respondents is illustrated in Table 3.3.

Table 3.3: Educational Status of the Respondents

S. No.	Status of Education	No. of Respondents	Percentage
1.	Up to high school	159	53.0
2.	Higher secondary	89	29.7
3.	Degree	28	9.3
4.	Others	24	8.0
	Total	**300**	**100.0**

Source: Primary Data

Table 3.3 represents that 53 per cent of the respondents have level of education up to high school followed by this 29.7 per cent have higher secondary education. The number of respondents who have degree education constitute 9.3 per cent. Only 3.3 per cent of the respondents have other educational qualification such as diploma and technical education. Thus, it reveals that most (53%) of the rural women entrepreneurs have only high school education.

MARITAL STATUS

The marital status of the respondents reveals the social status of an individual. In general, the need and commitment of the married persons are greater than the unmarried. Similarly, the status like separated and widowed determines different requirements in life. The marital status of the respondents is shown in Table 3.4.

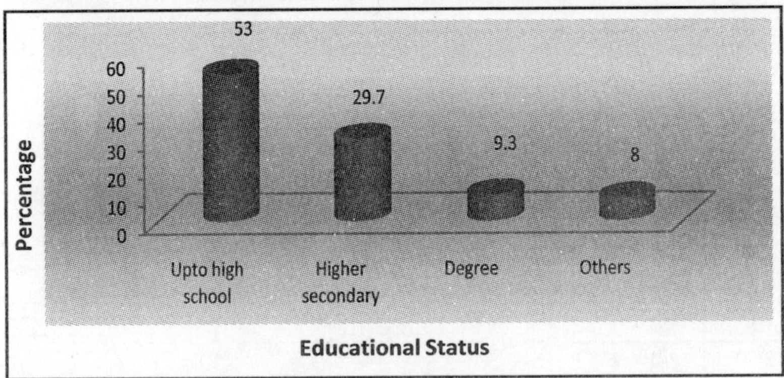

Fig. 3.2. Educational Status of the Respondents

Table 3.4: Marital Status of the Respondents

S. No.	Marital Status	No. of Respondents	Percentage
1.	Single	35	11.7
2.	Married	221	73.7
3.	Divorced	19	6.3
4.	Widowed	25	8.3
	Total	**300**	**100.0**

Source: Primary Data

Table 3.4 shows that of 73.7 per cent of the respondents are married whereas 11.7 per cent are unmarried. The number of respondents who are widowed constitute 8.7 per cent of the total respondents and only 1.6 per cent of the respondents are divorced. Table 3.4 reveals that most (73.7%) of the rural women entrepreneurs are married. This shows that married women are involved in the entrepreneurial activities.

RESPONDENT'S CHILDREN

Women entrepreneurs are key players in any developing country particularly in terms of their contribution to economic development. The number of children will also influence women to engage in entrepreneurship. Most of the women has one or two children and very few women have 3, 4 or above 5 children. Thus, in the present study, the number of children of respondents is confined up to 2 children, 3 to 5 children and above 5 children.

Table 3.5: Respondent's Children

S. No.	Number of Children	No. of Respondents	Percentage
1.	0-2	167	63.0
2.	3-5	88	33.2
3.	Above 5	10	3.8
	Total	**265**	**100.0**

Source: Primary Data

Table 3.5 furnishes the number of children of the respondents. A maximum of 63 per cent of the respondents are in the category of 0-2 children and 33.2 per cent are having 3-5 children. Only 3.8 per cent of the respondents are having more than 5 children. Table 3.5 reveals that the maximum number of rural women engaged in entrepreneurship have less number of children.

NATURE OF FAMILY

The nature of family indicates the family system adopted by the respondents. Both nuclear and joint family system has its own merits and demerits in developing entrepreneurial behaviour. The nuclear family system creates an urge among the people to stand on their own legs whereas the joint family system provides some moral and financial support to promote the entrepreneurial behaviour. The family system of the respondents is presented in Table 3.6.

Table 3.6: Nature of Family

S. No.	Nature of Family	No. of Respondents	Percentage
1.	Nuclear	207	69
2.	Joint	93	31
	Total	**300**	**100.0**

Source: Primary Data

The percentage of women entrepreneurs who belong to nuclear family system is 69 whereas 31 per cent of the respondents belong to joint family system. It indicates that a decline of joint family system even in rural areas.

RESPONDENT'S FAMILY SIZE

The most important social character of the respondents is the family size. The family size indicates the number of family members living together with respondents. The family size may be an asset or liability which depends upon the earning capacity of the family members. In general, the increase in family size leads to the financial and the social commitments to the respondents with few exceptions. These commitments may hinder the growth of entrepreneurship among the respondents. The family size is confined into less than 3, 3 to 5, 6 to 8 and above 8.

Table 3.7: Respondent's Family Size

S. No.	Family Size	No. of Respondents	Percentage
1.	Less than 3	28	9.3
2.	3-5	182	60.7
3.	6-8	73	24.3
4.	Above 8	17	5.7
	Total	**300**	**100.0**

Source: Primary Data

Table 3.7 depicts the family size of the respondents. A maximum of 60.7 per cent of the respondents have a family size of 3 to 5 members followed by 24.3 per cent of them have a family size of 6 to 8 members. The number of respondents who have less than 3 members and more than 8 members in the family constitute 9.3 and 5.7 per cent respectively. The dominant family size of the respondents is 3 to 5 members.

EARNING MEMBERS IN THE FAMILY OF RESPONDENTS

The earning members of the family earn either daily or weekly or monthly basis. The earning members per family increase the per capita income of the respondent's family. It provides a financial and moral support to the respondents in all respects. The higher the earning members per family, the support of the family members is also higher. Apart from that, the standard of living of the respondents can be increased by more earning members per family which is essential for entrepreneurship.

Table 3.8: Earning Members in the Family of Respondents

S. No.	Earning Members	No. of Respondents	Percentage
1.	0-1	97	32.3
2.	2-3	177	59.0
3.	4-5	22	7.3
4.	Above 5	4	1.4
	Total	**300**	**100.0**

Source: Primary Data

Table 3.8 illustrates the earning members in the family of the respondents. A maximum of 59 per cent of the respondents have only two or three earning members in the family followed by 32.3 per cent have only one earning member in the family. The number of respondents who have 4 to 5 and above 5 earning members in the family constitutes 7.3 and 1.4 per cent respectively.

FAMILY OCCUPATION OF THE RESPONDENTS

The family occupation of the respondents represents the occupation of the father or husband of the respondents in the present study. The family occupation provides a lot of ideas to start and manage the enterprises. It also mould the psychological behaviour of the respondents which is suitable towards enterprises. Sometimes, the family occupation provides some training to the respondents in the enterprises. In the present study, the family occupation is confined into business, government employee, private employee, agriculture and others.

Table 3.9: Family Occupation of the Respondents

S. No.	Occupation of Family	No. of Respondents	Percentage
1.	Business	197	65.7
2.	Private	42	14
3.	Agriculture	37	12.3
4.	Government employee	24	8.0
	Total	**300**	**100.0**

Source: Primary Data

Table 3.9 explains the family occupation of the respondents. The important family occupation is business, private employee and agriculture which constitute 65.7, 14 and 12.3 per cent respectively. Only 8 per cent of the family occupation is government employment. It is evident from Table 4.9 that majority (65.7%) of the respondents family occupation is business.

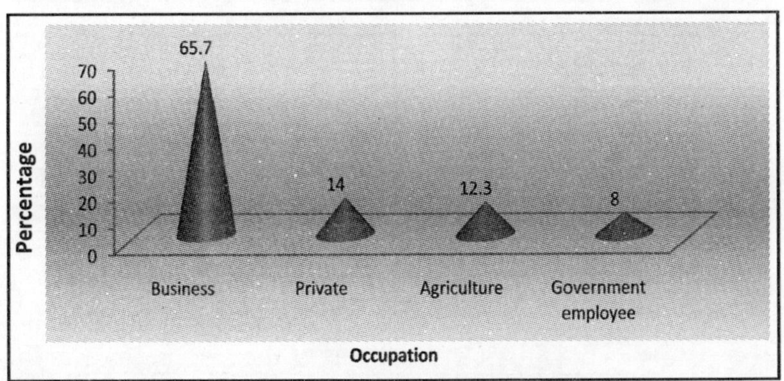

Fig. 3.3: Family Occupation of the Respondents

PRIMARY OCCUPATION OF THE RESPONDENTS

The primary occupation of the respondents represents the occupation done by them to earn their livelihood. It indicates the role of respondents in business. In the present study, the primary occupation is confined to business, private employee, agriculture and others. The primary occupation of the respondents is presented in Table 3.10.

Table 3.10: Primary Occupation of the Respondents

S. No.	Occupation	No. of Respondents	Percentage
1.	Business	210	70.0
2.	Agriculture	40	13.3
3.	Private	27	9.0
4.	Others	23	7.7
	Total	**300**	**100.0**

Source: Primary Data

A maximum of 70 per cent of the respondents are doing business as their primary occupation followed by 13.3 per cent of the respondents are doing agriculture as their primary occupation. Only 9 per cent of the rural women entrepreneurs are working as private employee followed by 7.7 per cent of respondents are doing other business such as finance and land business.

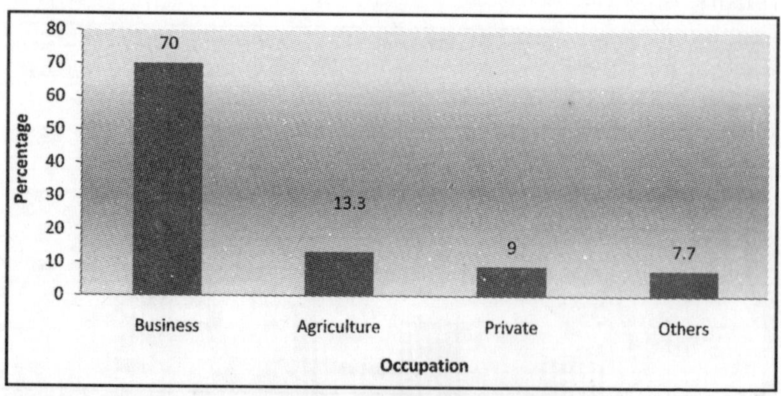

Fig. 3.4: Primary Occupation of the Respondents

FAMILY INCOME OF THE RESPONDENTS

The family income represents the total income earned by all earning members in the family through all sources per month. The higher family income leads to better standard of living and better education to the family members. The higher family income provides a base for finance to start the enterprise also. The respondents with better financial base may take risks in the enterprises. In the present study, the family income of the respondents is confined to less than ₹ 4000, ₹ 4001 to 8000, ₹ 8001 to 12000, and above ₹ 12,000. The distribution of respondents according to their family income is shown in Table 3.11.

Table 3.11: Family Income of the Respondents

S. No.	Family Income (in ₹)	No. of Respondents	Percentage
1.	Up to 4000	60	20.0
2.	4001-8000	75	25.0
3.	8001-12000	80	26.7
4.	Above 12000	85	28.3
	Total	**300**	**100.0**

Source: Primary Data

The number of respondents who have family monthly income of above ₹ 12,000 constitute 28.3 per cent followed by this, respondents who have income ₹ 8001 to 12,000 constitute 26.7 per cent. Among the rural women entrepreneurs, the number of respondents who have a family income of ₹ 4001 to 8000 constitute 26.7 per cent. Only 28.3 per cent of the respondents have an income up to ₹ 4000.

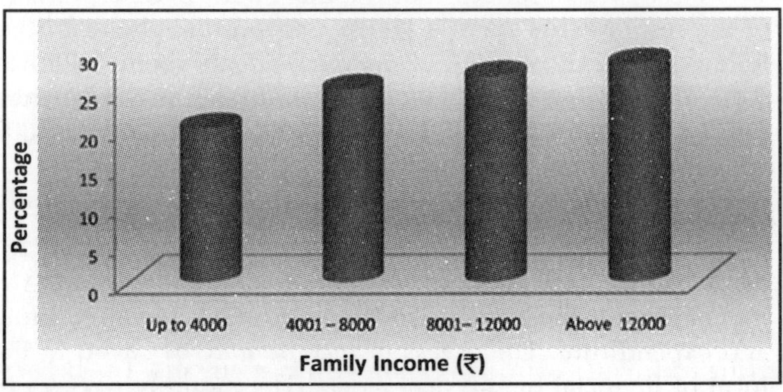

Fig. 3.5: Family Income of the Respondents

FAMILY EXPENDITURE OF THE RESPONDENTS

The family expenditure indicates the total expenses made on consumption by the respondents per month. The family expenditure may influence the nature of savings or indebtedness of the respondents. The savings or indebtedness directly affects the entrepreneurial behaviour of the respondents and also growth of enterprises of the respondents. The higher family expenditure may affect the saving potential of the respondents. In the present study, the family expenditure is classified into less than ₹ 2000, ₹ 2000 to 3000, ₹ 3001 to 4000, ₹ 4001 to 5000 and above ₹ 5000.

Table 3.12: Family Expenditure of the Respondents

S. No.	Family Expenditure (in ₹)	No. of Respondents	Percentage
1.	Up to 2000	4	1.3
2.	2001-3000	25	8.4
3.	3001-4000	31	10.4
4.	4001-5000	73	24.3
5.	Above 5000	167	55.7
	Total	**300**	**100.0**

Source: Primary Data

Table 3.12 describes that the maximum of 55.7 per cent of the respondents spent a family expenditure above ₹ 5000 followed by 24.3 per cent of the respondents spent ₹ 4001 to 5000. The number of rural women entrepreneurs who spent a family expenditure of ₹ 3001 to 4000 and ₹ 2000 to 3000 constitute 10.4 per cent and 8.4 per cent respectively. Only 1.3 per cent of the respondents spent up to ₹ 2000 as family expenditure per month.

SAVINGS OF THE RESPONDENTS

Savings is the outcome of the difference between revenue and expenditure. The excess of income may be saved in the form of financial or physical assets. The monthly savings of the respondents are calculated by the difference between the monthly income and expenditure of the respondents. The savings of the respondents may directly or indirectly influence the entrepreneurial behaviour and also the growth of enterprises of the entrepreneurs. In the present study, the monthly savings of the respondents are confined into negative, nil, up to ₹ 500, ₹ 501 to 1000, ₹ 1001 to 2000 and above ₹ 2000. The distribution of respondents according to their monthly savings is shown in Table 3.13.

Table 3.13: Savings of the Respondents

S. No.	Savings (in ₹)	No. of Respondents	Percentage
1.	Negative	24	8.0
2.	Nil	143	47.7
3.	Up to 1000	99	33.0
4.	1001-2000	16	5.3
5.	Above 2000	18	6.0
	Total	**300**	**100.0**

Source: Primary Data

Table 3.14 represents that 8 per cent of the respondents are indebted due to their excess family expenditure over the family income. A maximum of 47.7 per cent of the respondents have no savings at all. Only 33 per cent of the respondents have savings up to ₹ 1000. Among the rural women entrepreneurs, the respondents who saved more than ₹ 2000 and ₹ 1001 to 2000 constitute 6 per cent and 5.3 per cent respectively.

TYPE OF BUSINESS

Rural Women industries under the purview of KVIC are fragmented into six major groups except engineering and non conventional energy. Raw material based industry includes cottage pottery industry, limestone and other lime products industry, manufacture of bangles, paints, pigments, varnishes and distemper, manufacture of glass toys and glass decoration. Forest based industry includes bamboo and cane work, manufacture of paper cups, plates, paper containers, broom making, envelope making and manufacture of jute products. Agro based and food industry include packing and marketing of cereals, pulses, spices, condiments, masala, noodles making, sweets making, mini rice shelling unit, palm products industry, fruits and vegetable processing, pickles making, milk products and cattle feed, poultry feed making. Polymer and Chemical based industry includes soap industry, rubber goods, packing items of plastics, mehandi, essential oils, shampoos, hair oil, detergent and washing powder. Textile industry includes tailoring and preparation of readymade garments, embroidery, surgical bandages and stove wicks. Service industry includes laundry, barbar and tea stall.

Table 3.14: Distribution of Respondents According to the Type of Business

S. No.	Type of Business	No. of Respondents	Percentage
1.	Raw material based	30	10.0
2.	Forest based	43	14.3
3.	Agriculture and food product based	115	38.4
4.	Chemical/polymer based	37	12.3
5.	Textile based	45	15.0
6.	Service based	30	10.0
	Total	**300**	**100.0**

Source: Primary Data

A maximum of 38.4 per cent of the respondents engage in agriculture and food product based industries followed by 15 per cent engage in textile based industries. The number of respondents engages in forest based and chemical/polymer based and service based industries constitute 14.3 and 12.3 per cent respectively. Only 10 per cent of the respondents engage in raw material based industries and also service based industries.

NATURE OF BUSINESS

In general, nature of business is classified on the basis of work done by the business unit. The selection of business related to different line rest on the capability, opportunity and interest among the entrepreneurs. The selection of the business may show its impact on the performance. Hence, it is included as one of the profile variables of the organization. In the present study, the nature of business is classified into production, trading and service. Table 3.15 enumerates the nature of business of the respondents in the study area.

Table 3.15: Distribution of Respondents According to the Nature of Business

S. No.	Nature of Business	No. of Respondents	Percentage
1.	Production	133	44.3
2.	Trading	118	39.3
3.	Service	49	16.4
	Total	**300**	**100.0**

Source: Primary Data

The production based enterprise converts the raw-material into finished goods whereas no such activity is required in trading. Trading is mere buying the goods from dealers or wholesaler and sells it to the consumers. Service based enterprises sells their service at some cost to the needed consumers. Table 3.15 reveal that a maximum of 44.3 per cent of the rural women entrepreneurs are producing goods followed by this 39.3 per cent of the respondents are doing trading activities. Only 16.4 per cent of the entrepreneurs are involved in service providing activities.

FORMS OF BUSINESS ORGANIZATION

A sound organization is essential for the success of a business and it makes administration easy. It determines the activities to be undertaken for achieving the objectives. A business organization can be classified into sole trader, partnership and joint stock company. In the present study, the forms of organization are confined to sole-proprietorship, partnership and joint stock companies.

Table 3.16: Classification of Respondents According to Forms of Business Organization

S. No.	Nature of Business	No. of Respondents	Percentage
1.	Sole-proprietorship	180	60.0
2.	Partnership	120	40.0
3.	Joint Stock Company	Nil	–
	Total	**300**	**100**

Source: Primary Data

A maximum of 60 per cent of the respondents are involved in sole-proprietorship and only by 40 per cent of the respondents are doing business on partnership basis. There is no company form of organization run by rural women entrepreneurs.

NATURE OF BUSINESS PREMISES

The entrepreneurs run the enterprises according to their capability of finance, management, marketability and risk taking ability. The nature of business premises selected by them is influenced by their family occupation, scope of business, profitability and other aspects. In the present study, the nature of business premises is classified into business run at home, business run in the own building, rental building and others.

Table 3.17: Nature of Business Premises

S. No.	Nature of Business Premises	No. of Respondents	Percentage
1.	Home	138	46
2.	Own Building	93	31
3.	Rental Building	54	18
4.	Others	15	5
	Total	**300**	**100.0**

Source: Primary Data

Table 3.17 reveals that 46 per cent of the respondents have their enterprises in their home whereas 31 per cent of the respondents run their enterprises in their own building. The respondents, who run their enterprises in rental building, industrial estate, etc., constitute 23 per cent.

EXISTENCE OF BUSINESS

Existence of business unit gives information about the years of existence since its establishment. It indicates the life period of the business unit so far completed. Years of existence will influence the profitability and also the perception towards various problems encountered in the enterprise. In the present study, the existence of business is classified into up to 2 years, 3 to 4 years, 5 to 6 years, and above 6 years. The distribution of enterprises according to their existence is shown in Table 3.18.

Table 3.18: Existence of Business

S. No.	Years of Existence	No. of Respondents	Percentage
1.	Up to 2 years	45	15.0
2.	3-4 years	136	45.3
3.	5-6 years	83	27.7
4.	Above 6 years	36	12.0
	Total	**300**	**100.0**

Source: Primary Data

A maximum of 45.3 per cent of the enterprises have existence of 3 to 4 years followed by 27.7 per cent have an existence of 4 to 6 years. The number of enterprises which have an existence of up to 2 years and above 6 years constitute 15 per cent, and 12 per cent respectively.

SOURCE OF INSPIRATION

Competitiveness always brings the best out of people. The incidence of increasing competition in the present global scenario has forced many people to find out ways and means to innovate. The entrepreneurship is generally understood as a pursuit of opportunity without limiting oneself to the

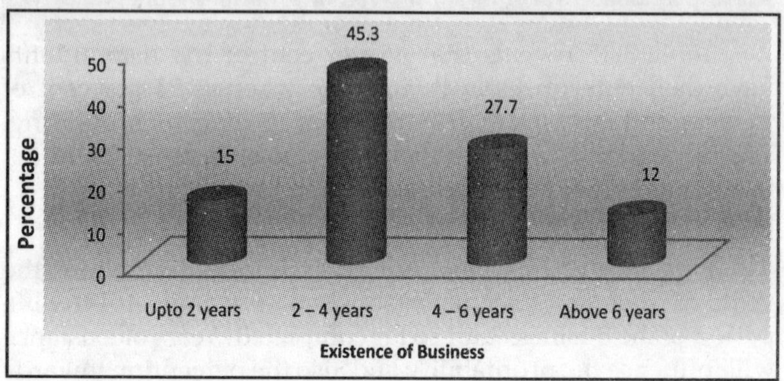

Fig. 3.6: Existence of Business

accepted norms of an organization. The sources of inspiration to start the enterprise is confined to self, family, friends and relatives, training institutions, government policies and programmes, successful entrepreneurs and others.

This section aims at assessing the source of inspiration to become an entrepreneur. The source of inspiration to become an entrepreneur as mentioned by Prof. R. K. Dixit in 'Women Entrepreneurship' (2012) has been classified as 'Self', 'Family', 'Friends and Relatives', 'Training Institutions', 'Government policies and programmes' and 'Successful entrepreneurs'.

Table 3.19: Sources of Inspiration to Become an Entrepreneur

S. No.	Sources	Mean	S.D	C.V.	't'-Value	Rank
1.	Self	3.98	1.04	26.17	16.68*	I
2.	Family	3.13	1.18	37.58	2.13*	II
3.	Friends and Relatives	3.09	1.18	38.20	1.69*	III
4.	Training Institutions	2.51	1.25	49.86	7.64*	V
5.	Government Policies and Programmes	2.42	1.20	49.62	9.17*	IV
6.	Successful Entrepreneurs	1.94	1.01	52.23	18.17*	VI

Table value with df (300-1) = 1.645

* Significant at 0.05 level.

Table 3.19 reveals that out of the six sources of inspiration which motivates a person to become an entrepreneur, the source 'Self', the co-efficient of variance (26.17) is the least, followed by the source 'Family' (37.58), 'Friends and Relatives' (38.20), 'Government Policies and Programmes' (49.62), 'Training Institutions' (49.86) and the source 'Successful Entrepreneurs' have the co-efficient of variation of 52.23. It is inferred from Table 3.19 that the self-motivation is ranked first compared to other sources of inspiration because of the low co-efficient of variation. So, it is evident that the self-motivation plays a vital role in inspiring the rural women to become entrepreneurs.

From the Table 3.19, it is found that the mean scores of the dimensions such as 'Self', 'Family', 'Friends and Relatives', 'Training Institutions', 'Government policies and programmes' and 'Successful entrepreneurs' are 3.98, 3.13, 3.09, 2.51, 2.42 and 1.94 respectively. Further, 't' values show that they are significant at 0.05 level. Hence it is concluded that the women entrepreneurs are influenced by the various sources of inspiration given in Table 3.19 to become an entrepreneur.

LEVELS OF SOURCES OF INSPIRATION

In order to study the level of sources of inspiration among the women entrepreneurs, the sample is grouped into three categories, namely: *(i)* low level, *(ii)* medium level and *(iii)* high level. The level of sources of inspiration (total) is determined by the score value calculated for 6 statements by adopting the scaling technique. The score values greater than or equal to $\overline{X} + S.D$ and score values less than or equal $\overline{X} + S.D$ to are classified respectively as high level and low level of sources of inspiration, while the score values in between $(\overline{X} + S.D)$ and $(\overline{X} + S.D)$ have been classified as medium level of sources of inspiration. The scores are given below.

Table 3.20: Sources of Inspiration Scores

Category	Low Level	High Level
Sources of inspiration (Total)	(Mean – Standard Deviation)	(Mean + Standard Deviation)
	17.08 - 2.62 = 14.46	17.08 + 2.62 = 19.70

To analyse the various sources of information, it is categorised into low, medium and high level scores. The source of information which falls below 14.46 is said to be in the low level and above that score is said to be high level. Based on the scores, the levels of sources of information can be measured.

ASSOCIATION BETWEEN LEVEL OF SOURCES OF INSPIRATION AND EDUCATIONAL QUALIFICATION OF WOMEN ENTREPRENEURS

Chi-square test is used to find the significance of educational qualification on the level of sources of inspiration of women entrepreneurs. The null hypothesis framed was "The level of sources of inspiration of women entrepreneurs is independent of their educational qualification". The result of Chi-square test is given in Table 3.21.

Table 3.21: Association Between Level of Sources of Inspiration and Educational Qualification of Women Entrepreneurs

Educational Qualification	Level of Sources of Inspiration			
	Low	Medium	High	Total
Up to high school	24	122	13	159
Higher secondary	12	62	15	89
Degree	7	11	10	28
Others	5	12	7	24
Total	**48**	**207**	**45**	**300**
Chi-square value	24.783			

Table value with df = (4-1) x (3-1) = 6 is 12.60 at 0.05 level of significance.

Table 3.21 shows that the calculated value of Chi-square is greater than the table value at 5 per cent level of significance. Hence, the null hypothesis, "The level of sources of inspiration of women entrepreneurs is independent of their educational qualification" is rejected. It is concluded that there is an association between the levels of sources of inspiration of women entrepreneurs and their educational qualification.

ASSOCIATION BETWEEN LEVEL OF SOURCES OF INSPIRATION AND FAMILY OCCUPATION OF WOMEN ENTREPRENEURS

Chi-square test is used to find the significance of family occupation of women entrepreneurs on the level of sources of inspiration of women entrepreneurs. The null hypothesis framed was "The level of sources of inspiration of women entrepreneurs is independent of their family occupation". The result of Chi-square test is given below.

Table 3.22: Association Between Level of Sources of Inspiration and Family Occupation of Women Entrepreneurs

Occupation of Family	Level of Sources of Inspiration			
	Low	Medium	High	Total
Business	29	151	17	197
Private	7	23	12	42
Agriculture	7	24	6	37
Others	5	9	10	24
Total	**48**	**207**	**45**	**300**
Chi-square value	29.110			

Table value with df = (4-1) x (3-1) = 6 is 12.60 at 0.05 level of significance.

Table 3.22 shows that the calculated value of Chi-square is greater than the table value at 5 per cent level of significance. Hence, the null hypothesis, "The level of sources of inspiration of women entrepreneurs is independent of their family occupation" is rejected. It is concluded that there is an association between the sources of inspiration of women entrepreneurs and their family occupation.

ASSOCIATION BETWEEN LEVEL OF SOURCES OF INSPIRATION AND OCCUPATION OF WOMEN ENTREPRENEURS

Chi-square test is used to find the significance of occupation of women entrepreneurs on the level of sources of inspiration of women entrepreneurs. The null hypothesis framed was

"The level of sources of inspiration of women entrepreneurs is independent of their occupation". The result of Chi-square test is given below.

Table 3.23: Association Between Level of Sources of Inspiration and Occupation of Women Entrepreneurs

Occupation of Respondents	Level of Sources of Inspiration			
	Low	Medium	High	Total
Business	21	161	28	210
Agriculture	10	24	6	40
Private	12	10	5	27
Others	5	12	6	23
Total	**48**	**207**	**45**	**300**
Chi-square value	30.573			

Table value with df = (4-1) x (3-1) = 6 is 12.60 at 0.05 level of significance.

Table 3.23 shows that the calculated value of Chi-square is greater than the table value at 5 per cent level of significance. Hence, the null hypothesis, "The level of sources of inspiration of women entrepreneurs is independent of their occupation" is rejected. It is concluded that there is an association between the sources of inspiration of women entrepreneurs and the occupation of women entrepreneurs.

ASSOCIATION BETWEEN LEVEL OF SOURCES OF INSPIRATION AND MONTHLY FAMILY INCOME OF WOMEN ENTREPRENEURS

Chi-square test is used to find the significance of family monthly income of women entrepreneurs on the level of sources of inspiration of women entrepreneurs. The null hypothesis framed was "The level of sources of inspiration of women entrepreneurs is independent of their family income". The result of Chi-square test is given below.

Table 3.24 shows that the calculated value of Chi-square is greater than the table value at 5 per cent level of significance. Hence, the null hypothesis, "The level of sources of inspiration

Table 3.24: Association Between Level of Sources of Inspiration and Monthly Family Income of Women Entrepreneurs

Family Monthly Income (in₹)	Level of Sources of Inspiration			
	Low	Medium	High	Total
Up to 4000	9	46	5	60
4001-8000	21	49	5	75
8001-12000	13	61	6	80
Above 12000	5	51	29	85
Total	**48**	**207**	**45**	**300**
Chi-square value	43.454			

Table value with df = (4-1) x (3-1) = 6 is 12.60 at 0.05 level of significance.

of women entrepreneurs is independent of their family income" is rejected. It is concluded that there is an association between the levels of sources of inspiration of women entrepreneurs and the monthly family income of women entrepreneurs.

ASSOCIATION BETWEEN LEVEL OF SOURCES OF INSPIRATION AND YEARS OF EXPERIENCE OF WOMEN ENTREPRENEURS

Chi-square test is used to find the significance of years of experience of women entrepreneurs on the level of sources of inspiration of women entrepreneurs. The null hypothesis framed was "The level of sources of inspiration of women entrepreneurs is independent of their years of experience". The result of Chi-square test is given below. (*See table on next page*)

Table 3.25 shows that the calculated value of Chi-square is greater than the table value at 5 per cent level of significance. Hence, the null hypothesis, "The level of sources of inspiration of women entrepreneurs is independent of their years of experience" is rejected. It is concluded that there is an association between the sources of inspiration of women entrepreneurs and the years of experience of women entrepreneurs.

Table 3.25: Association Between Level of Sources of Inspiration and years of Experience of Women Entrepreneurs

Years of Experience	Level of Sources of Inspiration			
	Low	Medium	High	Total
Up to 2 years	18	20	7	45
3-4 years	12	115	9	136
5-6 years	10	60	13	83
Above 6 years	8	12	16	36
Total	**48**	**207**	**45**	**300**
Chi-square value		64.962		

Table value with df = (4-1) x (3-1) = 6 is 12.60 at 0.05 level of significance.

INITIAL INVESTMENT IN THE BUSINESS

Investment is essential to invest on capital goods and also for working capital needs. The capital invested at the time of promotion is called as initial capital. In the present study, initial investment is confined to less than ₹ 10,000, ₹ 10,001 to 20,000, ₹ 20,001 to 30,000, ₹ 30,001 to 40,000, ₹ 40,001 to 50,000 and above ₹ 50,000.

Table 3.26: Initial Investment in the Business

S. No.	Initial Investment (in ₹)	No. of Respondents	Percentage
1.	Less than 10,000	160	53.3
2.	10,001-20,000	49	16.3
3.	20,001-30,000	19	6.3
4.	30,001-40,000	12	4.0
5.	40,001-50,000	8	2.7
6.	Above 50,000	52	17.3
	Total	**300**	**100.0**

Source: Primary Data

A maximum of 53.3 per cent of the respondents have invested less than ₹ 10,000 followed by 17.3 per cent of the respondents have invested above ₹ 50,000 in the initial stage. Among the rural women entrepreneurs, who have invested ₹ 10,001 to 20,000, ₹ 20,001 to 30,000 and ₹ 30,001 to 40,000 constitute 16.3 per cent, 6.3 per cent and 4 per cent respectively. Only 2.7 per cent of the respondents have invested ₹ 40,001 to 50,000.

INVESTMENT IN THE BUSINESS AT PRESENT

The capital requirements are growing day by day when the business activities are growing. Usually, increase in sales, debts, cost of raw materials, etc., requires an additional investment to manage the enterprises. The investment made on the enterprise in the present study is measured only at the time of survey. It is confined to less than ₹ 10,000, ₹ 10,001 to 20,000, ₹ 20,001 to 30,000, ₹ 30,001 to 40,000, ₹ 40,001 to 50,000 and above ₹ 50,000.

Table 3.27: Investment in the Business at Present

S. No.	Investment at Present (in ₹)	No. of Respondents	Percentage
1.	Less than 10,000	116	38.6
2.	10,000-20,000	66	22.0
3.	20,001-30,000	25	8.4
4.	30,001-40,000	16	5.3
5.	40,001-50,000	7	2.3
6.	Above 50,000	70	23.4
	Total	**300**	**100.0**

Source: Primary Data

A maximum of 38.6 per cent of the respondents have invested less than ₹ 10,000 followed by 23.4 per cent of the respondents have invested above ₹ 50,000. Among the rural women entrepreneurs, the respondents who have invested ₹ 10,001 to 20,000, ₹ 20,001 to 30,000 and ₹ 30,001 to 40,000 constitute 22 per cent, 8.4 per cent and 5 per cent respectively. Only 2 per cent of the respondents have invested ₹ 40,001 to 50,000.

SOURCES OF INVESTMENT

The sources of investment indicate where from the enterprises mobilise their capital. Since the source of investment determines the cost of capital and also the profitability of the enterprises, it is included in the present study. In the present study, the respondents are allowed to represent their response on the source of investment. The sources of investment in the study are confined to owned and borrowed.

Table 3.28: Sources of Investment

S. No.	Sources of Investment	No. of Respondents	Percentage
1.	Owned	190	63.3
2.	Borrowed	110	36.7
	Total	**300**	**100.0**

Source: Primary Data

Table 3.28 reveals that the important source of investment among the rural women entrepreneurs are owned and borrowed and their respective percentages are 63.3 per cent and 36.7 per cent. From the Table 3.28, it is clear that most of the rural women entrepreneurs use their own money as investment.

SOURCES OF BORROWINGS

The sources of borrowings in the study are confined to Friends and Relatives, Private Money Lenders, Banks, Non-Government Organizations, Micro-Credit Institutions, etc.

Table 3.29: Sources of Borrowings

S. No.	Source of Borrowings	No. of Respondents	Percentage
1.	Friends and relatives	47	42.8
2.	Private money lenders	14	12.7
3.	Banks	26	23.6
4.	Non-Government organizations	11	10.0
5.	Micro-Credit institutions	12	10.9
	Total	**110**	**100.0**

Source: Primary Data

Table 3.29 reveals that the important source of borrowings among the rural women entrepreneurs is friends and relatives who constitute 42.8 per cent followed by 23.6 per cent of the respondents have borrowed from banks. The number of respondents who have borrowed from Private Money Lenders, Micro-Credit Institutions and Non-Government Organizations constitute 12.7 per cent, 10.9 per cent and 10 per cent respectively.

MONTHLY INCOME FROM THE BUSINESS

The monthly income from the business indicates the net income from the enterprise. In the present study, the monthly income from the business is confined to less than ₹ 5,000, ₹ 5,000 to 10,000, ₹ 10,001 to 15,000 and more than ₹ 15,000.

Table 3.30: Monthly Income from the Business

S. No.	Monthly Income (in ₹)	No of Respondents	Percentage
1.	Less than 5,000	103	34.3
2.	5,000-10,000	133	44.3
3.	10,001-15,000	30	10.0
4.	More than 15,000	34	11.4
	Total	**300**	**100.0**

Source: Primary Data

A maximum of 44.3 per cent of the respondents earn an income of ₹ 5,000 to 10,000 followed by this 34.3 per cent earn ₹ 5,000 to 10,000. Among the rural women entrepreneurs, the respondents who earn more than ₹ 10,000 and 10,001 to ₹ 15,000 constitute 11.4 per cent and 10 per cent respectively. (*See fig. 3.7 on next page*)

PROFIT EARNED FROM THE BUSINESS

The performance of the enterprise is assessed in terms of profit earned from the business. The entrepreneurs are asked to give the profit earned from the business at the time of survey. The distribution of respondents according to the profit earned from the business is shown in Table 3.31. (*See table on next page*)

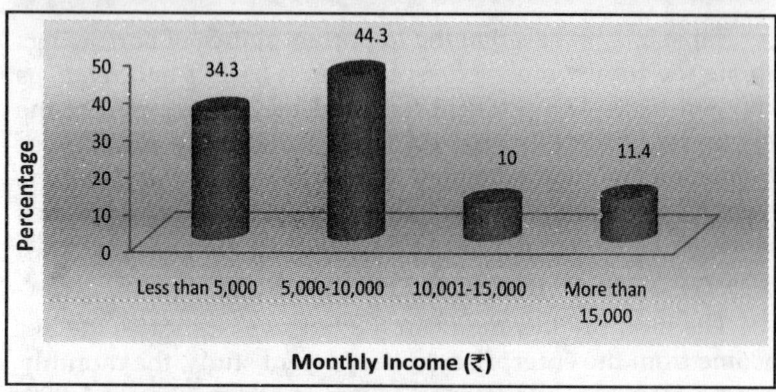

Fig. 3.7: Monthly Income from the Business

Table 3.31: Profit Earned from the Business

S. No	Profit (in ₹)	No of Respondents	Percentage
1.	Less than 2,000	25	8.3
2.	2,000-4,000	40	13.4
3.	4,000-6,000	124	41.3
4.	6,000-8,000	62	20.7
5.	8,000-10,000	37	12.3
6.	Above 10,000	12	4.0
	Total	**300**	**100.0**

Source: Primary Data

Nearly 41.3 per cent of the enterprises have earned ₹ 4000 to 5000 as profit every month whereas enterprises which earned profit of ₹ 6000 to 8000 constitute 20.7 per cent. The enterprises which earned profit of ₹ 2000 to 4000 and less than ₹ 2000 constitute 13.4 per cent and 8.3 per cent respectively. The enterprises which earned a profit of above ₹ 8000 constitute 16.3 per cent.

RESPONDENTS AWARENESS ABOUT GOVERNMENT ASSISTANCE

Majority of rural women entrepreneurs say that the present policy provisions are not sufficient. So, there is a need to formulate policies which should remove this misunderstanding among rural women entrepreneurs. The reality is that awareness about the various benefits provided under different schemes is also very low. In the present study, awareness of the respondents about government assistance is tested by yes or no question.

Table 3.32: Respondents Awareness about Government Assistance

S. No	Awareness	No of Respondents	Percentage
1.	Yes	72	24
2.	No	228	76
	Total	**300**	**100.0**

Source: Primary Data

Table 3.32 reveals that 76 per cent of the respondents are not aware of the government assistance and 24 per cent of the respondents are aware of the various benefits provided under different schemes offered by the government.

ASSISTANCE RECEIVED BY THE RESPONDENTS

The respondents who are aware of the government assistance may or may not receive any assistance through various schemes offered by the government. Thus, in the present study, whether the assistance received or not by the rural women entrepreneurs was enquired. The response given by the respondents is shown in Table 3.33.

TAble 3.33: Assistance Received by the Respondents

S. No.	Response	No of Respondents	Percentage
1.	Yes	64	21.3
2.	No	236	78.7
	Total	**300**	**100.0**

Source: Primary Data

Table 3.33 exhibits that 78.7 per cent of the respondents have not received any assistance and 21.3 per cent have received assistance through various schemes of government.

NUMBER OF WORKERS ENGAGED IN THE BUSINESS

The purpose of entrepreneurship is to promote self-employment and to create employment opportunities. Even in the case of rural enterprises, the employment opportunities are visible. In order to analyse this aspect, the number of employees engaged in business unit is collected from the rural women entrepreneurs. In the present study, the number of workers engaged by rural women entrepreneurs is confined to one, two, three and above three.

Table 3.34: Number of Workers Engaged in the Business

S. No	Number of Workers	No of Respondents	Percentage
1.	One	81	50.3
2.	Two	43	26.7
3.	Three	18	11.2
4.	Above three	19	11.8
	Total	**161**	**100.0**

Source: Primary Data

Table 3.34 exhibits the number of employment opportunities provided by the respondents through their business units. The number of respondents who provide an additional employment constitute 50.3 per cent. It is followed by 26.7 per cent of the respondents who provide employment to two persons. Only 23 per cent of the respondents provide three or more additional employment. The remaining 139 respondents which are not shown in the Table 3.34 are doing their business solely.

TYPE OF WORKERS EMPLOYED

In the present study, type of workers employed is confined to skilled, semi skilled and unskilled. (Table 3.35)

A maximum of 77.01 per cent of the workers employed are skilled workers followed by this 10.55 per cent of the workers are semiskilled. Only 12.4 per cent of the workers are unskilled. Table 3.35 shows that most (77%) of the skilled workers are employed by the rural women entrepreneurs.

Table 3.35: Type of Workers Employed

S. No.	Type of Workers	No. of Respondents	Percentage
1.	Skilled	124	77.0
2.	Semiskilled	17	10.6
3.	Unskilled	20	12.4
	Total	**161**	**100.0**

Source: Primary Data

SOURCE OF WORKERS

The availability of the workers is also significant for the success of the enterprise. The workers may be available either from the nearby places or from faraway places. In the present study, source of workers are confined to local, nearby place and neighbouring districts.

Table 3.36: Source of Workers

S. No.	Source of Workers	No. of Respondents	Percentage
1.	Local	134	83.2
2.	Nearby Placed	19	11.8
3.	Neighboring Districts	8	5.0
	Total	**161**	**100.0**

Source: Primary Data

A maximum of 83.2 per cent of the workers are from local places followed by 11.8 per cent of the workers are from nearby places. Only 5 per cent of the workers are from neighbouring districts.

Rural women's entrepreneurship can contribute to economic growth in developing countries and clearly represents an untapped potential. For many rural women, entrepreneurship is part of a broader livelihood strategy, often undertaken on a part-time basis, and where it production and reproduction tasks, as well as market and non-market work are separated. With few employment choices, women often start businesses in highly saturated sectors, in the informal economy and in low-productivity and low return activities, where they would be benefited.

The socio-economic profile of rural women entrepreneurs are considered very important as rural enterprises had employed very few employees and operate with less formality and reflect to a greater degree of attitudes of the entrepreneur. The study shows that the women entrepreneurs themselves have played a significant motivational role in running their enterprises.

Entrepreneurial Skills of Rural Women Entrepreneurs

Entrepreneur is human being who has his dignity, self-respect, values, sentiments, aspirations, dreams apart from economic status. Indeed, economic betterment and social upliftment motivates a person to distinguish from others. The possession of certain skills or abilities results in superior performance. An entrepreneur may possess certain skills and at the same time it is possible to develop these through training, experience and guidance. Various skills required for superior performance as mentioned by Vasant Desai in 'The Dynamics of Entrepreneurial Development and Management' (2010) are technical, business management, personal entrepreneurial, enterprise, behavioural, communication, listening and soft skills.

ASSESSMENT OF ENTREPRENEURIAL SKILLS

In this section, an attempt is made to assess the skills necessary to become an entrepreneur. A mean score above the neutral point indicates that the respondents have developed the significant skills and vice-versa. It is needless to point out however that a mean score of, say 15, just one point above the neutral point do not indicate definite assessment, as the little difference between the mean and the neutral point may be due to error variance that is bound to occur in any investigation, more so in educational and psychological research. Hence, mean score and the neutral point was tested for significance by applying 't' test.

The different entrepreneurial skills necessary to perform entrepreneurial activities have been identified as 'Technical Skills', 'Business Management Skills', 'Personal Entrepreneurial Skills', 'Enterprise Skills', 'Behavioural Skills', 'Communication Skills', 'Listening Skills' and 'Soft Skills'. The skills are presented in Table 4.1.

Table 4.1: Different Dimensions of Entrepreneurial Skills

S. No.	Entrepreneurial Skills	Mean	S.D.	C.V.	't'-Value	Rank
1.	Technical Skills	36.89	2.35	6.37	77.85*	V
2.	Business Management Skills	41.86	1.30	3.11	179.92*	I
3.	Personal Entrepreneurial Skills	28.33	1.96	6.92	90.62*	VI
4.	Enterprise Skills	50.45	2.32	4.60	96.01*	II
5.	Behavioural Skills	39.34	2.01	5.11	114.11*	III
6.	Communication Skills	28.67	1.60	5.58	63.98*	IV
7.	Listening Skills	15.31	1.20	7.84	52.39*	VIII
8.	Soft Skills	27.87	2.17	7.78	45.49*	VII

Table value with df (300-1) = 1.645

* Significant at 0.05 level.

Table 4.1 reveals that out of the eight skills of entrepreneur considered for performing entrepreneurial activities 'the co-efficient of variance of the 'Business Management Skills' is the least (3.11), followed by 'Enterprise Skills' (4.60), 'Behavioural Skills' (5.11), 'Communication Skills' (5.58), 'Technical Skills' (6.37), 'Personal Entrepreneurial Skills' (6.92), 'Soft Skills' (7.78) and 'Listening Skills' (7.84). From Table 4.1,

'Business Management Skills' is ranked in the first place as it influences the respondents to become an entrepreneur to the greatest extent.

From Table 4.1, it is found that the mean scores of the dimensions such as 'Business Management Skills', 'Enterprise Skills', 'Behavioural Skills', 'Communication Skills', 'Technical Skills', 'Personal Entrepreneurial Skills', 'Soft Skills' and 'Listening Skills' are 41.86, 50.45, 39.34, 28.67, 36.89, 28.33, 27.87 and 15.31 respectively, which are above the neutral point. Further, 't' values show that they are significant at 0.05 level. As all the entrepreneurial skills tested are significant, it is concluded that all the skills have a bearing on the entrepreneurship.

LEVELS OF ENTREPRENEURIAL SKILLS

In order to study the level of entrepreneurial skills among the women entrepreneurs, the sample is grouped into three categories, namely: *(i)* low, *(ii)* medium and *(iii)* high level. The scores were calculated by adopting scaling technique for all the skills. The score values greater than or equal to $\overline{X} + S.D$ and score values less than or equal $\overline{X} - S.D$ to are classified respectively as high level and low level of entrepreneurial skills, while the score values in between $(\overline{X} + S.D)$ and $(\overline{X} - S.D)$ have been classified as medium level of entrepreneurial skills. The scores are given below.

Table 4.2: Entrepreneurial Skill Scores

Category	Low Level	High Level
	(Mean – Standard Deviation)	(Mean + Standard Deviation)
Entrepreneurial Skills (Total)	268.72 - 5.38 = 263.34	268.72 + 5.38 = 274.10

To analyse the various entrepreneurial skills, it is categorised into low, medium and high level scores. The skills which fall below 263.34 are said to be in the low level and above the score are said to be high level. Based on the scores, the levels of entrepreneurial skills can be measured.

ASSOCIATION BETWEEN LEVEL OF ENTREPRENEURIAL SKILLS AND EDUCATIONAL QUALIFICATION OF RURAL WOMEN ENTREPRENEURS

Chi-square test is used to find the significance of educational qualification on the level of entrepreneurial skills of rural women entrepreneurs. The null hypothesis framed was "The level of entrepreneurial skills of rural women entrepreneurs is independent of their educational qualification". The results of Chi-square test are given in Table 4.3.

Table 4.3: Association Between Level of Entrepreneurial Skills and Educational Qualification of Rural Women Entrepreneurs

Educational Qualification	Level of Entrepreneurial Skills			
	Low	Medium	High	Total
Up to high school	28	119	12	159
Higher secondary	8	74	7	89
Degree	6	13	9	28
Others	5	9	10	24
Total	**47**	**215**	**38**	**300**
Chi-square value	41.407			

Table value with df = (4-1) x (3-1) = 6 is 12.60 at 0.05 level of significance

Table 4.3 shows that the calculated value of Chi-square is greater than the table value at 5 per cent level of significance. Hence, the null hypothesis, "The level of entrepreneurial skills of rural women entrepreneurs is independent of their educational qualification" is rejected. It is concluded that there is an association between the levels of entrepreneurial skills of rural women entrepreneurs and their educational qualification.

ASSOCIATION BETWEEN LEVEL OF ENTREPRENEURIAL SKILLS AND FAMILY OCCUPATION OF RURAL WOMEN ENTREPRENEURS

Chi-square test is used to find the significance of family occupation on the level of entrepreneurial skills of rural women entrepreneurs. The null hypothesis framed was "The level of entrepreneurial skills of rural women entrepreneurs is independent of their family occupation". The results of Chi-square test are given in Table 4.4.

Table 4.4: Association Between Level of Entrepreneurial Skills and Family Occupation of Rural Women Entrepreneurs

Occupation of Family	Level of Entrepreneurial Skills			
	Low	Medium	High	Total
Business	24	157	16	197
Private	9	26	7	42
Agriculture	9	22	6	37
Others	5	10	9	24
Total	**47**	**215**	**38**	**300**
Chi-square value	26.505			

Table value with df = (4-1) x (3-1) = 6 is 12.60 at 0.05 level of significance

Table 4.4 shows that the calculated value of Chi-square is greater than the table value at 5 per cent level of significance. Hence, the null hypothesis, "The level of entrepreneurial skills of rural women entrepreneurs is independent of their family occupation" is rejected. It is concluded that there is an association between the levels of entrepreneurial skills of rural women entrepreneurs and their family occupation of the rural women entrepreneurs.

ASSOCIATION BETWEEN LEVEL OF ENTREPRENEURIAL SKILLS AND OCCUPATION OF RURAL WOMEN ENTREPRENEURS

Chi-square test is used to find the significance of occupation on the level of entrepreneurial skills of rural women entrepreneurs. The null hypothesis framed was "The level of entrepreneurial skills of rural women entrepreneurs is independent of their occupation". The results of Chi-square test are given in Table 4.5. (*See table on next page*)

Table 4.5 shows that the calculated value of Chi-square is greater than the table value at 5 per cent level of significance. Hence, the null hypothesis, "The level entrepreneurial skills

Table 4.5: Association Between Level of Entrepreneurial Skills and Occupation of Women Entrepreneurs

Occupation of Respondents	Level of Entrepreneurial Skills			
	Low	Medium	High	Total
Business	15	178	17	210
Agriculture	13	20	7	40
Private	12	7	8	27
Others	7	10	6	23
Total	**47**	**215**	**38**	**300**
Chi-square value	66.132			

Table value with df = (4-1) x (3-1) = 6 is 12.60 at 0.05 level of significance

of rural women entrepreneurs are independent of their occupation" is rejected. It is concluded that there is an association between the levels of entrepreneurial skills of rural women entrepreneurs and the occupation of rural women entrepreneurs.

ASSOCIATION BETWEEN LEVEL OF ENTREPRENEURIAL SKILLS AND MONTHLY FAMILY INCOME OF RURAL WOMEN ENTREPRENEURS

Chi-square test is used to find the significance of family income on the level of entrepreneurial skills of rural women entrepreneurs. The null hypothesis framed was "The level of entrepreneurial skills of rural women entrepreneurs is independent of their family income". The results of Chi-square test are given in Table 4.6.

Table 4.6 shows that the calculated value of Chi-square is greater than the table value at 5 per cent level of significance. Hence, the null hypothesis, "The level of entrepreneurial skills of rural women entrepreneurs is independent of their family income" is rejected. It is concluded that there is an association between the levels of entrepreneurial skills of rural women entrepreneurs and the monthly family income of rural women entrepreneurs.

Table 4.6 Association Between Level of Entrepreneurial Skills and Monthly Family Income of Rural Women Entrepreneurs

Monthly Family Income	Level of Entrepreneurial Skills			
	Low	Medium	High	Total
Up to ₹4000	25	28	7	60
₹ 4001-8000	6	61	8	75
₹ 8001-12000	10	60	10	80
Above ₹12000	6	66	13	85
Total	**47**	**215**	**38**	**300**
Chi-square value	40.743			

Table value with df = (4-1) x (3-1) = 6 is 12.60 at 0.05 level of significance

ASSOCIATION BETWEEN LEVEL OF ENTREPRENEURIAL SKILLS AND YEARS OF EXPERIENCE OF RURAL WOMEN ENTREPRENEURS

Chi-square test is used to find the significance of years of experience of rural women entrepreneurs on the level of entrepreneurial skills of women entrepreneurs. The null hypothesis framed was "The level of entrepreneurial skills of rural women entrepreneurs is independent of their years of experience". The result of Chi-square test is given in Table 4.7.

Table 4.7: Association between Level of Entrepreneurial Skills and Years of Experience of Rural Women Entrepreneurs

Years of Experience	Level of Entrepreneurial Skills			
	Low	Medium	High	Total
Up to 2 years	15	22	8	45
2-4 years	14	115	7	136
4-6 years	12	58	13	83
Above 6 years	6	20	10	36
Total	**47**	**215**	**38**	**300**
Chi-square value	33.401			

Table value with df = (4-1) x (3-1) = 6 is 12.60 at 0.05 level of significance

Table 4.7 shows that the calculated value of Chi-square is greater than the table value at 5 per cent level of significance. Hence, the null hypothesis, "The level of entrepreneurial skills of rural women entrepreneurs is independent of their years of experience" is rejected. It is concluded that there is an association between the levels of entrepreneurial skills of rural women entrepreneurs and the years of experience of rural women entrepreneurs.

ANALYSIS OF VARIANCE AMONG ENTREPRENEURIAL SKILLS AND AGE OF RURAL WOMEN ENTREPRENEURS

In order to analyse the entrepreneurial skills and age of rural women entrepreneurs, a null hypothesis has been framed. The null hypothesis set for this purpose was, "There is no significant difference among the mean scores of entrepreneurial skills in total and in different dimensions such as technical skills, business management skills, personal entrepreneurial skills, enterprise skills, behavioural skills, communication skills, listening skills and soft skills of women entrepreneurs with respect to the variable age.

Since the calculated 'F' values are less than the table value in the entrepreneurial skills dimensions such as Technical skills, Business Management Skills, Behavioural Skills and Listening Skills, the null hypothesis is accepted. So, it is found that there is no significant difference among the mean scores of entrepreneurial skills and the individual skills such as Technical skills, Business Management Skills, Behavioural Skills and Listening Skills of women entrepreneurs with respect to their age. But, it is found that there is significant difference among the mean scores of entrepreneurial skills in total and in different dimensions such as Personal Entrepreneurial skills, Enterprise skills, Communication skills and Soft skills of rural women entrepreneurs with respect to their age.

Personal Entrepreneurial Skills of Women Entrepreneurs with Respect to Age

Since the 'F' ratio of Personal Entrepreneurial Skills is greater than that of the table value, the Scheffe test is applied.

Table 4.8: Analysis of Variance among the Mean Scores of Entrepreneurial Skills in Total and its Different Dimensions with Respect to Age of the Respondents

Dimensions	Source of Variance	Sum of Squares	df	Mean of Squares	F-Value	Remarks at 0.05 Level
Overall	Between	417.3275	3	139.1092	4.9237	Sig
	Within	8362.9384	296	28.2532		
Technical Skills	Between	24.3388	3	8.1129	1.4689	N.S.
	Within	1634.8947	296	5.5233		
Business Management Skills	Between	10.4030	3	3.4677	2.0609	N.S.
	Within	498.0438	296	1.6826		
Personal Entrepreneurial Skills	Between	80.6111	3	26.8704	7.2603	Sig
	Within	1095.5042	296	3.7010		
Enterprise Skills	Between	43.9077	3	14.6359	2.7405	Sig
	Within	1580.8463	296	5.3407		
Behavioural Skills	Between	8.0783	3	2.6928	0.6621	N.S.
	Within	1203.8055	296	4.0669		
Communication Skills	Between	45.8636	3	15.2879	6.2111	Sig
	Within	728.5638	296	2.4614		
Listening Skills	Between	5.0789	3	1.6930	1.1777	N.S.
	Within	425.4889	296	1.4375		
Soft Skills	Between	170.0419	3	56.6806	12.9511	Sig
	Within	1295.4502	296	4.3765		

Table value required for df 3, 296 is 2.636

Table 4.9: Scheffe's Post HOC Test for the Mean Scores of Personal Entrepreneurial Skills of Rural Women Entrepreneurs with Respect to Age

Age (in Years)				Mean Difference	C.I. Value	Result at 5% Level
Up to 25	26-35	36-45	Above 45			
267.500	270.126			2.626	3.052	N.S.
267.500		269.361		1.861	3.329	N.S.
267.500			265.303	2.197	3.841	N.S.
	270.126	269.361		0.765	2.107	N.S.
	270.126		265.303	4.823	2.848	Sig.
		269.361	265.303	4.058	3.142	Sig.

Table 4.9 reveals that significant differences are found between the rural women entrepreneurs in the age group of 26-35 years and above 45 years, and 36-45 years and above 45 years. Further, it reveals that the rural women entrepreneurs in the age group 26-35 years have higher personal entrepreneurial skills than the other age groups. But significant differences are not found between the rural women entrepreneurs in the age group of up to 25 years and 26-35 years, 25 years and 36-45 years, 25 years and above 45 years, and 26-35 years and 36-45 years.

Enterprise Skills of Rural Women Entrepreneurs with Respect to Age

Since the 'F' ratio of the Enterprise Skills is greater than that of the table value, the Scheffe test is applied.

Table 4.10 reveals that significant differences are found between the rural women entrepreneurs in the age group of upto 25 years and 26-35, up to 25 years and 36-45 years, and upto 25 years and above 45 years. Further, it reveals that the rural women entrepreneurs in the age group of up to 25 years have higher enterprise skills than the other age groups. But significant differences are not found between the rural women entrepreneurs in the age group of 26-35 years and 36-45 years, 26-35 years, and above 45 years, and 36-45 years and above 45 years.

Table 4.10: Scheffe's Post HOC Test for the Mean Scores of Enterprise Skills of Women Entrepreneurs with Respect to Age

Age (in Years)				Mean Difference	C.I. Value	Result at 5% Level
Up to 25	26-35	36-45	Above 45			
52.393	50.341			2.052	1.327	Sig.
52.393		50.236		2.157	1.447	Sig.
52.393			49.636	2.757	1.670	Sig.
	50.341	50.236		0.105	0.916	N.S.
	50.341		49.636	0.705	1.238	N.S.
		50.236	49.636	0.600	1.366	N.S.

Communication Skills of Rural Women Entrepreneurs with Respect to Age

Since the 'F' ratio of the Communication Skills is greater than that of the table value, the Scheffe test is applied.

Table 4.11: Scheffe's Post HOC Test for the Mean Scores of Communication Skills of Rural Women Entrepreneurs with Respect to Age

Age (in Years)				Mean Difference	C.I. Value	Result at 5% Level
Up to 25	26-35	36-45	Above 45			
28.571	28.401			0.170	0.901	N.S.
28.571		29.028		0.456	0.983	N.S.
28.571			29.364	0.792	1.134	N.S.
	28.401	29.028		0.627	0.622	Sig.
	28.401		29.364	0.962	0.840	Sig.
		29.028	29.364	0.336	0.927	N.S.

Table 4.11 reveals that significant differences are found between the age group of 26-35 years and above 45 years, and 26-35 years and 36-45 years. Further, it reveals that the rural women entrepreneurs in the age group of above 45 years have higher communication skills than the women entrepreneurs in

the age groups such as up to 25 years, 26-35 and 36-45 years. But significant differences are not found between the rural women entrepreneurs in the age group of up to 25 years and 26-35 years, up to 25 years and 36-45 years, up to 25 years and above 45 years, and 36-45 years and above 45 years.

Soft Skills of Rural Women Entrepreneurs with Respect to Age

Since the 'F' ratio of Soft Skills is greater than that of the table value, the Scheffe test is applied.

Table 4.12 Scheffe's Post HOC Test for the Mean Scores of Soft Skills of Rural Women Entrepreneurs With Respect to Age

Age (in Years)				Mean Difference	C.I. Value	Result at 5% Level
Up to 25	26-35	36-45	Above 45			
27.000	28.275			1.275	1.201	Sig.
27.000		27.875		0.875	1.310	N.S.
27.000			26.515	0.485	1.512	N.S.
	28.275	27.875		0.400	0.829	N.S.
	28.275		26.515	1.760	1.121	Sig.
		27.875	26.515	1.360	1.237	Sig.

Table 4.12 reveals that significant differences are found between the women entrepreneurs in the age group up to 25 years and 26-35 years, 26-35 years and above 45 years, and 36-45 years and above 45 years. Further, it reveals that the rural women entrepreneurs in the age group of 26-35 years have higher soft skills than the women entrepreneurs in the age groups such as up to 25 years, 36-45 years and above 45 years. But significant differences are not found between the women entrepreneurs in the age group of up to 25 years and 36-45 years, up to 25 years and above 45 years, and 26-35 years and 36-45 years.

ANALYSIS OF VARIANCE AMONG ENTREPRENEURIAL SKILLS AND EDUCATIONAL QUALIFICATION

Null Hypothesis

There is no significant difference among the mean scores of entrepreneurial skills in total and in different dimensions

Table 4.13 Analysis of Variance among the Mean Scores of Entrepreneurial Skills in Total and in Different Dimensions of Rural Women Entrepreneurs with Respect to Educational Qualification

Dimensions	Source of Variance	Sum of Squares	df	Mean of Squares	F-Value	Remarks at 0.05 Level
Overall	Between	250.1462	3	83.3821	2.9272	Sig
	Within	8431.7694	296	28.4857		
Technical Skills	Between	69.0384	3	23.0128	4.2830	Sig
	Within	1590.4349	296	5.3731		
Business Management Skills	Between	5.9942	3	1.9981	1.1776	N.S.
	Within	502.2122	296	1.6967		
Personal Entrepreneurial Skills	Between	102.6660	3	34.2220	9.5152	Sig
	Within	1064.5771	296	3.5965		
Enterprise Skills	Between	48.0463	3	16.0154	2.9950	Sig
	Within	1582.8072	296	5.3473		
Behavioural Skills	Between	11.2122	3	3.7374	0.9227	N.S.
	Within	1198.9740	296	4.0506		
Communication Skills	Between	13.0634	3	4.3545	1.7115	N.S.
	Within	753.1017	296	2.5443		
Listening Skills	Between	8.1965	3	2.7322	1.9091	N.S.
	Within	423.6252	296	1.4312		
Soft Skills	Between	41.6632	3	13.8877	3.0050	Sig
	Within	1367.9792	296	4.6216		

Table value required for df 3, 296 is 2.636

such as technical skills, business management skills, personal entrepreneurial skills, enterprise skills, behavioural skills, communication skills, listening skills and soft skills of women entrepreneurs with respect to their educational qualification.

Since the calculated 'F' values are less than the table value in the entrepreneurial skills dimensions such as Business Management Skills, Behavioural Skills, Communication Skills and Listening Skills, the null hypothesis is accepted. So, it is found that there is no significant difference among the mean scores of entrepreneurial skills dimensions such as Business Management Skills, Behavioural Skills, Communication Skills and Listening Skills of rural women entrepreneurs with respect to their educational qualification. But, it is found that there is significant difference among the mean scores of entrepreneurial skills in total and in different dimensions such as Technical skills, Personal Entrepreneurial skills, Enterprise skills and Soft skills of rural women entrepreneurs with respect to their educational qualification.

Entrepreneurial Skills (Total) of Rural Women Entrepreneurs with Respect to Educational Qualification

Since the 'F' ratio of Entrepreneurial Skills (Total) is greater than that of the table value, the Scheffe test is applied.

Table 4.14: Scheffe's Post HOC Test for the Mean Scores of Entrepreneurial Skills (Total) of Rural Women Entrepreneurs with Respect to Educational Qualification

Educational Qualification				Mean Difference	C.I. Value	Result at 5% Level
High School	Higher Secondary	Degree	Others			
266.943	270.843			3.899	1.987	Sig.
266.943		269.429		2.485	3.076	N.S.
266.943			268.875	1.932	3.287	N.S.
	270.843	269.429		1.414	3.252	N.S.
	270.843		268.875	1.968	3.452	N.S.
		269.429	268.875	0.554	4.175	N.S.

Table 4.14 reveals that significant differences are found between the women entrepreneurs having educational qualification up to high school and higher secondary. Further, it reveals that the women entrepreneurs having higher secondary qualification have higher entrepreneurial skills than the women entrepreneurs having high school, degree and other qualification. But significant differences are not found between the women entrepreneurs of having educational qualification high school and degree, high school and others, higher secondary and others, higher secondary and degree, and degree and others.

Technical Skills of Rural Women Entrepreneurs with Respect to Educational Qualification

Since the 'F' ratio of Technical Skills is greater than that of the table value, the Scheffe test is applied.

Table 4.15: Scheffe's Post HOC Test for the Mean Scores of Technical Skills of Women Entrepreneurs with Respect to Educational Qualification

Educational Qualification				Mean Difference	C.I. Value	Result at 5% Level
High School	Higher Secondary	Degree	Others			
36.484	37.483			0.999	0.863	Sig.
36.484		37.000		0.516	1.336	N.S.
36.484			37.250	0.766	1.427	N.S.
	37.483	37.000		0.483	1.412	N.S.
	37.483		37.250	0.233	1.499	N.S.
		37.000	37.250	0.250	1.813	N.S.

Table 4.15 reveals that significant differences are found between the women entrepreneurs having educational qualification up to high school and higher secondary. Further, it reveals that the women entrepreneurs having higher secondary qualification have higher technical skills than the women entrepreneurs having high school, degree and other qualification. But significant differences are not found between the women entrepreneurs having educational qualification of

high school and degree, high school and others, higher secondary and others, higher secondary and degree, and degree and others.

Personal Entrepreneurial Skills of Rural Women Entrepreneurs with Respect to Educational Qualification

Since the 'F' ratio of Personal Entrepreneurial Skills is greater than that of the table value, the Scheffe test is applied.

Table 4.16 Scheffe's Post HOC Test for the Mean Scores of Personal Entrepreneurial Skills of Rural Women Entrepreneurs with Respect to Educational Qualification

Educational Qualification				Mean Difference	C.I. Value	Result at 5% Level
High School	Higher Secondary	Degree	Others			
27.830	28.978			1.147	0.706	Sig.
27.830		28.750		0.920	1.093	N.S.
27.830			28.708	0.878	1.168	N.S.
	28.978	28.750		0.227	1.156	N.S.
	28.978		28.708	0.269	1.227	N.S.
		28.750	28.708	0.042	1.484	N.S.

Table 4.16 reveals that significant differences are found between the women entrepreneurs having educational qualification up to high school and higher secondary. Further, it reveals that the women entrepreneurs having higher secondary qualification have higher personal entrepreneurial skills than the women entrepreneurs having educational qualification of high school, degree and others. But significant differences are not found between the women entrepreneurs having educational qualification of high school and degree, high school and others, higher secondary and others, higher secondary and degree, and degree and others.

Enterprise Skills of Rural Women Entrepreneurs with Respect to Educational Qualification

Since the 'F' ratio of Enterprise Skills is greater than that of the table value, the Scheffe test is applied.

Table 4.17: Scheffe's Post HOC Test for the Mean Scores of Enterprise Skills of Rural Women Entrepreneurs with Respect to Educational Qualification

Education Qualification				Mean Difference	C.I. Value	Result at 5% Level
High School	Higher Secondary	Degree	Others			
50.648	51.449			0.802	0.861	N.S.
50.648		48.607		2.041	1.333	Sig.
50.648			50.083	0.564	1.424	N.S.
	51.449	48.607		2.842	1.409	Sig.
	51.449		50.083	1.366	1.496	N.S.
		48.607	50.083	1.476	1.809	N.S.

Table 4.17 reveals that significant differences are found between the women entrepreneurs having educational qualification up to high school and degree, and higher secondary and degree. Further, it reveals that the women entrepreneurs having higher secondary qualification have higher enterprise skills than the women entrepreneurs having educational qualification of high school, degree and others. But significant differences are not found between the women entrepreneurs having educational qualification of high school and higher secondary, high school and degree, high school and others, higher secondary and others, higher secondary and others, and degree and others.

Soft Skills of Rural Women Entrepreneurs with Respect to Educational Qualification

Since the 'F' ratio of Soft Skills is greater than that of the table value, the Scheffe test is applied. (*See table on next page*)

Table 4.18 reveals that significant differences are found between the women entrepreneurs having educational qualification up to high school and degree, high school and higher secondary, and higher secondary and others. Further, it reveals that the women entrepreneurs having higher secondary qualification have higher soft skills than the women entrepreneurs having educational qualification of high school,

Table 4.18 Scheffe's Post HOC Test for the Mean Scores of Soft Skills of Rural Women Entrepreneurs with Respect to Educational Qualification

Education Qualification				Mean Difference	C.I. Value	Result at 5% Level
High School	Higher Secondary	Degree	Others			
26.554	29.303			2.750	0.800	Sig.
26.554		28.250		1.697	1.239	Sig.
26.554			27.875	1.322	1.324	N.S.
	29.303	28.250		1.053	1.310	N.S.
	29.303		27.875	1.428	1.390	Sig.
		28.250	27.875	0.375	1.682	N.S.

degree and others. But significant differences are not found between the women entrepreneurs having educational qualification of higher secondary and degree, high school and others, and degree and others.

ANALYSIS OF VARIANCE AMONG ENTREPRNEURIAL SKILLS AND MARITAL STATUS

Null Hypothesis

There is no significant difference among the mean scores of entrepreneurial skills in total and in different dimensions such as technical skills, business management skills, personal entrepreneurial skills, enterprise skills, behavioural skills, communication skills, listening skills and soft skills of women entrepreneurs with respect to marital status.

Since the calculated 'F' values are less than the Table 4.19 value in the entrepreneurial skills dimensions such as technical skills, business management skills, personal entrepreneurial skills, enterprise skills, behavioural skills, communication skills, listening skills and soft skills of women entrepreneurs, the null hypothesis is accepted. So, it is found that there is no significant difference among the mean scores of entrepreneurial skills of rural women entrepreneurs with respect to marital status.

Table 4.19: Analysis of Variance among the Mean Scores of Entrepreneurial Skills in Total and in Different Dimensions of Rural Women Entrepreneurs with Respect to Marital Status

Dimensions	Source of Variance	Sum of Squares	df	Mean of Squares	F-Value	Remarks at 0.05 Level
Overall	Between	25.5167	3	8.5056	0.2915	N.S.
	Within	8635.6572	296	29.1745		
Technical Skills	Between	17.6233	3	5.8744	1.0643	N.S.
	Within	1633.7601	296	5.5195		
Business Management Skills	Between	3.7970	3	1.2657	0.7426	N.S.
	Within	504.4970	296	1.7044		
Personal Entrepreneurial Skills	Between	30.1392	3	10.0464	2.6188	N.S
	Within	1135.5246	296	3.8362		
Enterprise Skills	Between	35.0492	3	11.6831	2.1914	N.S.
	Within	1578.0907	296	5.3314		
Behavioural Skills	Between	29.5284	3	9.8428	2.4428	N.S.
	Within	1192.6637	296	4.0293		
Communication Skills	Between	7.3217	3	2.4406	0.9510	N.S.
	Within	759.6286	296	2.5663		
Listening Skills	Between	5.3250	3	1.7750	1.2318	N.S.
	Within	426.5222	296	1.4410		
Soft Skills	Between	1.5256	3	0.5085	0.1073	N.S.
	Within	1403.3019	296	4.7409		

Table value required for df 3, 296 is 2.636

Further, the mean scores show that the dimensions of entrepreneurial skills such as Behavioural skills, personal Entrepreneurial skills, Enterprise skills of married women entrepreneurs are better than the unmarried women entrepreneurs.

ANALYSIS OF VARIANCE AMONG ENTREPRNEURIAL SKILLS AND NATURE OF FAMILY

Null Hypothesis

There is no significant difference between the mean scores of entrepreneurial skills of women entrepreneurs in total and in different dimensions such as Technical Skills, Business Management Skills, Personal Entrepreneurial Skills, Enterprise Skills, Behavioural Skills, Communication Skills, Listening Skills and Soft Skills with respect to nature of family.

Table 4.20 shows that there is no significant difference in the entrepreneurial skills of women entrepreneurs in total and in dimensions of various skills with respect to nature of family.

It also revealed in the Table 4.20 that there is significant difference exists in the dimensions of entrepreneurial skills such as Technical Skills, Business Management Skills, Personal Entrepreneurial Skills, Enterprise Skills, Communication Skills, Listening Skills and Soft Skills with respect to nature of family. The mean scores show that the entrepreneurial skills such as Technical skills, Business management skills, Personal entrepreneurial skills and soft skills of joint family women entrepreneurs are better than the nuclear family women entrepreneurs. Further, the mean scores show that the entrepreneurial skills dimensions such as Enterprise skills, Communication skills and Listening skills of nuclear family women entrepreneurs are better than the joint family women entrepreneurs.

ENTREPRNEURIAL SKILLS AND FAMILY OCCUPATION OF RURAL WOMEN ENTREPRENEURS

Null Hypothesis

There is no significant difference among the mean scores of entrepreneurial skills in total and in different dimensions

Table 4.20: Analysis of Variance among the Mean Scores of Entrepreneurial Skills in Total and in Different Dimensions of Rural Women Entrepreneurs with Respect to Nature of Family

Dimensions	Nature of Family	Number	Mean	SD	C.R. Value	Remarks at 0.05 Level
Total	Joint	202	269.33	4.66	1.44	N.S.
	Nuclear	88	268.36	5.50		
Technical Skills	Joint	202	37.16	2.35	2.96	Sig
	Nuclear	88	36.30	2.27		
Business Management Skills	Joint	202	41.73	1.08	2.26	Sig
	Nuclear	88	42.15	1.56		
Personal Entrepreneurial Skills	Joint	202	28.84	1.72	6.88	Sig
	Nuclear	88	27.15	2.01		
Enterprise Skills	Joint	202	50.21	2.25	2.85	Sig
	Nuclear	88	51.03	2.26		
Behavioural Skills	Joint	202	39.38	1.69	1.03	N.S.
	Nuclear	88	39.66	2.31		
Communication Skills	Joint	202	28.43	1.29	2.89	Sig
	Nuclear	88	29.10	2.02		
Listening Skills	Joint	202	15.20	0.86	2.74	Sig
	Nuclear	88	15.67	1.50		
Soft Skills	Joint	202	28.38	1.65	4.28	Sig
	Nuclear	88	27.31	2.07		

Table value for df 298 is 1.96 at 0.05 level of significance.

Table 4.21: Analysis of Variance among the Mean Scores of Entrepreneurial Skills in Total and in Different Dimensions of Rural Women Entrepreneurs with Respect to Occupation of Family

Dimensions	Source of Variance	Sum of Squares	df	Mean of Squares	F-Value	Remarks at 0.05 Level
Overall	Between	80.1810	3	26.7270	0.9224	N.S.
	Within	8576.8021	296	28.9757		
Technical Skills	Between	2.8493	3	0.9498	0.1705	N.S.
	Within	1648.5368	296	5.5694		
Business Management Skills	Between	16.9820	3	5.6607	3.3862	Sig
	Within	494.8239	296	1.6717		
Personal Entrepreneurial Skills	Between	61.1211	3	20.3737	5.4946	Sig
	Within	1097.5530	296	3.7079		
Enterprise Skills	Between	57.8768	3	19.2923	3.6190	Sig
	Within	1577.9079	296	5.3308		
Behavioural Skills	Between	3.6585	3	1.2195	0.2993	N.S.
	Within	1206.1749	296	4.0749		
Communication Skills	Between	14.6802	3	4.8934	1.9180	N.S.
	Within	755.1747	296	2.5513		
Listening Skills	Between	6.3162	3	2.1054	1.4676	N.S.
	Within	424.6507	296	1.4346		
Soft Skills	Between	8.9625	3	2.9875	0.6334	N.S.
	Within	1396.0734	296	4.7165		

Table value required for df 3, 296 is 2.636

such as technical skills, business management skills, personal entrepreneurial skills, enterprise skills, behavioural skills, communication skills, listening skills and soft skills of women entrepreneurs with respect to family occupation.

Since the calculated 'F' values are less than the table value in the entrepreneurial skills dimensions such as Technical Skills, Behavioural Skills, Communication Skills, Listening Skills and Soft Skills, the null hypothesis is accepted. So, it is found that there is no significant difference among the mean scores of entrepreneurial skills dimensions of women entrepreneurs with respect to the family occupation. But, it is found that there is significant difference among the mean scores of entrepreneurial skills in total and in different dimensions such as Business Management skills, Personal Entrepreneurial skills and Enterprise skills of women entrepreneurs with respect to the variable occupation of family.

Business Management Skills of Rural Women Entrepreneurs with Respect to Family Occupation

Since the 'F' ratio of Business Management Skills is greater than that of the table value, the Scheffe test is applied.

Table 4.22: Scheffe's Post HOC Test for the Mean Scores of Business Management Skills of Rural Women Entrepreneurs with Respect to Family Occupation

Occupation of Family				Mean Difference	C.I. Value	Result at 5% Level
Business	Private	Agri-culture	Others			
42.970	41.786			1.184	0.618	Sig.
42.970		40.324		2.645	0.651	Sig.
42.970			41.917	1.053	0.786	Sig.
	41.786	40.324		1.461	0.820	Sig.
	41.786		41.917	0.131	0.930	N.S.
		40.324	41.917	1.592	0.953	Sig.

Table 4.22 reveals that significant differences are found between the women entrepreneurs' family doing business and

agriculture, business and private occupation, business and others, and agriculture and other occupation. Further, it reveals that the women entrepreneurs' family doing business have higher business management skills than the women entrepreneurs doing private occupation, agriculture and others. But significant differences are not found between the women entrepreneurs of private and of other occupations.

Personal Entrepreneurial Skills of Rural Women Entrepreneurs with Respect to Family Occupation

Since the 'F' ratio of Personal Entrepreneurial Skills is greater than that of the table value, the Scheffe test is applied.

Table 4.23: Scheffe's Post HOC Test for the Mean Scores of Personal Entrepreneurial Skills of Rural Women Entrepreneurs with Respect to Family Occupation

Occupation of Family				Mean Difference	C.I. Value	Result at 5% Level
Business	Private	Agri-culture	Others			
28.279	27.643			0.636	0.920	N.S.
28.279		28.649		0.369	0.970	N.S.
28.279			29.417	1.138	1.171	N.S.
	27.643	28.649		1.006	1.221	N.S.
	27.643		29.417	1.774	1.386	Sig.
		28.649	29.417	0.768	1.419	N.S.

Table 4.23 reveals that no significant differences are found between women entrepreneurs' family doing business and agriculture, business and private occupation, business and others, private occupation and others, and agriculture and others. Further, it reveals that the women entrepreneurs doing other occupation such as finance and land business have higher personal entrepreneurial skills than the women entrepreneurs' family doing private occupation, agriculture and business. But significant differences are found between the women entrepreneurs families engaged in private and other occupation.

Enterprise Skills of Rural Women Entrepreneurs with Respect to Family Occupation

Since the 'F' ratio of Enterprise Skills is greater than that of the table value, the Scheffe test is applied.

Table 4.24: Scheffe's Post HOC Test for the Mean Scores of Enterprise Skills of Rural Women Entrepreneurs with Respect to Occupation of Family

Occupation of Family				Mean Difference	C.I. Value	Result at 5% Level
Business	Private	Agri-culture	Others			
51.635	50.500			1.135	1.103	Sig.
51.635		48.946		2.689	1.163	Sig.
51.635			49.583	2.051	1.404	Sig.
	50.500	48.946		1.554	1.464	Sig.
	50.500		49.583	0.917	1.661	N.S.
		48.946	49.583	0.637	1.702	N.S.

Table 4.24 reveals that significant differences are found between the women entrepreneurs' family doing business and agriculture, business and private occupation, business and others, and private occupation and agriculture. Further, it reveals that the women entrepreneurs doing family business have higher enterprise skills than the women entrepreneurs' family doing private occupation, agriculture and others. But significant differences are not found between the women entrepreneurs' family doing private occupation and others, agriculture and other occupations.

ENTREPRNEURIAL SKILLS AND OCCUPATION OF RESPONDENTS

Null Hypothesis

There is no significant difference among the mean scores of entrepreneurial skills in total and in different dimensions such as technical skills, business management skills, personal entrepreneurial skills, enterprise skills, behavioural skills, communication skills, listening skills and soft skills of women rural entrepreneurs with respect to their occupation.

Table 4.25: Analysis of Variance among the Mean Scores of Entrepreneurial Skills in Total and in Different Dimensions of Rural Women Entrepreneurs with Respect to Occupation

Dimensions	Source of Variance	Sum of Squares	df	Mean of Squares	F-Value	Remarks at 0.05 Level
Overall	Between	2328.1711	3	776.0570	32.3697	Sig
	Within	7096.5411	296	23.9748		
Technical Skills	Between	312.4541	3	104.1514	21.2789	Sig
	Within	1448.7985	296	4.8946		
Business Management Skills	Between	38.3772	3	12.7924	7.9014	Sig
	Within	479.2264	296	1.6190		
Personal Entrepreneurial Skills	Between	101.5657	3	33.8552	9.5377	Sig
	Within	1050.6873	296	3.5496		
Enterprise Skills	Between	64.9983	3	21.6661	4.0667	Sig
	Within	1577.0095	296	5.3277		
Behavioural Skills	Between	16.2412	3	5.4137	1.3403	N.S.
	Within	1195.6213	296	4.0393		
Communication Skills	Between	219.6197	3	73.2066	35.6744	Sig
	Within	607.4152	296	2.0521		
Listening Skills	Between	8.6385	3	2.8795	2.0097	N.S.
	Within	424.1189	296	1.4328		
Soft Skills	Between	705.3248	3	235.1083	75.2189	Sig
	Within	925.1942	296	3.1257		

Table value required for df 3, 296 is 2.636

Since the calculated 'F' values are less than the table value in respect of Behavioural Skills and Listening Skills, the null hypothesis is accepted. So, it is found that there is no significant difference among the mean scores of Behavioural Skills and Listening Skills of women entrepreneurs with respect to their occupation. But, it is found that there is significant difference among the mean scores of entrepreneurial skills in total and in different dimensions such as Technical Skills, Business Management Skills, Personal Entrepreneurial Skills, Enterprise Skills, Communication Skills and Soft Skills of women entrepreneurs with respect to the their occupation.

Entrepreneurial Skills (Total) of Rural Women Entrepreneurs with Respect to Occupation

Since the 'F' ratio of Entrepreneurial Skills (Total) is greater than that of the table value, the Scheffe test is applied.

Table 4.26: Scheffe's Post HOC Test for the Mean Scores of Entrepreneurial Skills (Total) of Rural Women Entrepreneurs with Respect to Occupation

Occupation of Respondents				Mean Difference	C.I. Value	Result at 5% Level
Business	Agri-culture	Private	Others			
269.871	266.150			3.721	2.375	Sig.
269.871		262.667		7.205	2.815	Sig.
269.871			269.783	0.089	3.024	N.S.
	266.150	262.667		3.483	3.430	Sig.
	266.150		269.783	3.633	3.603	Sig.
		262.667	269.783	7.116	3.907	Sig.

Table 4.26 reveals that significant differences are found between women entrepreneurs doing business and agriculture, business and private occupation, business and others, agriculture and others, and private occupation and others. Further, it reveals that the women entrepreneurs doing business have higher Entrepreneurial Skills in total than the women entrepreneurs doing private occupation, agriculture and others. But significant differences are not found between the women entrepreneurs doing business and other occupation.

Technical Skills of Rural Women Entrepreneurs with Respect to Occupation

Since the 'F' ratio of Technical Skills is greater than that of the table value, the Scheffe test is applied.

Table 4.27: Scheffe's Post HOC Test for the Mean Scores of Technical Skills of Rural Women Entrepreneurs with Respect to Occupation

Occupation of Respondents				Mean Difference	C.I. Value	Result at 5% Level
Business	Agri-culture	Private	Others			
37.348	35.550			1.798	1.073	Sig.
37.348		35.111		2.237	1.272	Sig.
37.348			37.130	0.217	1.366	N.S.
	35.550	35.111		0.439	1.550	N.S.
	35.550		37.130	1.580	1.628	N.S.
		35.111	37.130	2.019	1.765	Sig.

Table 4.27 reveals that significant differences are found between women entrepreneurs doing business and agriculture, business and private occupation, agriculture and other occupation. Further, it reveals that the women entrepreneurs doing business have higher technical skills than the women entrepreneurs doing private occupation, agriculture and other occupation. But significant differences are not found between the women entrepreneurs doing private occupation and others, business and others, private occupation and agriculture.

Business Management Skills of Rural Women Entrepreneur with Respect to Occupation of Respondents

Since the 'F' ratio of Business Management Skills is greater than that of the table value, the Scheffe test is applied.

Table 4.28 reveals that significant differences are found between women entrepreneurs doing business and agriculture, private occupation and agriculture, and agriculture and other occupation. Further, it reveals that the women entrepreneurs

Table 4.28: Scheffe's Post HOC Test for the Mean Scores of Business Management Skills of Rural Women Entrepreneurs with Respect to Occupation

Occupation of Respondents				Mean Difference	C.I. Value	Result at 5% Level
Business	Agri-culture	Private	Others			
41.971	41.825			0.146	0.617	N.S.
41.971		40.889		1.083	0.732	Sig.
41.971			42.044	0.072	0.786	N.S.
	41.825	40.889		0.936	0.891	Sig.
	41.825		42.044	0.218	0.936	N.S.
		40.889	42.044	1.155	1.015	Sig.

doing business have higher Business Management Skills than the women entrepreneurs doing private occupation, agriculture and other occupation. But significant differences are not found between the women entrepreneurs doing business and private occupation, business and other occupation, private occupation and other occupation.

Personal Entrepreneurial Skills of Rural Women Entrepreneurs with Respect to Occupation

Since the 'F' ratio of Personal Entrepreneurial Skills is greater than that of the table value, the Scheffe test is applied.

Table 4.29: Scheffe's Post HOC Test for the Mean Scores of Personal Entrepreneurial Skills of Rural Women Entrepreneurs with Respect to Occupation

Occupation of Respondents				Mean Difference	C.I. Value	Result at 5% Level
Business	Agri-culture	Private	Others			
28.410	28.250			0.160	0.914	N.S.
28.410		26.778		1.632	1.083	Sig.
28.410			29.522	1.112	1.164	N.S.
	28.250	26.778		1.472	1.320	Sig.
	28.250		29.522	1.272	1.386	N.S.
		26.778	29.522	2.744	1.503	Sig.

Table 4.29 reveals that significant differences are found between women entrepreneurs doing business and agriculture, private occupation and agriculture, agriculture and other occupation, private occupation and others. Further, it reveals that the women entrepreneurs doing business have higher Personal Entrepreneurial Skills than the women entrepreneurs doing private occupation, agriculture and other occupation. But significant differences are not found between the women entrepreneurs doing business and private occupation, business and other occupation, private occupation and other occupation.

Enterprise Skills of Rural Women Entrepreneurs with Respect to Occupation

Since the 'F' ratio of Enterprise Skills is greater than that of the table value, the Scheffe test is applied.

Table 4.30: Scheffe's Post HOC Test for the Mean Scores of Enterprise Skills of Rural Women Entrepreneurs with Respect to Occupation

Occupation of Respondents				Mean Difference	C.I. Value	Result at 5% Level
Business	Agri-culture	Private	Others			
51.638	50.075			1.563	1.120	Sig.
51.638		50.333		1.305	1.327	N.S.
51.638			48.478	3.160	1.426	Sig.
	50.075	50.333		0.258	1.617	N.S.
	50.075		48.478	1.597	1.699	N.S.
		50.333	48.478	1.855	1.842	Sig.

Table 4.30 reveals that significant differences are found between women entrepreneurs doing business and private occupation, business and other occupation, agriculture and other occupation, private occupation and other occupation. Further, it reveals that the women entrepreneurs doing business have higher Enterprise Skills than the women entrepreneurs doing private occupation, agriculture and other occupation. But significant differences are not found between

the women entrepreneurs doing business and agriculture, private occupation and agriculture, and private occupation and other occupation.

Soft Skills of Rural Women Entrepreneurs with Respect to Occupation

Since the 'F' ratio of Soft Skills is greater than that of the table value, the Scheffe test is applied.

Table 4.31: Scheffe's Post HOC Test for the Mean Scores of Soft Skills of Rural Women Entrepreneurs with Respect to Occupation

Occupation of Respondents				Mean Difference	C.I. Value	Result at 5% Level
Business	Agri-culture	Private	Others			
28.471	26.750			1.721	0.858	Sig.
28.471		24.296		4.175	1.016	Sig.
28.471			28.470	0.007	1.092	N.S.
	26.750	24.296		2.454	1.238	Sig.
	26.750		28.470	1.728	1.301	Sig.
		24.296	28.470	4.182	1.411	Sig.

Table 4.31 reveals that significant differences are found between women entrepreneurs doing business and private occupation, business and agriculture, agriculture and other occupation, private occupation and agriculture, and private occupation and other occupation. Further, it reveals that the women entrepreneurs doing business have higher Soft Skills than the women entrepreneurs doing private occupation, agriculture and other occupation. But significant differences are not found between the women entrepreneurs doing business and other occupation.

ENTREPRNEURIAL SKILLS AND YEARS OF EXPERIENCE OF RURAL WOMEN ENTREPRENEURS

Null Hypothesis

There is no significant difference among the mean scores of entrepreneurial skills in total and in different dimensions

Table 4.32: Analysis of Variance among the Mean Scores of Entrepreneurial Skills in Total and in Different Dimensions of Rural Women Entrepreneurs with Respect to Years of Experience

Dimensions	Source of Variance	Sum of Squares	df	Mean of Squares	F-Value	Remarks at 0.05 Level
Overall	Between	302.0839	3	100.6946	3.5500	Sig
	Within	8396.0533	296	28.3650		
Technical Skills	Between	67.4903	3	22.4968	4.1951	Sig
	Within	1587.3300	296	5.3626		
Business Management Skills	Between	43.9583	3	14.6528	9.3288	Sig
	Within	464.9293	296	1.5707		
Personal Entrepreneurial Skills	Between	345.6315	3	115.2105	40.6805	Sig
	Within	838.2956	296	2.8321		
Enterprise Skills	Between	452.2345	3	150.7448	37.0199	Sig
	Within	1205.3092	296	4.0720		
Behavioural Skills	Between	140.8464	3	46.9488	12.8963	Sig
	Within	1077.5850	296	3.6405		
Communication Skills	Between	26.6463	3	8.8821	3.5403	Sig
	Within	742.6163	296	2.5088		
Listening Skills	Between	5.6876	3	1.8959	1.3206	N.S.
	Within	424.9337	296	1.4356		
Soft Skills	Between	64.6785	3	21.5595	4.7540	Sig
	Within	1342.3572	296	4.5350		

Table value required for df 3, 296 is 2.636

such as technical skills, business management skills, personal entrepreneurial skills, enterprise skills, behavioural skills, communication skills, listening skills and soft skills of women entrepreneurs with respect to years of experience.

Since the calculated 'F' values are less than the Table 4.32 value in the Listening Skills, the null hypothesis is accepted. So, it is found that there is no significant difference among the mean scores of Listening Skills of women entrepreneurs with respect to their years of experience. But, it is found that there is significant difference among the mean scores of entrepreneurial skills in total and in different dimensions such as Technical Skills, Business Management Skills, Personal Entrepreneurial Skills, Enterprise Skills, Behavioural Skills, Communication Skills and Soft Skills of women entrepreneurs with respect to their years of experience.

Entrepreneurial Skills of Rural Women Entrepreneurs with Respect to Years of Experience

Since the 'F' ratio of Entrepreneurial Skills (Total) is greater than that of the table value, the Scheffe test is applied.

Table 4.33: Scheffe's Post HOC Test for the Mean Scores of Entrepreneurial Skills (Total) of Rural Women Entrepreneurs with Respect to Years of Experience

Years of Experience (in Years)				Mean Difference	C.I. Value	Result at 5% Level
Below 2	2-4	4-6	Above 6			
270.778	268.029			2.748	2.576	Sig.
270.778		268.627		2.151	2.773	N.S.
270.778			268.972	1.806	3.349	N.S.
	268.029	268.627		0.597	2.086	N.S.
	268.029		268.972	0.943	2.807	N.S.
		268.627	268.972	0.346	2.989	N.S.

Table 4.33 reveals that significant differences are found between the women entrepreneurs having an experience below 2 years and 2-4 years. Further, it reveals that the women

entrepreneurs having an experience of below 2 years have higher entrepreneurial skills in total than the women entrepreneurs having an experience of 2-4 years, 4-6 years and above 6 years. But significant differences are not found between the women entrepreneurs having an experience of below 2 years and 2-4 years, below 2 years and above 6 years, 2-4 years and 4-6 years, 2-4 years and above 6 years, and 4-6 years and above 6 years.

Technical Skills of Rural Women Entrepreneurs with Respect to Years of Experience

Since the 'F' ratio of Technical Skills is greater than that of the table value, the Scheffe test is applied.

Table 4.34: Scheffe's Post HOC Test for the Mean Scores of Technical Skills of Rural Women Entrepreneurs with Respect to Years of Experience

Years of Experience (in Years)				Mean Difference	C.I. Value	Result at 5% Level
Below 2	2-4	4-6	Above 6			
36.800	37.015			0.215	1.120	N.S.
36.800		36.313		0.487	1.206	N.S.
36.800			37.861	1.061	1.456	N.S.
	37.015	36.313		0.701	0.907	N.S.
	37.015		37.861	0.846	1.221	N.S.
		36.313	37.861	1.548	1.300	Sig.

Table 4.34 reveals that significant differences are found between the women entrepreneurs having an experience of 4-6 years and above 6 years. Further, it reveals that the women entrepreneurs having an experience above 6 years have higher technical skills than the women entrepreneurs having an experience below 2 years, 2-4 years and 4-6 years. But significant differences are not found between the women entrepreneurs having an experience below 2 years and 2-4 years, below 2 years and 4-6 years, below 2 years and above 6 years, 2-4 years and 4-6 years, 2-4 years and above 6 years.

Business Management Skills of Rural Women Entrepreneurs with Respect to Years of Experience

Since the 'F' ratio of Business Management Skills is greater than that of the table value, the Scheffe test is applied.

Table 4.35: Scheffe's Post HOC Test for the Mean Scores of Business Management Skills of Rural Women Entrepreneurs with Respect to Years of Experience

Years of Experience (in Years)				Mean Difference	C.I. Value	Result at 5% Level
Below 2	2-4	4-6	Above 6			
42.622	41.647			0.975	0.606	Sig.
42.622		42.012		0.610	0.652	N.S.
42.622			41.361	1.261	0.788	Sig.
	41.647	42.012		0.365	0.491	N.S.
	41.647		41.361	0.286	0.661	N.S.
		42.012	41.361	0.651	0.703	N.S.

Table 4.35 reveals that significant differences are found between the women entrepreneurs having an experience below 2 years and 2-4 years, and below 2 years and above 6 years. Further, it reveals that the women entrepreneurs having an experience 2-4 years have higher Business Management Skills than the women entrepreneurs having an experience of 2-4 years, 4-6 years and above 6 years. But significant differences are not found between the women entrepreneurs having an experience below 2 years and 4-6 years, 2-4 years and 4-6 years, 2-4 years and above 6 years, 4-6 years and above 6 years.

Personal Entrepreneurial Skills of Rural Women Entrepreneurs with Respect to Years of Experience

Since the 'F' ratio of Personal Entrepreneurial Skills is greater than that of the table value, the Scheffe test is applied.

Table 4.36 reveals that significant differences are found between the women entrepreneurs having an experience below 2 years and 4-6 years, below 2 years and above 6 years, 4-6 years and above 6 years, 2-4 years and 4-6 years, 2-4 years

Table 4.36: Scheffe's Post HOC Test for the Mean Scores of Personal Entrepreneurial Skills of Rural Women Entrepreneurs with Respect to Years of Experience

Years of Experience (in Years)				Mean Difference	C.I. Value	Result at 5% Level
Below 2 Years	2-4 Years	4-6 Years	Above 6 Years			
28.667	29.279			0.613	0.814	N.S.
28.667		27.265		1.402	0.876	Sig.
28.667			26.750	1.917	1.058	Sig.
	29.279	27.265		2.014	0.659	Sig.
	29.279		26.750	2.529	0.887	Sig.
		27.265	26.750	0.515	0.944	N.S.

and above 6 years. Further, it reveals that the women entrepreneurs having an experience of 2-4 years have higher Personal Entrepreneurial Skills than the women entrepreneurs having an experience below 2 years, 4-6 years and above 6 years. But significant differences are not found between the women entrepreneurs having an experience below 2 years and 2-4 years, 4-6 years and above 6 years.

Enterprise Skills of Rural Women Entrepreneurs with Respect to Years of Experience

Since the 'F' ratio of Enterprise Skills is greater than that of the table value, the Scheffe test is applied.

Table 4.37: Scheffe's Post HOC Test for the Mean Scores of Enterprise Skills of Rural Women Entrepreneurs with Respect to Years of Experience

Years of Experience (in Years)				Mean Difference	C.I. Value	Result at 5% Level
Below 2 Years	2-4 Years	4-6 Years	Above 6 Years			
50.822	49.213			1.609	0.976	Sig.
50.822		51.807		0.985	1.051	N.S.
50.822			51.500	0.678	1.269	N.S.
	49.213	51.807		2.594	0.790	Sig.
	49.213		51.500	2.287	1.064	Sig.
		51.807	51.500	0.307	1.132	N.S.

Table 4.37 reveals that significant differences are found between the women entrepreneurs having an experience below 2 years and 2-4 years, 2-4 years and 4-6 years, 2-4 years and above 6 years. Further, it reveals that the women entrepreneurs having an experience of 4-6 years have higher Enterprise Skills than the women entrepreneurs having an experience of below 2 years, 2-4 years and above 6 years. But significant differences are not found between the women entrepreneurs having an experience below 2 years and 4-6 years, below 2 years and above 6 years, 4-6 years and above 6 years.

Behavioural Skills of Rural Women Entrepreneurs with Respect to Years of Experience

Since the 'F' ratio of Behavioural Skills is greater than that of the table value, the Scheffe test is applied.

Table 4.38: Scheffe's Post HOC Test for the Mean Scores of Behavioural Skills of Rural Women Entrepreneurs with Respect to Years of Experience

Years of Experience (in Years)				Mean Difference	C.I. Value	Result at 5% Level
Below 2 Years	2-4 Years	4-6 Years	Above 6 Years			
39.867	38.662			1.205	0.923	Sig.
39.867		40.169		0.302	0.993	N.S.
39.867			39.361	0.506	1.200	N.S.
	38.662	40.169		1.507	0.747	Sig.
	38.662		39.361	0.699	1.006	N.S.
		40.169	39.361	0.808	1.071	N.S.

Table 4.38 reveals that significant differences are found between the women entrepreneurs having an experience below 2 years and 2-4 years, 2-4 years and 4-6 years. Further, it reveals that the women entrepreneurs having an experience of 4-6 years have higher Behavioural Skills than the women entrepreneurs having an experience of below 2 years, 2-4 years and above 6 years. But significant differences are not found between the women entrepreneurs having an experience below 2 years and 4-6 years, below 2 years and above 6 years, 4-6 years and above 6 years, 2-4 years and above 6 years.

Communication Skills of Rural Women Entrepreneurs with Respect to Years of Experience

Since the 'F' ratio of Communication Skills is greater than that of the table value, the Scheffe test is applied.

Table 4.39: Scheffe's Post HOC Test for the Mean Scores of Communication Skills of Rural Women Entrepreneurs with Respect to Years of Experience

Years of Experience (in Years)				Mean Difference	C.I. Value	Result at 5% Level
Below 2 Years	2-4 Years	4-6 Years	Above 6 Years			
28.400	29.978			1.578	0.766	Sig.
28.400		28.398		0.002	0.825	N.S.
28.400			27.500	0.900	0.996	N.S.
	29.978	28.398		1.580	0.620	Sig.
	29.978		27.500	2.478	0.835	Sig.
		28.398	27.500	0.898	0.889	Sig.

Table 4.39 reveals that significant differences are found between the women entrepreneurs having an experience below 2 years and 2-4 years, 2-4 years and 4-6 years, 4-6 years and above 6 years, 2-4 years and above 6 years. Further, it reveals that the women entrepreneurs having an experience of 2-4 years have higher Communication Skills than the women entrepreneurs having an experience of below 2 years, 4-6 years and above 6 years. But significant differences are not found between the women entrepreneurs having an experience of below 2 years and 4-6 years, below 2 years and above 6 years.

Soft Skills of Rural Women Entrepreneurs with Respect to Years of Experience

Since the 'F' ratio of Soft Skills is greater than that of the table value, the Scheffe test is applied.

Table 4.40 reveals that significant differences are found between the women entrepreneurs having an experience of 2-4 years and 4-6 years, below 2 years and 4-6 years.

Table 4.40: Scheffe's Post HOC Test for the Mean Scores of Soft Skills of Rural Women Entrepreneurs with Respect to Years of Experience

Years of Experience (in Years)				Mean Difference	C.I. Value	Result at 5% Level
Below 2 Years	2-4 Years	4-6 Years	Above 6 Years			
28.444	28.015			0.430	1.030	N.S.
28.444		27.169		1.276	1.109	Sig.
28.444			28.194	0.250	1.339	N.S.
	28.015	27.169		0.846	0.834	Sig.
	28.015		28.194	0.180	1.122	N.S.
		27.169	28.194	1.026	1.195	N.S.

Further, it reveals that the women entrepreneurs having an experience of below 2 years have higher Soft Skills than the women entrepreneurs having an experience of 2-4 years, 4-6 years and above 6 years. But significant differences are not found between the women entrepreneurs having an experience below 2 years and 2-4 years, below 2 years and above 6 years, 4-6 years and above 6 years, 2-4 years and above 6 years.

FACTORS INFLUENCING RURAL WOMEN ENTREPRENEURSHIP

Factor analysis is a technique by which a data set is analysed by creating one or more factors, each representing a cluster of interrelated variables within the data. The concentration variables are converted to logarithms and R-mode factor analysis is performed. It involved a comparison of the relations among variables in terms of samples (Mg len, 1992).

Principal axis factor analysis with varimax rotation was conducted to assess the underlying structure for the twenty items of factors influencing entrepreneurship and they are listed in the Table 4.41.

Table 4.41: Factors Influencing Entrepreneurship

Item	Factors Influencing Entrepreneurship
1.	Earn money
2.	Challenge seeking
3.	Social status
4.	Self-identity
5.	Family necessity
6.	Role model
7.	Employment
8.	Economic independence
9.	Financial assistance
10.	Aspiration about the children
11.	Traditional/Hereditary
12.	Urge to achieve
13.	Revival of sick unit
14.	Market potential
15.	More dependents in family
16.	Entrepreneurial experience
17.	Technical knowledge
18.	Use of idle funds
19.	Organizational skills
20.	Encouragement of family members

Table 4.42 displays the total variance explained among the factors influencing entrepreneurship.

In the R-mode factor analysis, eight factors account for about 64 percentage of the variance with first factor accounting for 9.55 per cent, second factor for 8.90 per cent, third factor for 8.68 per cent, fourth factor for 8.21 per cent, fifth factor for 7.83 per cent, sixth for 7.61 per cent, seventh for 7.13 per cent and eighth for 5.99 per cent.

Table 4.43 displays the items and factor loadings for the rotated factors. (*See table 4.43 on page 183*)

Table 4.42: Total Variance Explained

Factors	Initial Eigen Values			Rotated Sums of Squared Loadings		
	Total	% of Variance	Cumulative %	Total	% of Variance	Cumulative %
1	2	3	4	5	6	7
1.	2.463	12.317	12.317	1.909	9.545	9.545
2.	2.166	10.832	23.149	1.778	8.892	18.437
3.	1.816	9.082	32.231	1.735	8.677	27.114
4.	1.621	8.107	40.338	1.643	8.214	35.328
5.	1.347	6.734	47.072	1.566	7.831	43.159
6.	1.192	5.960	53.032	1.522	7.612	50.772
7.	1.104	5.518	58.550	1.427	7.133	57.904
8.	1.069	5.344	63.894	1.198	5.989	63.894
9.	0.939	4.695	68.589			
10.	0.908	4.539	73.127			
11.	0.778	3.891	77.018			
12.	0.736	3.680	80.698			
13.	0.689	3.443	84.141			

Contd...

1	2	3	4	5	6	7
14.	0.662	3.308	87.449			
15.	0.601	3.006	90.455			
16.	0.544	2.719	93.174			
17.	0.477	2.383	95.557			
18.	0.363	1.816	97.373			
19.	0.288	1.438	98.811			
20.	0.238	1.189	100.000			

Table 4.43: Factors Loadings for the Rotated Factors

Factors 1	Factors Loading 2								Cummunalities 3
	I	II	III	IV	V	VI	VII	VIII	
1.	**0.777**	-0.230	-0.237	0.134	-0.001	0.079	0.020	-0.007	0.74
2.	0.007	0.199	0.056	**0.729**	-0.075	0.112	-0.156	-0.037	0.62
3.	-0.039	**0.740**	0.140	-0.078	-0.234	0.113	-0.163	0.369	0.80
4.	-0.296	-0.225	0.119	**0.583**	0.134	0.018	0.139	0.049	0.43
5.	**0.682**	0.061	0.135	-0.243	-0.007	-0.069	-0.008	0.235	0.61
6.	0.030	0.048	-0.173	-0.222	**0.593**	0.097	0.225	0.077	0.50
7.	-0.074	**0.662**	0.049	0.016	0.194	0.128	0.376	-0.020	0.64
8.	-0.297	0.004	**0.761**	0.046	0.017	0.032	-0.078	-0.008	0.68
9.	0.043	**0.690**	0.022	0.055	0.341	-0.195	-0.034	-0.205	0.68
10.	-0.010	0.077	**0.538**	-0.492	0.029	-0.116	-0.021	0.109	0.57
11.	0.007	0.018	-0.031	0.114	-0.075	-0.153	**0.810**	-0.146	0.72
12.	-0.373	-0.087	0.050	0.267	-0.031	**0.751**	-0.103	0.027	0.80
13.	0.261	0.089	0.016	-0.031	-0.004	**0.852**	0.050	0.065	0.81
14.	0.004	0.018	-0.026	-0.177	0.066	0.107	**0.605**	0.219	0.46

Contd...

1	2								3
15.	0.261	0.087	**0.769**	0.087	0.001	0.074	0.026	-0.108	0.69
16.	-0.528	-0.173	-0.244	**0.508**	0.068	-0.062	-0.015	0.195	0.67
17.	-0.133	0.108	0.029	-0.068	**0.664**	-0.014	0.029	0.170	0.51
18.	0.074	0.038	-0.085	-0.004	0.129	0.085	0.029	**0.802**	0.68
19.	-0.224	-0.130	0.197	0.113	**0.636**	-0.103	-0.265	-0.010	0.60
20.	-0.163	0.281	-0.143	-0.312	0.324	0.235	-0.219	**0.533**	0.58
Eigen Values	2.46	2.17	1.82	1.62	1.35	1.19	1.10	1.07	
% of Variance	12.32	10.83	9.08	8.11	6.73	5.96	5.52	5.34	

Note: Loading > |0.5| are selected. Shaded numbers indicate loading factor

Table 4.43 shows that there are eight factors are loaded in the rotated factors. The first factor which seems to be 'Economic factors' loads most strongly on the statements 1 and 5 respectively with loading in the first column *(factor one)*. '(1) Earn money' has its highest loading on the first factor. The second factor which seems to be 'Social factors' is composed of 3 statements 3, 7 and 9 respectively with loading in the second column *(factor two)*. '(3) Social status' has the highest loading on the second factor. The third factor which seems to be 'Survival factors' is composed of 3 statements 8, 10 and 15 respectively with loading in the third column *(factor third)*. '(15) More dependents in family' has the highest loading on the third factor. The *factor fourth* which seems to be 'Entrepreneurial factors' is composed of 3 statements 2, 4 and 16 respectively with loading in the factor fourth. '(2) Challenge Seeking' has the highest loading on the fourth factor. The *factor fifth* which seems to be 'Organizational factors' is composed of 3 statements 6, 17 and 19 respectively with loading in the fifth factor. '(17) Technical knowledge' has the highest loading on the *factor fifth*. The *factor sixth* which seems to be 'Promotional factors' is composed of 2 statements 12 and 13 respectively with loading on the sixth factor. '(13) Revival of sick unit' has the highest loading on the sixth factor. The seventh factor which seems to be 'Historical factors' is composed of 2 statements 11 and 14 respectively with loading on the *factor seventh*. '(11) Traditional/ Hereditary' has the highest loading on the seventh factor. The last factor which seems to be 'Motivational factors' is composed of 2 statements 18 and 20 respectively with loading in the eighth column *(factor eight)*. '(18) Use of idle funds' has the highest loading on the eighth factor.

The skills of entrepreneurship constitute one of the major resources in the promotion of entrepreneurship, hence some skills specific to women were considered. A successful entrepreneur should possess the various entrepreneurial skills such as business management skills, enterprise skills, behavioural skills, communication skills, technical skills, personal entrepreneurial skills, soft skills and listening skills. Economic factors such as earn money and family necessity are the highest motivational factors that influence rural women to enter into entrepreneurship.

Problems Associated with Rural Women Entrepreneurs

Despite the fact that the Government has launched many developmental programmes for increasing entrepreneurship, the rural women entrepreneurship has not been able to achieve much. Hence, there exists a gap between what they possibly can and actual performing with the existing facilities. This implies that the women entrepreneurs are not able to exploit the resources at a fullest level which might be due to knowledge, social and psychological problems.

The main problems faced by women entrepreneurs are financial problems, over dependence on intermediaries, scarcity of raw materials, intense competition, high cost of production, low mobility, family ties and responsibilities, economical and social status, adverse effects of risk learning, lack of learning, lack of education and skill acquisition and low need for achievement. Due to their family responsibilities, women have less time. They have to look after both their children and business. Most of the women have lack of mobility and do not undergo additional training and they are handicapped by their inability to move from one place to another to their work. The problem in rural and remote areas is different from others.

The number of problems encountered is entrepreneurial, general, knowledge, social and psychological.

PROBLEMS OF RURAL WOMEN ENTREPRENEURS

This section aims at assessing the various problems faced by entrepreneurs. A mean score above the neutral point indicates that the respondents have developed the significant problems and vice-versa. It is needless to point out however that a mean score of, say 15, just one point above the neutral point do not indicate definite assessment, as the little difference between the mean and the neutral point may be due to error variance that is bound to occur in any investigation, more so in educational and psychological research. Hence, mean score and the neutral point was tested for significance by applying 't' test.

The different dimensions of entrepreneurial problems encountered by rural women entrepreneurs are 'Entrepreneurial problems', 'General Problems', 'Knowledge Problems', 'Economic Problems', 'Social Problems', and 'Psychological Problems'.

Table 5.1: Problems Encountered by Rural Women Entrepreneurs

S. No.	Problems	Mean	S.D	C.V.	't'-value	Rank
1.	Entrepreneurial Problems	29.99	2.66	8.87	63.59	V
2.	General Problems	32.87	3.09	9.40	57.81	VI
3.	Knowledge Problems	30.28	2.53	8.37	68.38	IV
4.	Economic Problems	24.55	1.22	4.96	102.82	I
5.	Social Problems	27.42	1.65	6.00	46.23	II
6.	Psychological Problems	23.37	1.68	7.20	8.41	III

Table value with df (300-1) = 1.645

* Significant at 0.05 level.

Table 5.1 reveals that out of the six problems of entrepreneur, the co-efficient of variance of 'Economic Problems' (4.96), is the least, followed by 'Social Problems' (6.00), 'Psychological Problems' (7.20, 'Knowledge Problems' (8.37), 'Entrepreneurial Problems' (8.87), and 'General Problems' (9.40). From the Table 5.1 that the 'Economic

Problems' is encountered by most of the rural women entrepreneurs as the standard deviation and co-efficient of variation for the economic problem is the least.

It is found that the mean scores of 'Economic Problems', 'Social Problems', 'Psychological Problems', 'Knowledge Problems', 'Entrepreneurial Problems', and 'General Problems' are 24.55, 27.42, 23.37, 30.28, 29.99 and 32.87 respectively. Further, 't' values shows that they are significant at 0.05 level. Hence it is concluded that all the problems taken into consideration have a significant bearing on their entrepreneurial activities.

LEVELS OF PROBLEMS FACED BY RURAL WOMEN ENTREPRENEURS

In order to study the magnitude of problems faced by the women entrepreneurs, the sample is grouped into three categories, namely: *(i)* low level, *(ii)* medium level and *(iii)* high level. The level of sources of information (total) is determined by the score value calculated for 6 problems (dimensions) by adopting the scaling technique. The score values greater than or equal $\overline{X} + S.D$ to and score values less than or equal to $\overline{X} - S.D$ are classified respectively as high level and low level of entrepreneurial skills, while the score values in between ($\overline{X} + S.D$) and ($\overline{X} - S.D$) have been classified as medium level of entrepreneurial skills. The scores are given below.

Table 5.2: Levels of Entrepreneurial Problem

Category	Low Level	High Level
	(Mean – Standard Deviation)	(Mean + Standard Deviation)
Entrepreneurial problems (Total)	168.48 – 6.08 = 162.00	168.48 + 6.08 = 174.96

To analyse the various problems faced by entrepreneurs, the problems are categorised into low, medium and high level. The problems which fall below 162.00 are said to be in the low level and above the score are said to be high level. Based on the scores, the levels of various problems can be measured.

ASSOCIATION BETWEEN LEVEL OF PROBLEMS AND EDUCATIONAL QUALIFICATION OF RURAL WOMEN ENTREPRENEURS

Chi-square test is used to find the significance of educational qualification on the problems of rural women entrepreneurs. The null hypothesis framed was "The level of problems of rural women entrepreneurs is independent of their educational qualification". The results of Chi-square test are given in Table 5.3.

Table 5.3: Association Between Level of Problems and Educational Qualification of Rural Women Entrepreneurs

Educational Qualification	Level of Problems			
	Low	Medium	High	Total
Up to 10th standard	23	123	13	159
12th Standard	8	70	11	89
UG Level	6	12	10	28
PG Level	5	7	12	24
Total	**42**	**212**	**46**	**300**
Chi-square value	46.470			

Table value with df = (4-1) x (3-1) = 6 is 12.60 at 0.05 level of significance

Table 5.3 shows that the calculated value of Chi-square is greater than that of the table value at 5 per cent level of significance. Hence, the null hypothesis, "The level of problems of rural women entrepreneurs is independent of their educational qualification" is rejected. It is concluded that there is an association between the levels of problems of rural women entrepreneurs and their educational qualification.

ASSOCIATION BETWEEN LEVEL OF PROBLEMS AND FAMILY OCCUPATION OF WOMEN ENTREPRENEURS

Chi-square test is used to find the significance of family occupation on the problems of rural women entrepreneurs. The null hypothesis framed was "The level of problems of rural women entrepreneurs is independent of their family occupation". The results of Chi-square test are given in Table 5.4.

Table 5.4: Association Between Level of Problems and Family Occupation of Rural Women Entrepreneurs

Occupation of Family	Level of Problems			
	Low	Medium	High	Total
Business	19	158	20	197
Private employment	11	24	7	42
Agriculture	7	21	9	37
Others	5	9	10	24
Total	**42**	**212**	**46**	**300**
Chi-square value	33.241			

Table value with df = (4-1) x (3-1) = 6 is 12.60 at 0.05 level of significance

Table 5.4 shows that the calculated value of Chi-square is greater than that of the table value at 5 per cent level of significance. Hence, the null hypothesis, "The level of problems of rural women entrepreneurs is independent of their family occupation" is rejected. It is concluded that there is an association between the levels of problems of rural women entrepreneurs and their family occupation.

ASSOCIATION BETWEEN LEVEL OF PROBLEMS AND OCCUPATION OF RURAL WOMEN ENTREPRENEURS

Chi-square test is used to find the significance of occupation of women entrepreneurs on the level of problems of rural women entrepreneurs. The null hypothesis framed was "The level of problems of rural women entrepreneurs is independent of their occupation". The result of Chi-square test is given in Table 5.5.

Table 5.5 shows that the calculated value of Chi-square is greater than that of the table value at 5 per cent level of significance. Hence, the null hypothesis, "The level of problems of rural women entrepreneurs is independent of their occupation" is rejected. It is concluded that there is an association between the levels of problems of women entrepreneurs and the occupation of rural women entrepreneurs.

Table 5.5: Association Between Level of Problems and Occupation of Rural Women Entrepreneurs

Occupation of Respondents	Level of Problems			
	Low	Medium	High	Total
Business	20	169	21	210
Agriculture	9	26	5	40
Private employment	8	10	9	27
Others	5	7	11	23
Total	**42**	**212**	**46**	**300**
Chi-square value	49.042			

Table value with df = (4-1) x (3-1) = 6 is 12.60 at 0.05 level of significance

ASSOCIATION BETWEEN LEVEL OF PROBLEMS AND MONTHLY FAMILY INCOME OF RURAL WOMEN ENTREPRENEURS

Chi-square test is used to find the significance of monthly family income of women entrepreneurs on the level of problems of rural women entrepreneurs. The null hypothesis framed was "The level of problems of rural women entrepreneurs is independent of their family income". The result of Chi-square test is given below.

Table 5.6: Association Between Level of Problems and Monthly Family Income of Rural Women Entrepreneurs

Family Monthly Income	Level of Problems			
	Low	Medium	High	Total
Up to ₹4000	11	32	17	60
₹ 4001-8000	8	58	9	75
₹ 8001-12000	10	56	14	80
Above ₹ 12000	13	66	6	85
Total	**42**	**212**	**46**	**300**
Chi-square value	16.441			

Table value with df = (4-1) x (3-1) = 6 is 12.60 at 0.05 level of significance

Table 5.6 shows that the calculated value of Chi-square is greater than that of the table value at 5 per cent level of significance. Hence, the null hypothesis, "The level of problems of rural women entrepreneurs is independent of their family income" is rejected. It is concluded that there is an association between the levels of problems of rural women entrepreneurs and their monthly family income.

ASSOCIATION BETWEEN LEVEL OF PROBLEMS AND YEARS OF EXPERIENCE OF RURAL WOMEN ENTREPRENEURS

Chi-square test is used to find the significance of years of experience of women entrepreneurs on the level of problems of women entrepreneurs. The null hypothesis framed was "The level of problems of women entrepreneurs is independent of their years of experience". The result of Chi-square test is given in Table 5.7.

Table 5.7: Association Between Level of Problems and Years of Experience of Rural Women Entrepreneurs

Years of Experience	Level of Problems			
	Low	Medium	High	Total
Up to 2	5	33	7	45
2-4	21	105	10	136
4-6	10	56	17	83
Above 6	6	18	12	36
Total	**42**	**212**	**46**	**300**
Chi-square value	18.745			

Table value with df = (4-1) x (3-1) = 6 is 12.60 at 0.05 level of significance

Table 5.7 shows that the calculated value of Chi-square is greater than that of the table value at 5 per cent level of significance. Hence, the null hypothesis, "The level of problems of women entrepreneurs is independent of their years of experience" is rejected. It is concluded that there is an association between the levels of problems of women entrepreneurs and their years of experience.

Table 5.8: Analysis of Variance among the Mean Scores of Problems in Total and in Different Dimensions of Rural Women Entrepreneurs with Respect to Age

Dimensions	Source of Variance	Sum of Squares	df	Mean of Squares	F-Value	Remarks at 0.05 Level
Overall	Between	134.3420	3	44.7807	1.2102	N.S.
	Within	10952.5095	296	37.0017		
Entrepreneurial Problems	Between	32.0738	3	10.6913	1.5163	N.S.
	Within	2087.0597	296	7.0509		
General Problems	Between	42.2386	3	14.0795	1.4758	N.S.
	Within	2823.8933	296	9.5402		
Knowledge Problems	Between	163.7105	3	54.5702	8.9014	Sig
	Within	1814.6256	296	6.1305		
Economic Problems	Between	4.3456	3	1.4485	0.9727	N.S.
	Within	440.8183	296	1.4893		
Social Problems	Between	21.8375	3	7.2792	2.7284	Sig
	Within	789.7078	296	2.6679		
Psychological Problems	Between	20.1005	3	6.7002	2.3812	N.S.
	Within	832.8702	296	2.8138		

Table value required for df 3, 296 is 2.636

ANALYSIS OF VARIANCE AMONG PROBLEMS AND AGE OF THE RURAL WOMEN ENTREPRENEURS

Null Hypothesis

There is no significant difference among the mean scores of problems in total and in different dimensions such as entrepreneurial problems, general problems, knowledge problems, economic problems, social problems and psychological problems of women entrepreneurs with respect to their age.

Since the calculated 'F' values are less than the table value in the problems such as Entrepreneurial Problems, General Problems, Economic Problems and Psychological Problems, the null hypothesis is accepted. So, it is found that there is no significant difference among the mean scores of the dimensions of entrepreneurial problems with respect to age. But, it is found that there is significant difference among the mean scores of problems in total and in different dimensions such as Knowledge Problems and Social Problems of women entrepreneurs with respect to age.

Knowledge Problems of Rural Women Entrepreneurs with Respect to Age

Since the 'F' ratio of Knowledge Problems is greater than that of the table value, the Scheffe test is applied.

Table 5.9: Scheffe's Post HOC Test for the Mean Scores of Knowledge Problems of Rural Women Entrepreneurs with Respect to Age

Age				Mean Difference	C.I. Value	Result at 5% Level
Up to 25	26-35	36-45	Above 45			
29.357	30.677			1.320	1.422	N.S.
29.357		30.319		0.962	1.551	N.S.
29.357			29.000	0.357	1.789	N.S.
	30.677	30.319		0.357	0.982	N.S.
	30.677		29.000	1.677	1.326	Sig.
		30.319	29.000	1.319	1.464	N.S.

Table 5.9 reveals that significant differences are found between the women entrepreneurs in the age group of 26-35 years and above 45 years. Further, it reveals that the women entrepreneurs in the age group 36-45 years have higher knowledge problems than the other age groups. But significant differences are not found between the women entrepreneurs in the age group of upto 25 years and 26-35 years, upto 25 years and 36-45 years, upto 25 years and above 45 years, and 26-35 years and 36-45 years, 36-45 and above 45 years.

Social Problems of Rural Women Entrepreneurs with Respect to Age

Since the 'F' ratio of Social Problems is greater than that of the table value, the Scheffe test is applied.

Table 5.10 Scheffe's Post HOC Test for the Mean Scores of Social Problems of Rural Women Entrepreneurs with Respect to Age

Age				Mean Difference	C.I. Value	Result at 5% Level
Up to 25	26-35	36-45	Above 45			
28.179	28.383			0.205	0.938	N.S.
28.179		27.361		0.817	1.023	N.S.
28.179			26.121	2.057	1.180	Sig.
	28.383	27.361		1.022	0.648	Sig.
	28.383		26.121	2.262	0.875	Sig.
		27.361	26.121	1.240	0.966	Sig.

Table 5.10 reveals that significant differences are found between the women entrepreneurs in the age group of up to 25 years and above 45 years, 26-35 years and 36-45 years, 26-35 years and above 45 years, 36-45 and above 45 years. Further, it reveals that the women entrepreneurs in the age group 26-35 years have higher social problems than the other age groups. But significant differences are not found between the women entrepreneurs in the age group of upto 25 years and 26- 35 years, upto 25 years and 36-45 years.

Table 5.11: Analysis of Variance among the Mean Scores of Problems in Total and in Different Dimensions with Respect to Educational Qualification

Dimensions	Source of Variance	Sum of Squares	df	Mean of Squares	F-Value	Remarks at 0.05 Level
Overall	Between	115.3921	3	38.4640	1.0408	N.S.
	Within	10939.5616	296	36.9580		
Entrepreneurial Problems	Between	26.9637	3	8.9879	1.2695	N.S.
	Within	2095.6991	296	7.0801		
General Problems	Between	20.0955	3	6.6985	0.6995	N.S.
	Within	2834.6569	296	9.5765		
Knowledge Problems	Between	124.3451	3	41.4484	6.6947	Sig
	Within	1832.5998	296	6.1912		
Economic Problems	Between	9.6274	3	3.2091	2.1835	N.S.
	Within	435.0419	296	1.4697		
Social Problems	Between	4.7226	3	1.5742	0.5789	N.S.
	Within	804.9524	296	2.7194		
Psychological Problems	Between	45.6668	3	15.2223	5.5601	Sig
	Within	810.3808	296	2.7378		

Table value required for df 3, 296 is 2.636

ANALYSIS OF VARIANCE AMONG PROBLEMS AND EDUCATIONAL QUALIFICATION

Null Hypothesis

There is no significant difference among the mean scores of problems in total and in different dimensions such as entrepreneurial problems, general problems, knowledge problems, economic problems, social problems and psychological problems of women entrepreneurs with respect to the variable educational qualification.

Since the calculated 'F' values are more than the table value in the problems such as such as and Knowledge Problems and Psychological Problems, the null hypothesis is rejected. So, it is found that there exists a significant difference among the mean scores of Knowledge Problems and Psychological Problems with respect to educational qualification. But, it is found that there is no significant difference among the mean scores of problems in total and Entrepreneurial Problems, General Problems, Economic Problems and Social Problems of women entrepreneurs with respect to educational qualification.

Knowledge Problems of Rural Women Entrepreneurs with Respect to Educational Qualification

Since the 'F' ratio of Knowledge Problems is greater than that of the table value, the Scheffe test is applied.

Table 5.12: Scheffe's Post HOC Test for the Mean Scores of Knowledge Problems of Rural Women Entrepreneurs with Respect to Educational Qualification

Educational Qualification				Mean Difference	C.I. Value	Result at 5% Level
High School	Higher Secondary	Degree	Others			
32.786	30.742			0.955	0.926	Sig.
32.786		31.071		1.285	1.434	N.S.
32.786			30.958	1.172	1.532	N.S.
	30.742	31.071		0.330	1.516	N.S.
	30.742		30.958	0.217	1.609	N.S.
		31.071	30.958	0.113	1.946	N.S.

Table 5.12 reveals that significant differences are found between the women entrepreneurs having educational qualification up to high school and higher secondary. Further, it reveals that the women entrepreneurs having educational qualification of high school have higher knowledge problems than the other educational qualification considered in the study. But significant differences are not found between the women entrepreneurs having educational qualification of high school and degree, high school and other qualification, higher secondary and other qualification, higher secondary and degree, degree and other qualification.

Psychological Problems of Rural Women Entrepreneurs with Respect to Educational Qualification

Since the 'F' ratio of Psychological Problems is greater than that of the table value, the Scheffe test is applied.

Table 5.13: Scheffe's Post HOC Test for the Mean Scores of Psychological Problems of Rural Women Entrepreneurs with Respect to Educational Qualification

Educational Qualification				Mean Difference	C.I. Value	Result at 5% Level
High School	Higher Secondary	Degree	Others			
23.692	23.000			0.692	0.616	Sig.
23.692		22.929		0.763	0.954	N.S.
23.692			23.125	0.567	1.019	N.S.
	23.000	22.929		0.071	1.008	N.S.
	23.000		23.125	0.125	1.070	N.S.
		22.929	23.125	0.196	1.294	N.S.

Table 5.13 reveals that significant differences are found between the women entrepreneurs having educational qualification up to high school and higher secondary. Further, it reveals that the women entrepreneurs having educational qualification of high school level have higher knowledge problems than others. But significant differences are not found between the women entrepreneurs having educational

qualification of high school and degree, high school and other qualification, higher secondary and others, higher secondary and degree, and degree and other qualification.

ANALYSIS OF VARIANCE AMONG PROBLEMS AND MARITAL STATUS OF RURAL WOMEN ENTREPRENEURS

Null Hypothesis

There is no significant difference among the mean scores of problems in total and in different dimensions such as entrepreneurial problems, general problems, knowledge problems, economic problems, social problems and psychological problems of rural women entrepreneurs with respect to their marital status. (*See table 5.14 next page*)

Since the calculated 'F' values are less than the table value in all dimensions of problems such as entrepreneurial problems, general problems, knowledge problems, economic problems, social problems and psychological problems of women entrepreneurs, the null hypothesis is accepted. So, it is found that there is no significant difference among the mean scores of various dimensions of problems with respect to the marital status of rural women entrepreneurs.

ANALYSIS OF VARIANCE AMONG PROBLEMS AND NATURE OF FAMILY OF RURAL WOMEN ENTREPRENEURS

Null Hypothesis

There is no significant difference between the mean scores of entrepreneurial skills of women entrepreneurs in total and in different dimensions such as entrepreneurial problems, general problems, knowledge problems, economic problems, social problems and psychological problems with respect to nature of family. (*See table 5.15 on page 201*)

Table 5.15 shows that there is no significant difference in the problems of women entrepreneurs in total and dimensions of various problems such as Entrepreneurial Problems, General Problems and Economic Problems with respect to the variable nature of family.

Table 5.14: Analysis of Variance among the Mean Scores of Problems in Total and in Different Dimensions with Respect to Marital Status

Dimensions	Source of Variance	Sum of Squares	df	Mean of Squares	F-Value	Remarks at 0.05 Level
Overall	Between	51.9787	3	17.3262	0.4659	N.S.
	Within	11008.4545	296	37.1907		
Entrepreneurial Problems	Between	38.4858	3	12.8286	1.8167	N.S.
	Within	2090.1929	296	7.0615		
General Problems	Between	10.6319	3	3.5440	0.3687	N.S.
	Within	2844.9675	296	9.6114		
Knowledge Problems	Between	23.2165	3	7.7388	1.2073	N.S.
	Within	1897.3789	296	6.4101		
Economic Problems	Between	1.5907	3	0.5302	0.3545	N.S.
	Within	442.7468	296	1.4958		
Social Problems	Between	6.0800	3	2.0267	0.7445	N.S.
	Within	805.7710	296	2.7222		
Psychological Problems	Between	3.7528	3	1.2509	0.4392	N.S.
	Within	842.9759	296	2.8479		

Table value required for df 3, 296 is 2.636

Table 5.15: Analysis of Variance among the Mean Scores of Problems in Total and in Different Dimensions with Respect to Nature of Family

Dimensions	Nature of Family	Number	Mean	S.D	C.R. Value	Remarks at 0.05 Level
Overall	Joint	202	168.20	5.16	1.74	N.S.
	Nuclear	88	169.59	6.71		
Entrepreneurial Problems	Joint	202	29.81	2.57	1.64	N.S.
	Nuclear	88	30.38	2.78		
General Problems	Joint	202	32.98	2.95	1.30	N.S.
	Nuclear	88	32.44	3.30		
Knowledge Problems	Joint	202	30.81	2.19	3.82	Sig
	Nuclear	88	29.69	2.32		
Economic Problems	Joint	202	24.54	1.06	1.08	N.S.
	Nuclear	88	24.72	1.36		
Social Problems	Joint	202	27.15	1.34	4.41	Sig
	Nuclear	88	28.11	1.84		
Psychological Problems	Joint	202	22.92	1.33	6.42	Sig
	Nuclear	88	24.25	1.74		

Table value for df (300-2) 298 is 1.96.

It is also revealed that there is significant difference exists in the dimensions of problems such as Knowledge Problems, Social Problems and Psychological Problems with respect to nature of family. The mean scores show that the problems such as general problems and knowledge problems of joint family women entrepreneurs are better than the nuclear family women entrepreneurs.

ANALYSIS OF VARIANCE AMONG PROBLEMS AND FAMILY OCCUPATION OF RURAL WOMEN ENTREPRENEURS

Null Hypothesis

There is no significant difference among the mean scores of problems in total and in different dimensions such as entrepreneurial problems, general problems, knowledge problems, economic problems, social problems and psychological problems of women entrepreneurs with respect to their family occupation.

Since the calculated 'F' values are less than the table value in the problems such as Entrepreneurial Problems, Knowledge Problems and Psychological Problems, the null hypothesis is accepted. So, it is found that there is no significant difference among the mean scores of Entrepreneurial Problems, Knowledge Problems and Psychological Problems with respect to family occupation. But, it is found that there is significant difference among the mean scores of problems in total and in different dimensions such as General Problems, Economic Problems and Social Problems of women entrepreneurs with respect to family occupation.

Problems (Total) of Rural Women Entrepreneurs with Respect to Family Occupation

Since the 'F' ratio of the Problems (Total) is greater than that of the table value, the Scheffe test is applied. (*See table 5.17 on page 204*)

Table 5.17 reveals that significant differences are found between the families of women entrepreneurs doing business and agriculture. Further, it reveals that the women entrepreneurs' family doing other business such as finance,

Table 5.16: Analysis of Variance among the Mean Scores of Problems tn Total and in Different Dimensions with Respect to Family Occupation

Dimensions	Source of Variance	Sum of Squares	df	Mean of Squares	F-Value	Remarks at 0.05 Level
Overall	Between	383.9822	3	127.9941	3.4963	Sig
	Within	10836.1193	296	36.6085		
Entrepreneurial Problems	Between	44.6052	3	14.8684	2.1127	N.S.
	Within	2083.1169	296	7.0376		
General Problems	Between	79.2049	3	26.4016	2.7961	Sig
	Within	2794.9629	296	9.4424		
Knowledge Problems	Between	29.5895	3	9.8632	1.5451	N.S.
	Within	1889.5287	296	6.3835		
Economic Problems	Between	13.1320	3	4.3773	2.9741	Sig
	Within	435.6517	296	1.4718		
Social Problems	Between	20.4360	3	6.8120	2.5548	N.S.
	Within	789.2468	296	2.6664		
Psychological Problems	Between	47.7139	3	15.9046	5.7997	Sig
	Within	811.7308	296	2.7423		

Table value required for df 3, 296 is 2.636

Table 5.17: Scheffe's Post HOC Test for the Mean Scores of Problems (Total) of Rural Women Entrepreneurs with Respect to Family Occupation

Occupation of Family				Mean Difference	C.I. Value	Result at 5% Level
Business	Private	Agri-culture	Others			
169.061	169.000			0.061	2.892	N.S.
169.061		165.946		3.115	3.049	Sig.
169.061			166.958	2.103	3.679	N.S.
	169.000	165.946		3.054	3.836	N.S.
	169.000		166.958	2.042	4.354	N.S.
		165.946	166.958	1.012	4.459	N.S.

land business has more problems than the family of women entrepreneurs doing business, private occupation and agriculture. But significant differences are not found between the women entrepreneurs' family doing private occupation and other occupation, business and private occupation, business and other occupation, and agriculture and other occupation.

General Problems of Rural Women Entrepreneurs with Respect to Family Occupation

Since the 'F' ratio of General Problems is greater than that of the table value, the Scheffe test is applied.

Table 5.18: Scheffe's Post HOC Test for the Mean Scores of General Problems of Rural Women Entrepreneurs with Respect to Family Occupation

Occupation of Family				Mean Difference	C.I. Value	Result at 5% Level
Business	Private	Agri-culture	Others			
33.056	34.191			1.135	1.469	N.S.
33.056		30.784		2.272	1.548	Sig.
33.056			32.417	0.639	1.868	N.S.
	34.191	30.784		3.407	1.948	Sig.
	34.191		32.417	1.774	2.211	N.S.
		30.784	32.417	1.633	2.265	N.S.

Table 5.18 reveals that significant differences are found between the families of women entrepreneurs doing business and agriculture. Further, it reveals that the women entrepreneurs' family doing other business such as finance, land business have more general problems than the family of women entrepreneurs doing other occupations. But significant differences are not found between the women entrepreneurs' family doing private occupation and others, business and private occupation, business and others, and agriculture and others.

Economical Problems of Rural Women Entrepreneurs with Respect to Occupation of Family

Since the 'F' ratio of Economical Problems is greater than that of the table value, the Scheffe test is applied.

Table 5.19: Scheffe's Post HOC Test for the Mean Scores of Economical Problems of Rural Women Entrepreneurs with Respect to Occupation of Family

Occupation of Family				Mean Difference	C.I. Value	Result at 5% Level
Business	Private	Agri-culture	Others			
24.655	25.524			0.869	0.580	Sig.
24.655		23.162		1.493	0.611	Sig.
24.655			24.375	0.280	0.738	N.S.
	25.524	23.162		2.362	0.769	Sig.
	25.524		24.375	1.149	0.873	Sig.
		23.162	24.375	1.213	0.894	Sig.

Table 5.19 reveals that significant differences are found between the families of women entrepreneurs doing business and private occupation, business and agriculture, private occupation and agriculture, private occupation and others, agriculture and others. Further, it reveals that the women entrepreneurs' family doing private occupation has more economic problems than the family of women entrepreneurs doing business, agriculture and others. But significant differences are not found between the women entrepreneurs' family is doing, business and other occupation.

Psychological Problems of Rural Women Entrepreneurs with Respect to Family Occupation

Since the 'F' ratio of Psychological Problems is greater than that of the table value, the Scheffe test is applied.

Table 5.20 Scheffe's Post HOC Test for the Mean Scores of Psychological Problems of Rural Women Entrepreneurs with Respect to Family Occupation

Occupation of Family				Mean Difference	C.I. Value	Result at 5% Level
Business	Private	Agri-culture	Others			
23.472	23.691			0.218	0.791	N.S.
23.472		23.135		0.337	0.834	N.S.
23.472			22.333	1.139	1.007	Sig.
	23.691	23.135		0.555	1.050	N.S.
	23.691		22.333	1.357	1.192	Sig.
		23.135	22.333	0.802	1.221	N.S.

Table 5.20 reveals that significant differences are found between the families of women entrepreneurs doing private occupation and others, business and others. Further, it reveals that the women entrepreneurs doing private occupation have more psychological problems than the family of women entrepreneurs doing business, agriculture and other occupation. But significant differences are not found between the women entrepreneurs' family doing business and private occupation, business and agriculture, private occupation and agriculture, agriculture and other occupation.

ANALYSIS OF VARIANCE AMONG PROBLEMS AND OCCUPATION OF RURAL WOMEN ENTREPRENEURS

Null Hypothesis

There is no significant difference among the mean scores of problems in total and in different dimensions such as entrepreneurial problems, general problems, knowledge problems, economic problems, social problems and psychological problems of women entrepreneurs with respect to the occupation of respondents.

Table 5.21: Analysis of Variance among the Mean Scores of Problems in Total and in Different Dimensions with Respect to Occupation of Respondents

Dimensions	Source of Variance	Sum of Squares	df	Mean of Squares	F-Value	Remarks at 0.05 Level
Overall	Between	1470.3311	3	490.1104	14.1588	Sig
	Within	10246.0918	296	34.6152		
Entrepreneurial Problems	Between	60.4578	3	20.1526	2.8912	Sig
	Within	2063.2369	296	6.9704		
General Problems	Between	140.4200	3	46.8067	4.9964	Sig
	Within	2772.9518	296	9.3681		
Knowledge Problems	Between	869.3092	3	289.7697	67.3436	Sig
	Within	1273.6452	296	4.3029		
Economic Problems	Between	25.2857	3	8.4286	5.8220	Sig
	Within	428.5215	296	1.4477		
Social Problems	Between	28.9103	3	9.6368	3.6120	Sig
	Within	789.7178	296	2.6680		
Psychological Problems	Between	40.3706	3	13.4569	4.9446	Sig
	Within	805.5660	296	2.7215		

Table value required for df 3, 296 is 2.636

Since the calculated 'F' values are more than the table value in the various dimensions of problems such as entrepreneurial problems, general problems, knowledge problems, economic problems, social problems and psychological problems, the null hypothesis is rejected. So, it is found that there is significant difference among the mean scores of the dimensions of problems and their occupation.

Problem (Total) of Rural Women Entrepreneurs with Respect to their Occupation

Since the 'F' ratio of the Problems (Total) is greater than that of the table value, the Scheffe test is applied.

Table 5.22: Scheffe's Post HOC Test for the Mean Scores of Problem (Total) of Rural Women Entrepreneurs with Respect to Occupation

Occupation of Respondents				Mean Difference	C.I. Value	Result at 5% Level
Business	Agri-culture	Private Employ-ment	Others			
169.486	166.400			3.086	2.854	Sig.
169.486		164.630		4.856	3.383	Sig.
169.486			167.478	2.007	3.634	N.S.
	166.400	164.630		1.770	4.121	N.S.
	166.400		167.478	1.078	4.330	N.S.
		164.630	167.478	2.849	4.695	N.S.

Table 5.22 reveals that significant differences are found between the mean scores of problems of women entrepreneurs doing business and private occupation, business and agriculture. Further, it reveals that the women entrepreneurs doing business have more problems in total than the women entrepreneurs doing private occupation, agriculture and others. But significant differences are not found between the women entrepreneurs doing private and other occupation, business and other occupation, agriculture and private occupation, agriculture and other occupation.

Entrepreneurial Problems of Rural Women Entrepreneurs with Respect to Occupation

Since the 'F' ratio of Entrepreneurial Problems is greater than that of the table value, the Scheffe test is applied.

Table 5.23: Scheffe's Post HOC Test for the Mean Scores of Entrepreneurial Problems of Rural Women Entrepreneurs with Respect to Occupation

Occupation of Respondents				Mean Difference	C.I. Value	Result at 5% Level
Business	Agri-culture	Private Employ-ment	Others			
30.129	29.250			0.879	1.281	N.S.
30.129		31.630		1.501	1.518	N.S.
30.129			28.217	1.911	1.631	Sig.
	29.250	31.630		2.380	1.849	Sig.
	29.250		28.217	1.033	1.943	N.S.
		31.630	28.217	3.412	2.107	Sig.

Table 5.23 reveals that significant differences are found between the problems of women entrepreneurs doing business and other occupation, agriculture and private occupation. Further, it reveals that the women entrepreneurs doing private occupation have more entrepreneurial problems than the women entrepreneurs doing business, agriculture, and other occupation. But significant differences are not found between the women entrepreneurs doing business and agriculture, business and private occupation and agriculture and other occupation.

General Problems of Rural Women Entrepreneurs with Respect to Occupation

Since the 'F' ratio of General Problems is greater than that of the table value, the Scheffe test is applied. (*See table on next page*)

Table 5.24 reveals that significant differences are found between the problems of women entrepreneurs doing business and agriculture, business and private occupation.

Table 5.24: Scheffe's Post HOC Test for the Mean Scores of General Problems of Rural Women Entrepreneurs with Respect to Occupation

Occupation of Respondents				Mean Difference	C.I. Value	Result at 5% Level
Business	Agri-culture	Private Employ-ment	Others			
34.157	32.400			1.757	1.485	Sig.
34.157		30.444		3.713	1.760	Sig.
34.157			32.696	1.461	1.890	N.S.
	32.400	30.444		1.956	2.144	N.S.
	32.400		32.696	0.296	2.252	N.S.
		30.444	32.696	2.251	2.442	N.S.

Further, it reveals that the women entrepreneurs doing business have more general problems than the women entrepreneurs doing private occupation, agriculture, and other occupation. But significant differences are not found between the women entrepreneurs doing agriculture and others, business and others, agriculture and private occupation, private occupation and other occupation.

Knowledge Problems of Rural Women Entrepreneurs with Respect to Occupation

Since the 'F' ratio of Knowledge Problems is greater than that of the table value, the Scheffe test is applied.

Table 5.25 reveals that significant differences are found between the problems of women entrepreneurs doing business and agriculture, business and private occupation and agriculture and other occupation, agriculture and private occupation, private occupation and other occupation. Further, it reveals that the women entrepreneurs doing business have more knowledge problems than the women entrepreneurs doing private occupation, agriculture, and other occupation. But significant differences are not found between the women entrepreneurs doing business and other occupation.

Table 5.25: Scheffe's Post HOC Test for the Mean Scores of Knowledge Problems of Rural Women Entrepreneurs with Respect to Occupation

Occupation of Respondents				Mean Difference	C.J. Value	Result at 5% Level
Business	Agri-culture	Private Employ-ment	Others			
30.871	29.525			1.346	1.006	Sig.
30.871		25.889		4.983	1.193	Sig.
30.871			31.391	0.520	1.281	N.S.
	29.525	25.889		3.636	1.453	Sig.
	29.525		31.391	1.866	1.526	Sig.
		25.889	31.391	5.502	1.655	Sig.

Economic Problems of Rural Women Entrepreneurs with Respect to Occupation

Since the 'F' ratio of Economic Problems is greater than that of the table value, the Scheffe test is applied.

Table 5.26: Scheffe's Post HOC Test for the Mean Scores of Economic Problems of Rural Women Entrepreneurs with Respect to Occupation

Occupation of Respondents				Mean Difference	C.I. Value	Result at 5% Level
Business	Agri-culture	Private Employ-ment	Others			
24.691	24.050			0.640	0.584	Sig.
24.691		24.407		0.283	0.692	N.S.
24.691			24.348	0.343	0.743	N.S.
	24.050	24.407		0.357	0.843	N.S.
	24.050		24.348	0.298	0.885	N.S.
		24.407	24.348	0.060	0.960	N.S.

Table 5.26 reveals that significant differences are found between the problems of women entrepreneurs doing business and agriculture. Further, it reveals that the women

entrepreneurs doing business have more economic problems than the women entrepreneurs doing private occupation, agriculture, and other occupation. But significant differences are not found between the women entrepreneurs doing business and others, business and private occupation and agriculture and other occupation, agriculture and private occupation, private occupation and other occupation.

Social Problems of Rural Women Entrepreneurs with Respect to Occupation

Since the 'F' ratio of Social Problems is greater than that of the table value, the Scheffe test is applied.

Table 5.27: Scheffe's Post HOC Test for the Mean Scores of Social Problems of Rural Women Entrepreneurs with Respect to Occupation

Occupation of Respondents				Mean Difference	C.I. Value	Result at 5% Level
Business	Agri-culture	Private Employ-ment	Others			
26.319	27.425			1.106	0.792	Sig.
26.319		29.222		2.903	0.939	Sig.
26.319			27.435	1.116	1.009	Sig.
	27.425	29.222		1.797	1.144	Sig.
	27.425		27.435	0.010	1.202	N.S.
		29.222	27.435	1.787	1.303	Sig.

Table 5.27 reveals that significant differences are found between the problems of women entrepreneurs doing business and agriculture, business and other occupation, business and private occupation, agriculture and private occupation, private occupation and other occupation. Further, it reveals that the women entrepreneurs doing private occupation have more social problems than the women entrepreneurs doing business, agriculture, and other occupation. But significant differences are not found between the women entrepreneurs doing agriculture and other occupation.

Psychological Problems of Rural Women Entrepreneurs with Respect to Occupation

Since the 'F' ratio of Psychological Problems is greater than that of the table value, the Scheffe test is applied.

Table 5.28: Scheffe's Post HOC Test for the Mean Scores of Psychological Problems of Rural Women Entrepreneurs with Respect to Occupation

Occupation of Respondents				Mean Difference	C.I. Value	Result at 5% Level
Business	Agri-culture	Private Employ-ment	Others			
23.319	23.750			0.431	0.800	N.S.
23.319		24.037		0.718	0.948	N.S.
23.319			22.391	0.928	1.019	N.S.
	23.750	24.037		0.287	1.155	N.S.
	23.750		22.391	1.359	1.214	Sig.
		24.037	22.391	1.646	1.316	Sig.

Table 5.28 reveals that significant differences are found between the problems of women entrepreneurs doing private occupation and other occupation, agriculture and other occupation. Further, it reveals that the women entrepreneurs doing agriculture have more psychological problems than the women entrepreneurs doing business, private occupation, and other occupation. But significant differences are not found between the women entrepreneurs doing business and other occupation, business and private occupation, agriculture and private occupation, business and agriculture.

ANALYSIS OF VARIANCE AMONG PROBLEMS AND FAMILY MONTHLY INCOME OF RURAL WOMEN ENTREPRENEURS

Null Hypothesis

There is no significant difference among the mean scores of problems in total and in different dimensions such as entrepreneurial problems, general problems, knowledge

Table 5.29: Analysis of Variance among the Mean Scores of Problems in Total and in Different Dimensions with Respect to Monthly Family Income

Dimensions	Source of Variance	Sum of Squares	df	Mean of Squares	F-Value	Remarks at 0.05 Level
Overall	Between	289.2386	3	96.4129	2.6505	Sig
	Within	10766.9412	296	36.3748		
Entrepreneurial Problems	Between	90.8658	3	30.2886	4.4313	Sig
	Within	2023.2127	296	6.8352		
General Problems	Between	92.3719	3	30.7906	3.2990	Sig
	Within	2762.6783	296	9.3334		
Knowledge Problems	Between	103.5108	3	34.5036	5.6209	Sig
	Within	1816.9668	296	6.1384		
Economic Problems	Between	27.1340	3	9.0447	6.4170	Sig
	Within	417.2089	296	1.4095		
Social Problems	Between	5.3848	3	1.7949	0.6609	N.S.
	Within	803.9116	296	2.7159		
Psychological Problems	Between	36.5367	3	12.1789	4.4512	Sig
	Within	809.8806	296	2.7361		

Table value required for df 3, 296 is 2.636

problems, economic problems, social problems and psychological problems of women entrepreneurs with respect to the variable monthly family income.

Since the calculated 'F' values are less than the table value in the various dimensions of problems such as Entrepreneurial Problems, Knowledge Problems, General Problems, Economic Problems and Psychological Problems, the null hypothesis is accepted. So, it is found that there is no significant difference among the mean scores of the dimensions of entrepreneurial problems with respect to monthly family income. But, it is found that there is significant difference among the mean scores of problems in total and in different dimensions such as Social Problems of women entrepreneurs with respect to the variable occupation of monthly family income.

Problem (Total) of Rural Women Entrepreneurs with Respect to Monthly Family Income

Since the 'F' ratio of the Problems (Total) is greater than that of the table value, the Scheffe test is applied.

Table 5.30: Scheffe's Post HOC Test for the Mean Scores of Problem (Total) of Rural Women Entrepreneurs with Respect to Monthly Family Income

Family Monthly Income				Mean Difference	C.I. Value	Result at 5% Level
Up to ₹ 4000	₹ 4001-8000	₹ 8001-12000	Above ₹ 12000			
170.050	168.840			1.210	2.938	N.S.
170.050		169.350		0.700	2.897	N.S.
170.050			165.953	4.097	2.860	Sig.
	168.840	169.350		0.510	2.726	N.S.
	168.840		165.953	2.887	2.687	Sig.
		169.350	165.953	3.397	2.642	Sig.

Table 5.30 reveals that significant differences are found between the women entrepreneurs who have family income up to ₹ 4000 and above 12000, ₹ 4001-8000 and above ₹ 12000, ₹ 8001-12000 and above ₹ 12000. Further, it reveals that the

women entrepreneurs who have family income up to ₹ 4000 have higher problems in total than the other income groups. But significant differences are not found between the women entrepreneurs who have family income up to ₹ 4000 and ₹ 4001-8000, up to ₹ 4000 and ₹ 8001-12000, ₹ 4001-8000 and ₹ 8001-12000.

Entrepreneurial Problems of Rural Women Entrepreneurs with Respect to Monthly Family Income

Since the 'F' ratio of Entrepreneurial Problems is greater than that of the table value, the Scheffe test is applied.

Table 5.31: Scheffe's Post HOC Test for the Mean Scores of Entrepreneurial Problems with Respect to Monthly Family Income

Family Monthly Income				Mean Difference	C.I. Value	Result at 5% Level
Up to ₹ 4000	₹ 4001-8000	₹ 8001-12000	Above ₹ 12000			
30.033	30.320			0.287	1.273	N.S.
30.033		30.525		0.492	1.256	N.S.
30.033			29.153	0.880	1.240	N.S.
	30.320	30.525		0.205	1.182	N.S.
	30.320		29.153	1.167	1.165	Sig.
		30.525	29.153	1.372	1.145	Sig.

Table 5.31 reveals that significant differences are found between the women entrepreneurs who have family income ₹ 4001-8000 and above ₹ 12000, ₹ 8001-12000 and above ₹ 12000. Further, it reveals that the women entrepreneurs who have family income ₹ 8001-12000 have more entrepreneurial problems than the other income groups. But significant differences are not found between the women entrepreneurs who have family income up to ₹ 4000 and ₹ 4001-8000, up to ₹ 4000 and ₹ 8001-12000, up to ₹ 4000 and above ₹ 12000, ₹ 4001-8000 and ₹ 8001-12000.

General Problems of Rural Women Entrepreneurs with Respect to Monthly Family Income

Since the 'F' ratio of General Problems is greater than that of the table value, the Scheffe test is applied.

Table 5.32 Scheffe's Post HOC Test for the Mean Scores of General Problems of Rural Women Entrepreneurs with Respect to Monthly Family Income

Family Monthly Income				Mean Difference	C.I. Value	Result at 5% Level
Up to ₹ 4000	₹ 4001-8000	₹ 8001-12000	Above ₹ 12000			
33.467	32.293			1.173	1.488	N.S.
33.467		34.450		0.983	1.467	N.S.
33.467			31.400	2.067	1.449	Sig.
	32.293	34.450		2.157	1.381	Sig.
	32.293		31.400	0.893	1.361	N.S.
		34.450	31.400	3.050	1.338	Sig.

Table 5.32 reveals that significant differences are found between the women entrepreneurs who have family income up to ₹ 4000 and above ₹ 12000, ₹ 4001-8000 and ₹ 8001-12000, ₹ 8001-12000 and above ₹ 12000. Further, it reveals that the women entrepreneurs who have family income ₹ 8001-12000 have more entrepreneurial problems than the other income groups. But significant differences are not found between the women entrepreneurs who have family income up to ₹ 4000 and ₹ 8001-12000, up to ₹ 4000 and ₹ 4001-8000, ₹ 4001-8000 and above ₹ 12000.

Knowledge Problems of Rural Women Entrepreneurs with Respect to Monthly Family Income

Since the 'F' ratio of Knowledge Problems is greater than that of the table value, the Scheffe test is applied. (*See table on next page*)

Table 5.33 reveals that significant differences are found between the women entrepreneurs who have family income up to ₹ 4000 and ₹ 4001-8000, up to ₹ 4000 and above ₹ 12000. Further, it reveals that the women entrepreneurs who have family income of above ₹ 12000 have more knowledge problems than the other income groups.

Table 5.33: Scheffe's Post HOC Test for the Mean Scores of Knowledge Problems of Rural Women Entrepreneurs with Respect to Monthly Family Income

Family Monthly Income				Mean Difference	C.I. Value	Result at 5% Level
Up to ₹ 4000	₹ 4001-8000	₹ 8001-12000	Above ₹ 12000			
29.217	30.520			1.303	1.207	Sig.
29.217		30.238		1.021	1.190	N.S.
29.217			30.871	1.654	1.175	Sig.
	30.520	30.238		0.282	1.120	N.S.
	30.520		30.871	0.351	1.104	N.S.
		30.238	30.871	0.633	1.085	N.S.

But significant differences are not found between the women entrepreneurs who have family income up to ₹ 4000 and ₹ 8001-12000, ₹ 4001-8000 and above ₹ 12000, ₹ 4001-8000 and ₹ 8001-12000, ₹ 8001-12000 and above ₹ 12000.

Economical Problems of Rural Women Entrepreneurs with Respect to Monthly Family Income

Since the 'F' ratio of Economical Problems is greater than that of the table value, the Scheffe test is applied.

Table 5.34: Scheffe's Post HOC Test for the Mean Scores of Economical Problems of Rural Women Entrepreneurs with respect to Monthly Family Income

Family Monthly Income				Mean Difference	C.I. Value	Result at 5% Level
Up to ₹ 4000	₹ 4001-8000	₹ 8001-12000	Above ₹ 12000			
24.783	24.947			0.163	0.578	N.S.
24.783		24.363		0.421	0.570	N.S.
24.783			24.224	0.560	0.563	N.S.
	24.947	24.363		0.584	0.537	Sig.
	24.947		24.224	0.723	0.529	Sig.
		24.363	24.224	0.139	0.520	N.S.

Table 5.34 reveals that significant differences are found between the women entrepreneurs who have family income ₹ 4001-8000 and ₹ 8001-12000, ₹ 4001-8000 and above ₹ 12000. Further, it reveals that the women entrepreneurs who have family income up to ₹ 4000 have more economic problems than the other income groups. But significant differences are not found between the women entrepreneurs who have family income up to ₹ 4000 and ₹ 4001-8000, up to ₹ 4000 and ₹ 8001-12000, up to ₹ 4000 and above ₹ 12000, ₹ 8001-12000 and above ₹ 12000.

Psychological Problems of Rural Women Entrepreneurs with Respect to Monthly Family Income

Since the 'F' ratio of Psychological Problems is greater than that of the table value, the Scheffe test is applied.

Table 5.35: Scheffe's Post HOC Test for the Mean Scores of Psychological Problems of Rural Women Entrepreneurs with Respect to Monthly Family Income

Family Monthly Income				Mean Difference	C.I. Value	Result at 5% Level
Up to ₹ 4000	₹ 4001-8000	₹ 8001-12000	Above ₹ 12000			
23.967	23.200			0.767	0.806	N.S.
23.967		23.475		0.492	0.794	N.S.
23.967			23.000	0.967	0.784	Sig.
	23.200	23.475		0.275	0.748	N.S.
	23.200		23.000	0.200	0.737	N.S.
		23.475	23.000	0.475	0.725	N.S.

Table 5.35 reveals that significant differences are found between the women entrepreneurs who have family income up to ₹ 4000 and above ₹ 12000. Further, it reveals that the women entrepreneurs who have family income up to ₹ 4000 have more psychological problems than the other income groups. But significant differences are not found between the women who have family income up to ₹ 4000 and ₹ 4001-8000, up to ₹ 4000 and ₹ 8001-12000, ₹ 8001-12000 and above ₹ 12000, ₹ 4001-8000 and ₹ 8001-12000, ₹ 4001-8000 and above ₹ 12000.

Table 5.36: Analysis of Variance among the Mean Scores of Problems in Total and in Different Dimensions with Respect to Years of Experience

Dimensions	Source of Variance	Sum of Squares	df	Mean of Squares	F-Value	Remarks at 0.05 Level
Overall	Between	416.6284	3	138.8761	3.8561	Sig
	Within	10660.4870	296	36.0152		
Entrepreneurial Problems	Between	8.8608	3	2.9536	0.4153	N.S.
	Within	2105.3930	296	7.1128		
General Problems	Between	176.0492	3	58.6831	6.4097	Sig
	Within	2709.9855	296	9.1554		
Knowledge Problems	Between	9.5663	3	3.1888	0.4938	N.S.
	Within	1911.4116	296	6.4575		
Economic Problems	Between	98.1562	3	32.7187	26.7493	Sig
	Within	362.0565	296	1.2232		
Social Problems	Between	39.4828	3	13.1609	5.0278	Sig
	Within	774.8178	296	2.6176		
Psychological Problems	Between	77.9721	3	25.9907	9.9626	Sig
	Within	772.2124	296	2.6088		

Table value required for df 3, 296 is 2.636

ANALYSIS OF VARIANCE AMONG PROBLEMS AND YEARS OF EXPERIENCE OF RURAL WOMEN ENTREPRENEURS

Null Hypothesis

There is no significant difference among the mean scores of problems in total and in different dimensions such as entrepreneurial problems, general problems, knowledge problems, economic problems, social problems and psychological problems of women entrepreneurs with respect to the variable years of experience.

Since the calculated 'F' values are less than the table value in the Entrepreneurial Problems and Knowledge Problems, the null hypothesis is accepted. So, it is found that there is no significant difference among the mean scores of the Entrepreneurial Problems and Knowledge Problems with respect to the years of experience. But, it is found that there is significant difference among the mean scores of problems in total and in different dimensions such as General Problems, Economic Problems and Psychological Problems and Social Problems of women entrepreneurs with respect to the variable years of experience.

Problem (Total) of Rural Women Entrepreneurs with Respect to Years of Experience

Since the 'F' ratio of the Problems (Total) is greater than that of the table value, the Scheffe test is applied.

Table 5.37: Scheffe's Post HOC Test for the Mean Scores of Problem (Total) of Rural Women Entrepreneurs with Respect to Years of Experience

Years of Experience				Mean Difference	C.I. Value	Result at 5% Level
Below 2	2-4	4-6	Above 6			
168.356	167.368			0.988	2.902	N.S.
168.356		170.048		1.693	3.124	N.S.
168.356			169.250	0.894	3.774	N.S.
	167.368	170.048		2.681	2.351	Sig.
	167.368		169.250	1.882	3.163	N.S.
		170.048	169.250	0.798	3.368	N.S.

Table 5.37 reveals that significant differences are found between the women entrepreneurs having an experience of 2-4 years and 4-6 years. Further, it reveals that the women entrepreneurs having an experience 2-4 years are facing more problems in total than the women entrepreneurs having an experience below 2 years, 4-6 years and above 6 years. But significant differences are not found between the women entrepreneurs having an experience below 2 years and 4-6 years, below 2 years and above 6 years, below 2 years and 2-4 years, 4-6 years and above 6 years, 2-4 years and above 6 years.

General Problems of Rural Women Entrepreneurs with Respect to Years of Experience

Since the 'F' ratio of General Problems is greater than that of the table value, the Scheffe test is applied.

Table 5.38: Scheffe's Post HOC Test for the Mean Scores of General Problems of Rural Women Entrepreneurs with Respect to Years of Experience

Years of Experience				Mean Difference	C.I. Value	Result at 5% Level
Below 2	2-4	4-6	Above 6			
31.400	33.368			1.968	1.463	Sig.
31.400		33.072		1.672	1.575	Sig.
31.400			32.333	0.933	1.903	N.S.
	33.368	33.072		0.295	1.185	N.S.
	33.368		32.333	1.034	1.595	N.S.
		33.072	32.333	0.739	1.698	N.S.

Table 5.38 reveals that significant differences are found between the women entrepreneurs having an experience below 2 years and 2-4 years, below 2 years and 4-6 years. Further, it reveals that the women entrepreneurs having an experience of 2-4 years are facing more general problems than the women entrepreneurs having an experience of below 2 years, 4-6 years and above 6 years. But significant differences are not found between the women entrepreneurs having an experience below 2 years and above 6 years, 2-4 years and 4-6 years, 4-6 years and above 6 years, 2-4 years and above 6 years.

Economical Problems of Rural Women Entrepreneurs with Respect to Years of Experience

Since the 'F' ratio of Economical Problems is greater than that of the table value, the Scheffe test is applied.

Table 5.39: Scheffe's Post HOC Test for the Mean Scores of Economical Problems of Rural Women Entrepreneurs with Respect to Years of Experience

Years of Experience				Mean Difference	C.I. Value	Result at 5% Level
Below 2	2-4	4-6	Above 6			
24.956	23.985			0.970	0.535	Sig.
24.956		24.976		0.020	0.576	N.S.
24.956			25.222	0.267	0.695	N.S.
	23.985	24.976		0.991	0.433	Sig.
	23.985		25.222	1.237	0.583	Sig.
		24.976	25.222	0.246	0.621	N.S.

Table 5.39 reveals that significant differences are found between the women entrepreneurs having an experience below 2 years and 2-4 years, 2-4 years and 4-6 years, 2-4 years and above 6 years. Further, it reveals that the women entrepreneurs having an experience of 4-6 years are facing more economic problems than the women entrepreneurs having an experience of below 2 years, 2-4 years and above 6 years. But significant differences are not found between the women entrepreneurs having an experience below 2 years and 4-6 years, below 2 years and above 6 years, 4-6 years and above 6 years.

Social Problems of Rural Women Entrepreneurs with Respect to Years of Experience

Since the 'F' ratio of Social Problems is greater than that of the table value, the Scheffe test is applied. (*See table on next page*)

Table 5.40 reveals that significant differences are found between the women entrepreneurs having an experience below 2 years and 2-4 years. Further, it reveals that the women

Table 5.40: Scheffe's Post HOC Test for the Mean Scores of Social Problems of Rural Women Entrepreneurs with Respect to Years of Experience

Years of Experience				Mean Difference	C.I. Value	Result at 5% Level
Below 2	2-4	4-6	Above 6			
28.178	27.169			1.009	0.782	Sig.
28.178		27.422		0.756	0.842	N.S.
28.178			27.444	0.733	1.017	N.S.
	27.169	27.422		0.253	0.634	N.S.
	27.169		27.444	0.275	0.853	N.S.
		27.422	27.444	0.023	0.908	N.S.

entrepreneurs having an experience of below 2 years are facing more social problems than the women entrepreneurs having an experience of 2-4 years, 4-6 years and above 6 years. But significant differences are not found between the women entrepreneurs having an experience 2-4 years and 4-6 years, 2-4 years and above 6 years below 2 years and 4-6 years, below 2 years and above 6 years, 4-6 years and above 6 years.

Psychological Problems of Women Entrepreneurs with Respect to Years of Experience

Since the 'F' ratio of Psychological Problems is greater than that of the table value, the Scheffe test is applied.

Table 5.41: Scheffe's Post HOC Test for the Mean Scores of Psychological Problems of Rural Women Entrepreneurs with Respect to Years of Experience

Years of Experience				Mean Difference	C.I. Value	Result at 5% Level
Below 2	2-4	4-6	Above 6			
23.422	22.875			0.547	0.781	N.S.
23.422		24.048		0.626	0.841	N.S.
23.422			23.611	0.189	1.016	N.S.
	22.875	24.048		1.173	0.633	Sig.
	22.875		23.611	0.736	0.851	N.S.
		24.048	23.611	0.437	0.906	N.S.

Table 5.41 reveals that significant differences are found between the women entrepreneurs having an experience 2-4 years and 4-6 years. Further, it reveals that the women entrepreneurs having an experience of 4-6 years are facing more psychological problems than the women entrepreneurs having an experience below 2 years, 2-4 years and above 6 years. But significant differences are not found between the women entrepreneurs having an experience below 2 years and 2-4 years, below 2 years and 4-6 years, below 2 years and above 6 years, 2-4 years and above 6 years, 4-6 years and above 6 years.

The individual rural women entrepreneur single handedly faces a plethora of endless problems. In fact, from the moment an entrepreneur conceives the idea to start her own unit; she has to work hard against heavy odds. This chapter has elaborated a number of problems and hurdles faced by upcoming women entrepreneurs who could have done much better in their chosen field, if the circumstances has been a little more favourable and encouraging.

A number of problems that have often affected their performance in the beginning of their career and the ever pinching, 'economic problems' ranked in the first place as it was faced by the respondents to the greatest extent. The availability of finance and its repayment both cause a lot of difficulties in maintaining and running their enterprises. Even if they succeed in getting over these problems, other problems such as social problems, psychological problems, knowledge problems, entrepreneurial problems and general problems do come in their way. Besides this, their own multiple commitments social as well as domestic often adversely affect their mobility which is very much needed in running any enterprise.

6

Summary of Findings and Suggestions

Rural Women play a significant role in the domestic and socio-economic life of the society and therefore, national development is not possible without developing this segment of the society. The objectives of the study were accomplished in analysing the profile of the rural women entrepreneurs and their enterprise. Moreover the entrepreneurial skills, motivating factors and the problems associated with them were also analysed in this study.

The methodology was formulated according to the objectives of the study with the help of comprehensive review of previous studies. For the primary data, 300 rural women entrepreneurs were selected from 19 blocks in the Tirunelveli district. Selected respondents were contacted in person and required data were collected with the help of a pre-tested comprehensive interview schedule. The secondary data were collected from the published as well as unpublished reports, handbooks, action plans and pamphlets from the office of the Director of Industries and Commerce, various books, journals, magazines, websites, etc. The collected data were analysed with the help of appropriate tools to assess the various sources of inspiration, the entrepreneurial skills possessed by them, factors influencing entrepreneurship and the problems faced by them.

FINDINGS

Findings based on the analysis and interpretations of the study are given below.

Findings Relating to Socio-economic Conditions of Rural Women Entrepreneurs

1. The age of the respondents reveals that most (80%) of the respondents are in the age group of 25 to 45 years. It implies that the entrepreneurs are involving themselves in the entrepreneurial activities in the age group of 25 to 45 years.
2. A maximum of 60.4 per cent of the total respondents are belonging to backward class and 17.3 per cent belong to most backward class. The number of respondents belonging to Schedule caste/Schedule tribe constitutes 12 per cent. The most dominant social class among the rural women entrepreneurs is backward class.
3. Majority (53%) of the respondents have only high school education.
4. A maximum of 73.7 per cent of the respondents are married whereas 11.7 per cent of the respondents are unmarried. The number of respondents who are widowed constitute 8.7 per cent of the total respondents.
5. The percentage of women entrepreneurs who are belonging to nuclear family system is 69 per cent whereas 31 per cent of the respondents belong to joint family system.
6. A maximum of 63 per cent of the respondents are in the category of 0-2 children and 33.2 per cent have 3-5 children. Only 3.8 per cent of the respondents have more than 5 children. It reveals that the maximum number of rural women engaged in entrepreneurship have less number of children.

7. Majority (60.7%) of the respondents has 3 to 5 members in their family and 24.3 per cent of them have 6 to 8 members. The number of respondents who have less than 3 members and more than 8 members in their family constitute 9.3 and 5.7 per cent respectively. The dominant family size of the respondents is 3 to 5 members.
8. A maximum of 59 per cent of the respondents have only two or three earning members in the family followed by 32.3 per cent have only one earning member in their family. The number of respondents who have 4 to 5 and above 5 earning members in the family constitutes 7.3 and 1.4 per cent respectively.
9. The important family occupation is business which constitutes 65.7 per cent whereas private employment and agriculture constitutes 14 and 12.3 per cent respectively. Only 8 per cent of the respondents' family is in government occupation.
10. A maximum of 70 per cent of the respondents are doing business as their primary occupation followed by this, 13.3 per cent of the respondents are doing agriculture as their primary occupation.
11. 28.3 per cent of the respondents have monthly family income of above ₹ 12,000 and 26.7 per cent have family income of ₹ 8,001 to 12,000.
12. A maximum of 55.7 per cent of the respondents spend above ₹ 5000 as family expenditure and 24.3 per cent are spending ₹ 4001 to 5000 as their family expenditure. Only 1.3 per cent of the respondents spend up to ₹ 2000 as their family expenditure per month.
13. 8 per cent of the respondents are indebted due to their excess family expenditure over the family income. A maximum of 47.7 per cent of the respondents have no savings. Only 33 per cent of the respondents have savings up to ₹ 1000. Among the rural women entrepreneurs, the respondents who are saving more than ₹ 2000 and ₹ 1001 to 2000 constitute 6 per cent and 5.3 per cent respectively.

14. A maximum of 38.4 per cent of the respondents engage in agriculture and food product based industries followed by this 15 per cent are engaged in textile based industries. The number of respondents engaged in forest based and chemical/polymer based service based industries constitute 14.3 and 12.3 per cent respectively. Only 10 per cent of the respondents are engaged in raw material based industries and also service based industries.
15. A maximum of 44.3 per cent of the rural women entrepreneurs are engaged in the production of goods followed by 39.3 per cent of the respondents are doing trading activities. Only 16.4 per cent of the entrepreneurs are involved in service based activities.
16. 60 per cent of the respondents have sole-proprietorship concern and only by 40 per cent of the respondents are doing business on partnership basis. There is no company form of organization run by rural women entrepreneurs.
17. 46 per cent of the respondents have their enterprises in their home whereas 31 per cent of the respondents run their enterprises in their own building. The respondents, who run their enterprises in rental building, industrial estate, etc., constitute 23 per cent.
18. 45.3 per cent of the enterprises 3 to 4 years old followed by this 27.7 per cent are 4 to 6 years old. The number of enterprises which have an existence of up to 2 years and above 6 years constitute 15 per cent, and 12 per cent respectively.
19. From the study the self-motivation is ranked first compared to other sources of inspirations because of the low co-efficient of variation. So it is evident that the self-motivation plays a vital role in inspiring the rural women to become entrepreneurs.
20. The analysis of the sources of inspiration reveals that there exists an association between the various sources of inspiration and the socio-economic variables such as educational qualification, occupation, income and years of experience.

21. 53.3 per cent of the respondents have invested less than 10,000 followed by 17.3 per cent of the respondents have invested above ₹ 50,000 as their investment in the business. Only 2.7 per cent of the respondents have invested ₹ 40,001 to 50,000.
22. The important source of investment among the rural women entrepreneurs are owned and borrowed and their respective percentages are 63.3 per cent and 36.7 per cent.
23. The important source of borrowings among the rural women entrepreneurs is friends and relatives which constitutes 42.8 per cent followed by this 23.6 per cent of the respondents have borrowed from banks. The number of respondents who have borrowed from Private Money Lenders, Micro-credit Institutions and Non-Government Organizations constitute 12.7 per cent, 10.9 per cent and 10 per cent respectively.
24. Among the rural women entrepreneurs, 44.3 per cent of the respondents are earning an income of ₹ 5,000 to 10,000 followed by 34.3 per cent are earning ₹ 5,000 to 10,000. The respondents who are earning more than ₹ 10,000 and ₹ 10,001 to 15,000 constitute 11.4 per cent and 10 per cent respectively.
25. Nearly 41.3 per cent of the enterprises are earning ₹ 4000 to 5000 as profit every month whereas enterprises which earned profit of ₹ 6000 to 8000 constitute 20.7 per cent. The enterprises which earned profit of ₹ 2000 to 4000 and less than ₹ 2000 constitute 13.4 per cent and 8.3 per cent respectively. The enterprises which earned a profit of above ₹ 8000 constitute 16.3 per cent.
26. A maximum of 76 per cent of the respondents are not aware of the government assistance and 24 per cent of the respondents are aware of the various assistances provided under different schemes offered by the government.
27. 78.7 per cent of the respondents have not received any assistance and 21.3 per cent have received assistance through various government schemes.

28. 50.3 per cent of the respondents are using only one person as worker. It is followed by 26.7 per cent of the respondents who provide employment to two persons. Only 23 per cent of the respondents provide three or more additional employment. 139 respondents are doing their business solely.
29. A maximum of 77.01 per cent of the workers employed are skilled workers followed by 10.55 per cent of the workers are semi-skilled. Only 12.4 per cent of the workers are unskilled.
30. 83.2 per cent of the workers are coming to the work from the local places followed by 11.8 per cent of the workers are coming from nearby places. Only 5 per cent of the workers are coming from neighbouring districts.

Findings Relating to Entrepreneurial Skills of Rural Women Entrepreneurs

31. Out of the eight entrepreneurial skills considered in this study the co-efficient of variance of the 'Business Management Skills' is the least (3.11) compared to other skills. Based on the co-efficient of variance, all the entrepreneurial skills are ranked. The business management skill which is the least among all the skills, ranked first. It reveals the necessity to possess the business management skill to perform the entrepreneurial activities.
32. The rural women entrepreneurs in the age group 26-35 years have higher personal entrepreneurial skills than the women entrepreneurs in the age groups such as up to 25 years, 36-45 years and above 45 years.
33. The rural women entrepreneurs in the age group of up to 25 years have higher enterprise skills than the women entrepreneurs in the age groups such as 26-35 years, 36-45 years and above 45 years.
34. The rural women entrepreneurs in the age group of 26-35 years have higher soft skills than the women entrepreneurs in the age groups such as up to 25 years, 36-45 years and above 45 years. But significant differences

are not found between the rural women entrepreneurs in the age group of up to 25 years and 36-45 years, up to 25 years and above 45 years, and 26-35 years and 36-45 years as regards the soft skill are concerned.

35. The rural women entrepreneurs having higher secondary qualification possess higher enterprise skills than the other education qualification.
36. The rural women entrepreneurs doing family business have higher business management skills than the family of women entrepreneurs doing private occupation, agriculture and others.
37. The rural women entrepreneurs doing family business have higher enterprise skills than the other categories.
38. The rural women entrepreneurs doing business as their primary occupation have higher technical skills than the women entrepreneurs doing private occupation, agriculture and other occupation.
39. As regards the business management skills are concerned, the rural women entrepreneurs doing business as the primary occupation have higher Business Management Skills than the other categories of respondents.
40. The analysis of personal entrepreneurial skills shows that the rural women entrepreneurs who are doing business as the primary occupation have higher Personal Entrepreneurial Skills than the other categories of the respondents.
41. The rural women entrepreneurs who are doing business as their primary occupation have higher Enterprise Skills than the other categories of respondents.
42. The rural women entrepreneurs doing business as their primary occupation have higher Soft Skills than the other categories of respondents.
43. The rural women entrepreneurs having more than 6 years as experience have higher technical skills than the women entrepreneurs having an experience below 2 years, 2-4 years and 4-6 years.

44. The rural women entrepreneurs having an experience of 2-4 years have higher Business Management Skills than the women entrepreneurs having an experience of 2-4 years, 4-6 years and above 6 years.
45. The rural women entrepreneurs having an experience of 4-6 years have higher Enterprise Skills than the women entrepreneurs having an experience below 2 years, 2-4 years and above 6 years.
46. The rural women entrepreneurs having an experience of 4-6 years have higher Behavioural Skills than the women entrepreneurs having an experience below 2 years, 2-4 years and above 6 years.
47. The rural women entrepreneurs having an experience of 2-4 years have higher Communication Skills than the women entrepreneurs having an experience below 2 years, 4-6 years and above 6 years.
48. The principle axis factor analysis with varimax rotation was conducted to assess the underlying structure of the twenty factors that influence entrepreneurship. The higher Eigen value shows the higher intensity of the factor explaining the variables together. By Eigen values, the most important factors that influence the respondents to start and manage the enterprises are earning money and family necessity since their Eigen value is 2.46.

Findings Relating to Problems Associated with Rural Women Entrepreneurs

49. Out of the six problems encountered by the rural women entrepreneurs, the co-efficient of variance of 'Economic Problems' scores the least (4.96) compared to other problems. It was ranked first as the co-efficient of variance of the economic problem is the least. It reveals that the economic problem prevails than the other problems as regards the rural entrepreneurs are concerned.
50. The rural women entrepreneurs in the age group of 36-45 years have higher knowledge problems than the

women entrepreneurs in the other age groups such as upto 25 years, 26-35 years and above 45 years.

51. The rural women entrepreneurs in the age group of 26-35 years have higher social problems than the women entrepreneurs in the other age groups such as up to 25 years, 36-45 years and above 45 years.
52. The rural women entrepreneurs having high school level of education have higher knowledge problems than the other categories of educational qualification.
53. The rural women entrepreneurs doing other business such as finance, land business have more general problems than the women entrepreneurs doing business, private occupation and agriculture as their occupation.
54. The rural women entrepreneurs doing private occupation have more economic problems than the women entrepreneurs doing business, agriculture and other occupations.
55. The rural women entrepreneurs doing private occupation have more psychological problems than the women entrepreneurs doing business, agriculture and other occupations.
56. The rural women entrepreneurs doing business have more general, knowledge and economic problems than the women entrepreneurs doing private occupation, agriculture and other occupations.
57. The rural women entrepreneurs doing private occupation have more social problems than the women entrepreneurs doing business, agriculture, and other occupations.
58. The rural women entrepreneurs doing agriculture as their occupation have more psychological problems than the women entrepreneurs doing business, private occupation, and other occupations.
59. The rural women entrepreneurs who have family income up to ₹ 4000 have higher problems in total than the women entrepreneurs who have family income ₹ 4001-8000, ₹ 8001-12000 and above ₹ 12000.

60. The rural women entrepreneurs who have family income ₹ 8001-12000 have entrepreneurial problems than the women entrepreneurs who have family income up to ₹ 4000, ₹ 4001-8000 and above ₹ 12000.
61. The rural women entrepreneurs who have family income of above ₹ 12000 have knowledge problems than the women entrepreneurs who have family income up to ₹ 4000, ₹ 4001-8000 and ₹ 8001-12000.
62. The rural women entrepreneurs who have family income up to ₹ 4000 have economic problems than the women entrepreneurs who have family income, ₹ 4001-8000 and ₹ 8001-12000, above ₹ 12000.
63. The rural women entrepreneurs who have family income up to ₹ 4000 have psychological problems than the women entrepreneurs who have family income, ₹ 4001-8000 and ₹ 8001-12000, above ₹ 12000.
64. The rural women entrepreneurs having an experience of 2-4 years are facing more general problems than the women entrepreneurs having an experience of below 2 years, 4-6 years and above 6 years.
65. The rural women entrepreneurs having an experience of 4-6 years are facing more economic problems than the women entrepreneurs having an experience of below 2 years, 2-4 years and above 6 years.
66. The rural women entrepreneurs having an experience below 2 years are facing more social problems than the women entrepreneurs having an experience of 2-4 years, 4-6 years and above 6 years.
67. The rural women entrepreneurs having an experience of 4-6 years are facing more psychological problems than the women entrepreneurs having an experience below 2 years, 2-4 years and above 6 years.

SUGGESTIONS

The researcher recommends the following on the basis of analysis and experience gained during the survey.

To The Policy-Makers

- Reorient policies to focus on developing existing rural industries would be of vital necessity. This shall help to achieve a rapid, all round and socially balanced economic growth and development.
- While framing the policies the real need of the target group should be taken in to consideration. As most of the women entrepreneurs are not able to meet the capital required the policy-makers could take in to account this need and frame the policies suit this need.
- The Government should chart out a plan to provide necessary training to the rural women entrepreneurs as regards the need for innovation and up gradation of technologies.
- Developing social networks could be one strategy. The culture of sharing and exchanging views and innovative ideas will go with preparing the rural women entrepreneurs to face the challenges of bigger players.
- The constraints faced by the rural women entrepreneurs differ from entrepreneurs of other areas. The problems faced by the rural women entrepreneurs vary according to their socio-economic criteria too. Hence, it is necessary to target the rural women entrepreneurs separately while framing the policies aiming at helping the rural women entrepreneurs.
- The policy-makers while framing the entrepreneurship models should focus on the key role of entrepreneurs such as to initiate, to establish, to build, to develop, to manage, to compete and to specialise. The EDP models have to be more dynamic, flexible and adequate booking to the needs of the rural areas. The efficiency of the model should be measured against a pre agreed bench mark because of different socio-economic strata existing in the country.

To The Supporting Institutions and Organizations

- Banks may grant working capital loans to Handloom and Power loom units, Artisans, Self-employed persons etc., under a flexible system.
- Though the government is supporting the rural women entrepreneurs the information about the various assistances are not known to the target people for whom the assistances are provided. Therefore this should be given due attention. The supporting organization which is responsible for implementing the government policies and programmes should take serious efforts to create the awareness about the government programmes among the target people. For this purpose a special task force needs to be created in the government nodal agencies for the awareness creation and the implementation of the programmes.
- As most of the supporting organizations are in the district head quarters, the nodal agencies are organizing the awareness programmes in the district head quarters. The branch of the supporting organization could be set up in the rural areas or frequent camps could be organized in the target areas.
- The supporting organizations need to shed their inhibition/ biased attitude towards the women entrepreneurs while granting loans and other facilities and incentives to the entrepreneurs.
- The NGOs which provides support to the nodal agencies must concentrate more on the rural women entrepreneurs and necessary micro credit could also be extended to the rural entrepreneurs.
- Rural Women Entrepreneurship Development Programmes (RWEDP) could be designed to develop and to nurture the rural women entrepreneurship.
- Separate Micro-credit Institution under the government nodal agencies could be set up to support the rural women entrepreneurs.

- Skill development training should be conducted at the rural areas. More NGOs should come forward to create networking among the rural women entrepreneurs and to provide necessary skill training to the rural women.
- By providing necessary skill training and developing income generating ventures in the rural areas the movement of women in search employment to other district could be curtailed. Any step in this direction will reduce the social evils for which the women are targeted.
- Trade associations for the rural women entrepreneurs could be created at the rural areas and necessary support should be provided to those associations by the government nodal agencies for organizing exhibition cum sale in the towns and the cities on a regular basis especially during the festival times to popularise the products produced by the rural women entrepreneurs.
- The entry of proxy women entrepreneurs need to be checked so that the benefits trickle down only to the genuine women entrepreneurs.

To The Rural Women Entrepreneurs

- The intending women entrepreneurs should attend the training programmes organized by the government nodal agencies to equip themselves with necessary skills which are necessary for a person to become an entrepreneur.
- The exposure visits to the nearby units and discussion with the successful entrepreneurs will also help the prospective women entrepreneurs to identify a suitable project idea.
- Survey of the local resources and its potentials will help the prospective rural women entrepreneurs to enter in to the right business.
- The use of internet and web based services should be used to gather information about the government schemes, programmes and assistances.
- Trade Associations could be created to have network among the women entrepreneurs as well as to protect the interest of the business of the rural women entrepreneurs.

- New marketing strategies should be evolved to increase the sale of goods produced by the rural women entrepreneurs.
- The potentials of the existing self-help groups' network could be used for marketing the goods produced by the rural women entrepreneurs.
- Government must take initiative to help the rural entrepreneurs to modernise their business and to introduce innovation in the business venture.

Women entrepreneurs faced many obstacles specifically in marketing their products. In order to overcome these obstacles, they must be given the same opportunities as men. In addition to this, in some countries, women experience obstacles with respect to holding property and entering contracts. Increased participation of women in the labour force is a prerequisite for improving the position of women in society and self-employed women. Particularly the entry of rural women in enterprises will have to be encouraged. Rural women can do wonders by their effectual and competent involvement in entrepreneurial activities. The rural women have basic indigenous knowledge, skill, potential and resources to establish and manage enterprise. Now, what is needed is the knowledge regarding accessibility to loans, various funding agencies procedure regarding certification, awareness on government welfare programmes, motivation, technical skill and support from family, government and other organization. Moreover, formation and strengthening of rural women entrepreneurs' network must be encouraged. Women entrepreneur networks are major sources of knowledge about women's entrepreneurship and they are increasingly recognised as a valuable tool for its development and promotion.

The present study will help the planners and the decision-makers who are involved in the development of rural entrepreneurship to review the existing policies and to make suitable suggestions to amend the provisions of the Act which governs the rural entrepreneurship. Based on the experience of the researcher the following important issues have identified for an in-depth study. The researcher will feel amply rewarded if the present study helps to undertake similar studies in the areas suggested below.

- Promotional efforts of government for the growth of rural women entrepreneurship.
- Impact of government assistance on the socio-economic empowerment of rural women entrepreneurs.
- The study of entrepreneurial skills on the growth of rural women entrepreneurship.
- The role of Self-Help Groups in the development of rural women entrepreneurship.
- A study on the role of Non-Government Organizations on the development of rural women entrepreneurship.

The multifaceted problems of rural women entrepreneurs should be dealt with by co-ordinating the efforts of the Government, supporting agencies and the rural women entrepreneurs to scale new heights in future.

Index

R

S

T